The Myths We Live By

Myths are no mere archaic relics but a potent force in everyday life, part of our collective unconscious. Old myths are constantly reworked and new myths continually created as people make sense of untidy and traumatic memories and give meaning to their lives. Yet myths have been strangely neglected by historians, and in these essays the authors challenge historians' traditional preoccupation with concrete realities, demanding recognition for the power of myth in shaping the actions and the imagination of the present.

The Myths We Live By uses the rich material of recorded life stories in a novel way, offering a rare view of how memory and tradition are continually reshaped and recycled to make sense of the past from the standpoint of the present. Focused primarily on recent memory, the examples stretch from the transient myths of contemporary Italian school children on strike, back to the family legends of classical Greece, and the traditional storytelling of Canadian Indians. Their range is international: from German-Dutch maids to Puerto Rican mothers in New York, from Australian soldiers to Swedish lumberjacks, from Cape Coloured martyrs of the Boer War to Nazi concentration camp survivors. Cumulatively, they advocate a transformed history, which actively relates subjective and objective, past and present, politics and poetry – history as a living force in the present.

This rich mixture of vivid material from the life stories of ordinary men and women is a landmark in oral history. It will appeal to anyone interested in oral history, memory, and myth, including students of social history, anthropology, cultural studies, psychology, and psychotherapy.

The editors

Raphael Samuel and Paul Thompson are internationally renowned oral and social historians. Raphael Samuel is editor of *Patriotism* (Routledge, 1989) and *East End Underworld* (Routledge & Kegan Paul, 1981). He is Tutor in Politics and Sociology, Ruskin College, Oxford.

Paul Thompson's books include *The Edwardians* (Weidenfeld & Nicolson, 1975, Paladin, 1977), and *The Voice of the Past* (OUP, 1978, 2nd edn 1988) and he is founder-editor of the journal *Oral History*. He is Research Professor in Social History at the University of Essex and Director of the National Life Story Collection at the National Sound Archive.

History Workshop Series
General Editor: Raphael Samuel
Ruskin College, Oxford

Metropolis: London
Histories and Representations since 1800
David Feldman and Gareth Stedman Jones (eds)

Patriotism: The Making and Unmaking of British National Identity
Volume 1: History and Politics
Volume 2: Minorities and Outsiders
Volume 3: National Fictions
Raphael Samuel

New Views of Co-operation
Stephen Yeo (ed.)

The Radical Soldier's Tale:
John Pearman 1819–1908
Carolyn Steedman

Slavery:
And Other Forms of Unfree Labour
Leonie Archer (ed.)

Socialism and the Intelligentsia 1880–1914
Carl Levy (ed.)

Disciplines of Faith:
Studies in Religion, Politics and Patriarchy
Jim Obelkevich et al. (eds)

The Enemy Within:
Pit Villages and the Miners' Strike of 1984–5
Raphael Samuel et al. (eds)

Voices of the People:
The Politics and Life of 'La Sociale' at the End of the Second Empire
Adrian Rifkin and Roger Thomas

Language, Gender and Childhood
Valerie Walkerdene et al. (eds)

The Progress of Romance:
The Politics of Popular Fiction
Jean Radford (ed.)

Theatres of the Left 1880–1935:
Workers' Theatre Movements in Britain and America
Raphael Samuel et al.

The Worst Street in North London:
Campbell Bunk, Islington, between the Wars
Jerry White

For Anarchism:
History, Theory, and Practice
David Goodway (ed.)

The Myths We Live By

edited by

Raphael Samuel

and

Paul Thompson

London and New York

First published 1990
by Routledge
11 New Fetter Lane, London EC4P 4EE

Simultaneously published in the USA and Canada by Routledge
a division of Routledge, Chapman and Hall, Inc.
29 West 35th Street, New York, NY 10001

Editorial material © Raphael Samuel and Paul Thompson 1990
Individual contributions © individual contributors 1990

Typeset in 10/11 Times by Saxon Typesetting Ltd, Derby
Printed in England by Clays Ltd., St Ives plc

British Library Cataloguing in Publication Data

The myths we live by. – (History workshop series)
1. Oral history
I. Samuel, Raphael II. Thompson, Paul III. Series
907'.2

Library of Congress Cataloging in Publication Data

The Myths we live by / edited by Raphael Samuel & Paul Thompson.
    p. cm. – (History workshop series)
    "Papers ... presented at the Sixth International Oral History Conference on 'Myth and History' held at St. John's College, Oxford, on 11–13 September 1987" –
    Includes bibliographical references.
    1. History–Errors, inventions, etc.–Congresses. 2. Oral history–Congresses. I. Samuel, Raphael. II. Thompson, Paul Richard, 1935– . III. International Oral History Conference on "Myth and History" (6th : 1987 : St. John's College) IV. Series.
    D3.A3157 1987
    907'.2–dc20   89-10962

    ISBN 0-415-03490-6
    ISBN 0-415-03609-7 (pbk.)

Contents

Acknowledgements

All the papers in this volume were originally presented at the Sixth International Oral History Conference on 'Myth and History', which was held at St John's College, Oxford, on 11–13 September 1987. John Byng-Hall led a workshop on his theme here as part of the conference. We should emphasize, however, our decision to concentrate here on a distinct and coherent theme which is more limited than that of the conference. Choosing from that abundant occasion was not easy, and many other papers than those here clearly deserved publication.

We wish to especially thank, among the many people whose help and support was vital to the conference itself, Brenda Corti of the University of Essex and Dwight Middleton of the History Workshop Centre for Social History: their roles were crucial to its success. Subsequently Alessandro Portelli's paper and an earlier version of Rosanna Basso's have appeared in *Oral History*, while the *Oral History Review* has published a substantially different variant of Rina Benmayor *et al*. Jean Peneff's paper has been published in French in *Societé*, and Luisa Passerini's in Italian in her *Storia e soggettivita: le fonti orali, la memoria* (La Nuova Italia, Florence, 1988). In the editing itself we owe a special debt to the suggestions and enthusiasm of Tony Morris while at Routledge. Terence Ranger also read the conference papers and helped us to evaluate them; Homi Bhabha and Timothy Ashplant made suggestions for the introduction; and Natasha Burchardt took an active part in the detailed editing. We warmly thank them all.

Paul Thompson

Notes on contributors

RAPHAEL SAMUEL is Tutor in Politics and Sociology at Ruskin College, Oxford. He is an editor of *History Workshop Journal* and his books include *Village Life and Labour* and *East End Underworld*.

PAUL THOMPSON is Research Professor in Social History at the University of Essex and Director of the National Life Story Collection at the National Sound Archive in London. He is an editor of *Oral History* and his books include *The Edwardians, Living the Fishing*, and *The Voice of the Past*.

ELIZABETH TONKIN teaches social anthropology at the Centre of West African Studies, University of Birmingham. She is interested in the social construction of oral history, and has worked on this and other aspects of the history and society of Eastern Liberia. She is also studying the construction and development of social anthropology as a discipline.

JEAN PENEFF is Professor of Sociology at the University of Aix-Marseille I, and taught earlier in Algiers and at Nantes. His fieldwork has been on French hospitals, the INSEE statistical centre, and in Algeria. His master's thesis was on autobiography, history, and sociology and he is author of *The Biographical Method*.

LUISA PASSERINI is Professor in the Methodology of Historical Research at the University of Turin. She has researched and published on oral sources, social movements, and the 1960s, and she is actively engaged in women's studies. She was founder-editor of *Fonti orali* and her books include *Fascism in Popular Memory*.

ROSANNA BASSO researches on the history of contemporary southern Italian society at the University of Lecce.

ALISTAIR THOMSON comes from Australia but now lives in Brighton, where he works for a community publisher QueenSpark

Books, and is finishing a doctorate about memory of the First World War in Australia, and historians' use of memory.

MARINELL ASH, who sadly died a year after the conference, came from California and worked for BBC educational broadcasting in Scotland.

ANNA BRAVO teaches history at the University of Turin. She is particularly interested in the history of the Resistance and in women's history and is presently researching on women's experience of the Second World War. She and Daniele Jalla edited *La Vita Offesa*. LILIA DAVITE, who worked with them in the editing, wrote her thesis on survival in the concentration camps. She teaches in a middle school. DANIELE JALLA works for the Piedmontese regional administration on local culture and history. He has researched and published on working-class families and associations and he is editor of the Italian national oral history bulletin *Fonti orali*.

BILL NASSON teaches economic history at the University of Cape Town. He has researched and published on South African social history, oral history, and education, and a book on the black experience of the Boer War.

ELLA JOHANSSON is teaching European anthropology and working on a dissertation on loggers in northern Swedish early industrialism at Lund University. She is also active in a museum project presenting children's history to children.

ALESSANDRO PORTELLI teaches American literature at the University of Rome, specializing in the nineteenth century and also in the literature of the working classes and minorities. He has written an oral history of Terni, *Biografia di una Città*, and edits a journal of popular culture and song, *I Giorni Cantati*.

ELENA CABEZALI, MARIA TERESA CHICOTE and MATILDE CUEVAS all teach contemporary history at the Complutense University of Madrid, belong to its seminar on oral sources, and have published on women in the Spanish Civil War. MATILDE CUEVAS has also written on city artisans in twentieth-century Spain. ELENA CABEZALI is currently working on domestic labour during the war, and MARIA TERESA CHICOTE on women in the countryside, while both are researching on the methodology of oral sources.

JULIE CRUIKSHANK now teaches anthropology at the University of British Columbia after working for several years with the Yukon Native Language Centre in Whitehorse, Yukon Territory.

RINA BENMAYOR is Research Director of the Culture and Oral History Task Forces at the Centro de Estudios Puertorriqueños, Hunter College, City University of New York. She wrote her dissertation at Berkeley on Spanish literature and is currently working on Puerto Rican women's life stories. CELIA ALVAREZ was a researcher at the Centro after her dissertation in sociolinguistics at Pennsylvania University, and now teaches in bilingual and bicultural education at Teachers College, Columbia University. ANA JUARBE became a researcher at the Centro after a degree in Latin American studies. She was born in Puerto Rico but has belonged to the New York Puerto Rican community from the age of four and now has a daughter, Andrea, aged five. BLANCA VASQUEZ studied education and journalism before becoming a researcher at the Centro, where she is editor of the *Centro Bulletin*. She is daughter of a Puerto Rican garment worker.

ROSALIND THOMAS teaches Ancient History at Royal Holloway and Bedford New College of the University of London. She is author of *Oral Tradition and Written Record in Classical Athens*.

JOHN BYNG-HALL is Consultant Child and Adolescent Psychiatrist at the Tavistock Clinic in London. He is a family therapist with a special interest in family myths, legends, and scripts, on which he has published over the last fifteen years.

BARBARA HENKES graduated in history and is now doing research on German maids in the Netherlands at the University of Groningen. She is also active in women's studies.

NATASHA BURCHARDT is Consultant Child and Adolescent Psychiatrist at Banbury in Oxfordshire. She has a longstanding interest in history and was an editor with Paul Thompson of the second international oral history conference papers, *Our Common History*.

Introduction

Raphael Samuel and Paul Thompson

Historians deal, by preference, with 'hard' realities – family, work, and home; politics and government; church and chapel. We cleave to precise locations, dateable periods, delimitable fields of study. Our chronologies are marked in numbered years rather than the succession of generations or lost golden ages. We are happier dealing with aggregates than with images, with functional interests rather than with fantasy selves. Legends are left to the antiquarians, nursery rhymes to the folklorists, proverbs and sayings to the etymologist. Our whole training predisposes us to give a privileged place to the factual, or what G. R. Elton, in *The Practice of History*, calls 'exact knowledge'.[1] We look for the reality content in our documents rather than what they may tell us about the symbolic categories through which reality is perceived. We build our arguments on empirically verifiable truths. As R.G. Collingwood put it, summing up the conventional wisdom of the profession, the historian's decisions 'shall follow inevitably from the evidence'.[2]

For anthropologists, by contrast, taking the supernatural seriously is a fundamental precept of their discipline. Skilled listeners practised in dealing with oral as well as documentary evidence, they look for the crucial clues for interpreting a society as much in myth and magic and shamanism as in matters of fact. Anthropology and history have drawn much closer over the last thirty years; yet despite some fruitful theoretical borrowings, and with the important exception of African history, this rapprochement has brought surprisingly little change in historical attitudes. The 'new' history, in its preoccupation with such matters as status, class, and social mobility is, if anything, even more attached to exact knowledge than the old, in both its favoured methods and its chosen fields of study. Quantification is its grand specific for the study of social 'structure', and latterly for understanding the ebb and flow of industrial militancy through measuring the periodicity of strikes. The historical demographers have been concerned with such measurable quantities as bastardy rates and family size: they have had a great deal to say about household structures, but very little about relationships or psychological attitudes, and nothing at all about such potent but indeterminate figures of folk narrative as the cruel stepmother or the bad son. Likewise in the history of popular movements, crowds are typically studied for their social composition rather than their ecstatic moments or their underlying fears. Popular religion is apt to be examined in terms of a belonging which emphasizes class or status rather than adherence to a spiritual view, be it mystical, millenarian, or salvationist. Contemporary oral history began in a similar spirit, practising a naïve realism which – at least until Luisa Passerini and Ron Grele began to challenge us – was all but taken for granted.[3] Inspired by the very abundance of the newly discovered sources in living memory which we had opened up, we made a fetish of everydayness, using 'thick' description, in the manner suggested by anthropologists, to reconstitute the small detail of domestic life: but we had little to say about dream-thoughts and the hidden sexuality of family relationships.

This volume, drawn from the sixth international oral history conference at Oxford, in itself suggests how far the concerns of oral historians have shifted over the last decade. When we listen now to a life story, the manner of its telling seems to us as important as what is told. We find ourselves exploring an interdisciplinary territory alongside others for whom the nature of narrative is a primary issue: among the anthropologists, psychoanalysts, historians like Haydon White who recognize history as itself a narrative construction, literary critics who read metaphors as clues to social consciousness. This new sensitivity can strengthen some of the earlier purposes of oral historians. Thus in giving voice to underprivileged minorities, we can at the same time bring recognition to spoken cultures, such as those of immigrants in societies dominated by the written word. But it has also brought a new and much broader potential. As soon as we recognize the value of the subjective in individual testimonies, we challenge the accepted categories of history. We reintroduce the emotionality, the fears and fantasies carried by the metaphors of memory, which historians have been so anxious to write out of their formal accounts. And at the same time the individuality of each life story ceases to be an awkward impediment to generalization, and becomes instead a vital document of the construction of consciousness, emphasizing both the variety of experience in any social group, and also how each individual story draws on a common culture: a defiance of the rigid categorization of private and public, just as of memory and reality. This is a matter of vital importance, not just to historians, but equally to those other disciplines focusing on narrative. For oral history, *The Myths We Live By* marks a crucial turning point, which has brought a new and as yet scarcely explored interdisciplinary significance.

We take myth for this volume in the broad and inclusive meaning which characterized the 1987 Oxford conference. Yet most commonly historians are apt to see myth, if they notice it at all, as an impediment to their true work. Childhood fables like the tale of Jack the Giant Killer would offend protocol if they were used as primary sources, though the 'Fee Fi Fo Fum' of Jack's terrifying adversary – already it seems a familiar catch in Shakespeare's time – must have been for many a 4- or 5-year-old the first intimation that they were of English blood. Likewise the figures of English national myth, with the outstanding exception of Robin Hood, who seems to fascinate Tory and Marxist alike, are the subject of 'antiquarian' interest rather than of scholarly research. Nell Gwynn, though she decorates the labels of the marmalade jars, is assigned to historical romance; Dick Whittington, a folk hero to generations of apprentices, is more familiar in pantomime than in the pages of urban history; Uncle Toby, the figure commemorated in a thousand pots and jugs, is left to the collectors of ceramics.

Such figures transcend the conventional categories of the historian. There is no body of records where they can be systematically studied, no statistics against which they can be measured, no prior reality to which they can be confidently referred. We do not know in many cases how or why they came into existence and we can only speculate on the reasons for their popular appeal. Chronologically they defy periodization, belonging, like the ballad heroes of old, to a past that never was. Geographically they inhabit a symbolic rather than a territorial space, so that even when they are given a precise location – the Wirral peninsula, say, in the case of *Sir Gawain and the Green Knight*, The East End of London in that of the Pearly Kings and Queens – it is a poetic fiction. Ideologically they are chameleon, being appropriated now by the Right, now by the Left, and also often by folk radicalism – the politics of the unpolitical.

These figures of national myth are creatures of excess and this is no doubt one of the sources of their popular appeal. Even when they take their name from real-life originals, they belong to the realm of the fabulous. Like the bowmen of Sherwood Forest, they perform legendary feats of strength. Like the poor boy made good, or the Cinderella figure translated from low to high estate, they cross class boundaries with apparently consummate ease. Like the fugitive Bonnie Prince Charlie they effect miraculous escapes. Like bluff King Hal, they consume prodigious quantities of food, swallow successions of mistresses or wives.

When we do encounter myth our first instinct, it seems, is to devalue it, to rob it of its mysteries, to bring it down to earth. Recently spurred on by the revelations of Eric Hobsbawn and Terence Ranger's *The Invention of Tradition* (1983), Anglo-Saxon historians seem happiest at work puncturing legends, proving the modernity of much of what passes for old, showing the artificiality of myth and its manipulable, plastic character. Highland dress was invented by a canny lowland tailor; the modern monarchy by far-seeing political strategists. 'All that is solid melts into air.'

Yet myth is a fundamental component of human thought. One has only to consider the magical feelings attaching to authority, or the glamour attributed to celebrities, or the power of divided historical origins and cultural traditions to set modern communities – in Ireland or Israel, Sri Lanka or the Lebanon – tearing themselves apart, to see that myth has lost neither its imaginative purchase nor its living power as a historical force today. Recent analyses of change in Britain – for example by Stuart Hall or Stanley Cohen[4] – have shown how the domestic dreams of the 'ideal home' behind the front door are matched in the view from the parlour windows of the outside world by recurrent episodes of 'moral panics' and fantasy fears of 'folk devils' who periodically disturb the peace. The advertisers peddle dreams; the politicians trade in both hopes and fears. In times of crisis they can also summon those sleeping fears which spring to life, for instance, in war fevers or invasion scares – those remembered traumas which make 'Never again!' the most potent of mobilizing cries. Historians themselves, however rationalistic in their method, are by no means insulated from the appeal of myth, as can be seen from the symbolic categories we employ (like 'the nation', or 'the common people'), the grand theories we subscribe to and, not least, our own fetishistic faith in facts. One could refer also to the idea of progress which, notwith-standing protestations to the contrary, and the use of such cognomens as 'genesis' and 'development' still very often serves as a unifying device for our narratives. In using titles like *The World We Have Lost*, we covertly play with myths of former golden ages which we assume our readers share. Most fundamentally of all, as Elizabeth Tonkin argues in our first chapter here, too many of us weigh evidence with an instinctive naïvety which rests on our failure to recognize rationalistic realism as the special myth of our own Western culture.

Yet if we turn to almost any historical field, this persistent blindness to myth undeniably robs us of much of our power to understand and interpret the past. Myth is, or ought to be, quite central to the study of popular movements, as it was for George Lefebvre when he wrote *The Great Fear of 1789*, a pioneering study of mass psychology, whose example his successors have yet to take up.[5] National sentiment, if we are to take account of it as an historical force, can hardly be studied without reference to the demonization of enemies both without and within. Likewise the history of economic development, at least in its capitalist forms, is incomprehensible without reference to those 'manias' and panics which, ever since the South Sea Bubble of 1720, have done so much to shape the direction of both home and foreign investment. And what role has the myth of human perfectibility under socialism played in the contemporary agony of socialist economics? Much the same might be asked of the role of fantasies of rebirth in religious revivals, or of creation myths in forging identities for growing organizations. And while the influence of the 'frontier myth' in the making of American society is part of the common currency of historical thought, the implications of British pride in 'splendid isolation' have been all too rarely aired by our own historians.

The potential value of a more sensitive approach to myth by historians lies above all in raising new questions: some of them deeply challenging. In identifying mythical elements in our own cultural or professional assumptions, we threaten our ethnocentric self-confidence. We discover a psychic dimension which recognizes the power of myth and unconscious desire as forces, not only in history, but in shaping our own lives. We open up a history which refuses to be safely boxed away in card indexes or computer programs: which instead pivots on the *active* relationship between past and present, subjective and objective, poetic and political.

In responding to this challenge oral historians have a special opportunity as well as special apprehensions. The memories with which we work bring us close to the processes of mythical construction and transmission. We can observe the displacements, omissions, and reinterpretations through which myths in personal and collective memory take shape. It was a fundamental proposition of the 1987 Oxford conference that we must look at life stories in this light. They should be seen, not as blurred experience, as disorderly masses of fragments, but as shaped accounts in which some incidents were dramatized, others contextualized, yet others passed over in silence, through a process of narrative shaping in which both conscious and unconscious, myth and reali▟ ▟▟▟▟ significant parts. But we need to go forward cautiousl▟ reasons.

The first is simple. We are arguing for the universality of myth as a constituent of human experience. It lies behind any historical evidence. Hence to identify the element of myth in oral sources is certainly *not* to say that we are working with memories of a false past. Furthermore, a high proportion of the rich detail in a typical life story remains objectively valid: sometimes demonstrably so, from other sources, and by extrapolation from such proven credibility sometimes the only good evidence we have from an undocumented, hidden world. But every life story is also potential evidence for the subjective, and even the unconscious. We do not have to chose one and jettison the other. Oral memory offers a double validity in understanding a past in which, as still today, myth was embedded in real experience: both growing from it, and helping to shape its perception.

The second is that it brings us up against the uncertain relationship between oral history and psychoanalysis. Once oral historians had discovered the 'different credibility' (as Sandro Portelli puts it)[6] of the subjective in memory, they became increasingly drawn towards psychoanalytic perspectives in its interpretation, seeking to learn from another profession which also listened acutely to personal memory. At the Oxford conference Karl Figlio argued that transference took place in our interviews too.[7] And in his own courageous and original autobiography, *In Search of a Past*, Ronald Fraser has juxtaposed and interwoven oral history interviews with the former servants of his childhood with his own memories unpicked in psychoanalysis. The outcome – including his recognition of second parents in the servants – is a rare synthesis of the social and the intimate. There is a compelling promise here.

Equally, it is important to recognize that some of the differences between the two disciplines remain fundamental. We may both recognize the validity of stories and even fantasies as forms of evidence. We may hope to bridge the historian's focus on the adult social and political world with the analyst's primary focus on the intimate, the individual, and the earliest years of life. But we can hardly blur our search for general causes with the analyst's for personal meaning; or the psychoanalytic assumption of universal mental processes with our own insistence on the need to locate change. Nor can we follow analysts in practical terms: we cannot ask our informants to lie down on a couch, or free-associate, or record their dreams for us. We have a different contract: sometimes informants will get attached to us, but we are neither qualified nor expected to work through their transference or to remove symptoms which are disturbing them. It will help nobody to confuse listening as a therapist with listening as a historian.

What we have begun to learn is to listen more acutely. We are more likely now to notice the silences in memory, the conscious or unconscious repressions: as with the Tanzanians who have forgotten part of their family story because 'if we tell it our lineage will be destroyed';[8] or victims still torn by traumatic past suffering like the concentration camp survivors who 'always want it to be told, but inside we are trying to forget';[9] or the militant Turinese workers who skip their humiliations under Fascism in a 'violent annihilation' of many years of their life stories which itself bears witness to the depth of their wounds.[10] Like Isabelle Bertaux-Wiame we can observe how the very language and grammar in which people tell their stories reflect unconscious assumptions: how women are more likely to speak as 'we' or 'one', and of relationships or groups, while men use the active 'I' and present themselves as the decision-makers in lives 'they have lived as *their own*'.[11] We can see how it is precisely where memory diverges most clearly from fact that 'imagination, symbolism, desire break in'.[12] The idealization and demonization of characters become clues to unrealized hopes or hidden fears; the fantasy of reconstructed events contributes to the dynamic influence of myth and rumour in social movements. We can learn to spot in these accounts the typical tricks of 'dream-work': the condensations, reversals, substitutions, metaphors, and word-play through which symbolic messages are conveyed, not only in dreams, but also in social customs like rough music, in jokes, in classic traditional myth, or in contemporary personal storytelling.

Let us return in this spirit to our life stories. Their spontaneity, above all when recorded in spoken form, gives them a special sense of authenticity. Yet as Freud first taught us, memory is inherently revisionist, an exercise in selective amnesia. What is forgotten may be as important as what is remembered. Some relationships will be retrospectively inflated in importance, others devalued. Chance meetings turn into epic encounters which have become momentous in the light of later years. As in a dream, whole sequences of events may be telescoped into a single moment, or conversely the exceptional translated into the habitual. Personal time is notoriously at odds with that of public history, and in a life history the disjunction is widened by the fact that one is faced, for the early years, with the changing time-scales of different phases of childhood. Those long-past summers seemed longer and hotter, winters colder, snows deeper. Brief interludes, such as holidays, stretched to an eternity; the long captivities of the classroom can sometimes shrink almost to nothing. Notions of social space are no less subject to the processes of condensation and displacement. Thus childhood is often remembered as a state of solitude, while in a different register it is remembered as being, to an extraordinary degree, gregarious, with troops of relatives and a choice of welcoming houses. In one version the family is a loved circle of familiar faces. In another it is an emotional wilderness. Like myth, memory requires a radical simplification of its subject matter. All recollections are told from a standpoint in the present. In telling, they need to make sense of the past. That demands a selecting, ordering, and simplifying, a construction of coherent narrative whose logic works to draw the life story towards the fable.

Psychoanalytic writing can point us towards other mythical elements. Freud's 'family romance' might encourage us to look at those other adults who, in a child's fantasy world, function as alternative parents, and offer it unlimited love – grandparents, uncles and aunts, teachers and mentors. It might also draw attention to those ancestor myths which figure so largely in English autobiography and which provided the family with idealized or make-believe pedigrees. Aristocratic origins, despite the realities of social mobility, were paradoxically so valued in the former English class system that prosperous middle-class families would prefer to have come down in the world than to suffer the stigma of being thought of as upstarts. In John Osborne's family, as he records in his autobiography, the grandparents on either side competed as to which had fallen furthest, one branch referring to a former landholding, the other to a liaison with a music-hall star.[13] A more recent turn in which oral history itself has played some part, conversely celebrates humble origins. Thus in the family history societies, a mushroom growth of recent years, it becomes a matter of pride to trace a pedigree back to a country parish and a family of common labourers. 'Gipsy' or Irish blood, rather than being a stigma, is dignified as exotic. In either case, however, patrician or plebeian, it is surely a version of the 'family romance' which we can see at work, in which a make-believe ancestry offers a second identity, a glamorous alternative to the present.

More generally one can note the ways in which personal history is informed and shaped by symbolic notions of the past. In one version of autobiography it is 'the good old days': a state of primal innocence corresponding in some sort to the Lost Eden of the Old Testament or the Golden Age of the poets, an enchanted space as remote as the 'once upon a time' of the fables. The past here functions as a kind of reverse image of the present, a time when 'everyone was neighbours', and life was more secure. There is no place in such accounts for sibling rivalry – a major theme of childhood experience – or the quarrels of husbands and wives. Humiliations, or what must have been humiliations at the time, appear as humorous incidents; hatreds are forgotten; and the whole is overlain or mediated by an overwhelming sense of loss.

In recent years, often on the initiative of oral history groups, there has been a spate of 'community' publications like this, in which old-timers look back on their childhood streets. Illustrated by grain photographs, and following in the wake of comprehensive clearance and redevelopment, these memoirs take on the character of an urban pastoral. The slum, for so many years a byword for poverty and deprivation, is transfigured into a warm and homely place, a little commonwealth where there was always a helping hand. The narrative of hard times becomes a record of courage and endurance. The characteristic note is elegiac, saying goodbye to what will never be seen again, an affectionate leave-taking. In such booklets – *The Good Old Bad Old Days* or *Poverty – Hardship but Happiness*[14] – the slum recaptures the symbolic space of 'the world we have lost'. Many, maybe most, of the facts will be true. It is the omissions and the shaping which make these stories also myth.

An alternative version of life history, more common perhaps in the written than the spoken word, charts a progress from darkness to light. Here the past serves as a kind of negative benchmark by which later achievement is judged, and the narrative is one of achievement rather than loss. As in the *Bildungsroman*, or novel of character, a great deal of attention is focused on the first stirrings of individuality, the awakening sense of a wider world. Anticipatory moments are seized on which appear retrospectively momentous. The woman who prides herself on being a 'born rebel' retraces her earliest steps towards independence. The self-made man dwells on his precocious and autonomous enterprise, both in autobiography, and – as Jean Peneff observes here – in recorded life stories; the aesthete focuses on his discovery of art. The spiritual autobiography, or conversion narrative, may insist on early signs of grace as well as darkness before the light was seen. Luisa Passerini has remarked on how many Turinese Communist militants recount their lives with a similar conversion imagery.[15] Life, in short, is conceptualized teleologically: 'Look, we have come through', is the guiding thread.

Childhood in these autobiographies may be portrayed as a time of captivity, with cold or distant parents, bullying teachers and in the case of the young servant or apprentice, brutal employers. Home life is an oppression; religion as in *Father and Son* or *The Way of All Flesh* a torment;[16] working conditions unrelievedly harsh. There is a morbid attention to remembered slights, as in Edmund Gosse's patrician indignation at his enforced companionship with a common village lad. For Charles Dickens, looking back from the pinnacle of later achievement and recalling his misfortune when, as a child of ten, he was set to work in a blacking factory, alongside common boys, the remembered humiliation was unbearable, and he returned to it obsessively and indignantly in his many fictions of the martyr-child.

Any life story, written or oral, more or less dramatically, is in one sense a personal mythology, a self-justification. And all embody and illustrate character ideals: the desire for independence, say, in those who celebrate their childhood for its moments of freedom, or filial loyalty for those who fetishize family tradition. In oral narratives in particular we come closer to traditional popular mythology in the conveying of moral values through the recounting of events. Such stories very commonly serve as parables, exemplifying courage or kindness or strength, and, like classic fable and myth, they can bear remarkable resemblances to one another. We are continually hearing the same story – or recognizable local variants of it – told by different people in different parts of the country and referring to different points of time: stock incidents which might be better understood in relation to narrativity than to some empiricist notion of truth. Very often, too, we seem to be dealing with fantasies (or as Sandro Portelli puts it 'daydreams' in which repressed wishes are represented as being fulfilled – revenge fantasies, for example, in which the persecuted turn the tables on, stand up to, or get the better of their oppressors. Thus in the poaching village of Headington Quarry a favourite story was of a policeman put, or nearly put (the accounts of old-timers differ) down a well; in the criminal district of Hoxton, East London, his metropolitan equivalent (according to a story collected by Jerry White) was allegedly put down a man-hole.[17]

Nor, below the surface of our narratives, is it difficult to find residues of a magical world view: notions of destiny and blood embodied in self-characterization, and the hand of fate in events, signs taken for wonders. Often, for instance, a story will pivot on a moment of revelation or truth, and in the talismanic importance attached to 'extraordinary coincidence' and 'pluck' it is possible to discern, concealed as in a memory trace, ideas of destiny and fate, a hidden hand guiding the subject forward. Treasure-trove stories abound in the narratives of those who were brought up poor, sometimes perhaps as a way of disguising theft. Small treats take on the character of feasts. Mysterious strangers appear to lend a helping hand – fairy godmothers or Scarlet Pimpernels who effect miraculous rescues. Inanimate objects take on a life of their own –

books, for the young autodidact deprived of real-life companionship; a hairbrush and a mirror, for the small-town girl who dreams
of bettering herself.[18]

Close scrutiny of the narrative may also suggest that we are
encountering not only remembered individuals' cultural stereotypes: 'ideal types', in Max Weber's sense of the term, people who
embody particular qualities. Great play may be made of 'characters'
who are sometimes realized more vividly than parents. Teachers
either discern hidden promise or else behave as brutes. Fathers are
similarly apt to be remembered as loving and affectionate, or as
domestic tyrants, though in a remarkable number of cases they
almost entirely disappear from the narrative. Mothers are either
omnipresent or (as in Mrs Thatcher's accounts of her Grantham
childhood) invisible. The selection of personalities, like that of
events, is in part symbolic, illustrating in one register the cruelties
and injustice of the world, and in another its fundamental benev-
olence. Any autobiographical narrative doubles as a morality: and
this can be discerned not only in its shaping, but in the mythical
elements which may be juxtaposed with unique personal memory.

The identification of repeated mythical elements in life stories
brings us close to the archetypal motifs of Jungian psychoanalytic
theory: an approach which Luisa Passerini develops especially here.
They could also be examined in another perspective to which
historians have also given too little serious attention: that of the
folklorist.

Folklorists, despised and ignored by professionally trained
historians (though occasionally raided for evidence), are in many
ways better equipped to deal with the figures of myth, and they are
also plainly – judging by the amount of work they produce on the
subject – fascinated by them. Indifferent to periodization, they will
follow legendary figures over millenia. Comparative in their
method, they will ignore the limits of national culture. The-
oretically, through the work of Vladimir Propp,[19] they also offer an
alternative interpretative framework, one which looks for family
likenesses between different figures, and 'tale types' to which the
individual narratives can be shown to conform.

Folklore invites us to think of those we record as storytellers
rather than 'informants', and to enter their own imaginative world.
It directs attention to the formulaic motifs in our narratives; the
stock characters; the standard legends. It might alert us to the
hidden morality of our testimonies, the parallels with the 'points' of
traditional narrative. It might remind us that, however local and
particular the circumstances of oral history work, we have stum-
bled, if not on a grand Jungian collective unconscious, at least on

specific cultural universals. Thus the 'big hewer' of coalfield legend, and the heroic loggers discussed in this volume, seem to have their equivalent in every species of workplace lore, and beyond that in warrior ballads too. The procedures of the folklorists parallel those of the psychoanalysts in encouraging us to take an essential first step: to relate the myths we find not to 'reality' but rather to other myths, and to the imaginative complexes which sustain them.

The example of folklore might also encourage us to pay more attention to stories, and to give much more space or time for them, allowing descriptive or documentary detail to appear, as it were, in the interstices of the narrative rather than making it the chief object of our work. *The Dillen*,[20] one of the very best books to have been produced by British oral history, is also a rare example of one which seems of a piece with folk narrative. It has recommended itself to the historian by the earthiness of its language ('It's a poor hen as can't scrat'); by the immediacy of remembered detail; and above all by the fact that it comes from the most exotic (if not the most uncharted), of terrains, The Lower Depths. But the real genius of the book is that Angela Hewins, the compiler (granddaughter of the narrator) has respected the storyteller's arts and given free play to his fantasies. George Hewins, the narrator, tells his life in a series of adventures. The pages are filled, as in a novel, with *dialogue:* whether remembered, invented, or reinvented it is impossible to say, but in any event making the characters protagonists in the drama rather than shadows. The chapters, as in any good story, are complete in themselves, and built up around particular excitements – here a windfall, there a sexual conquest, recounted in best bar-room style, somewhere else a comedy of errors. Chance and luck, as in a fable, play a crucial part in the narrative. Mysteries come and go, sometimes resolved to the narrator's satisfaction, sometimes left hanging in the air. Characters flit in and out of the story without so much as a placing word – no background detail, no let-up in pace, no pause for retrospection or reflection.

The Dillen begins with a creation myth, in which the narrator appears to have been witness to his own conception and birth. In a brilliant metaphor, the River Avon is transformed into a kind of water of life, flanked by 'emerald green banks'; George himself – a foundling – is a 'Love child' a Moses found (or at least conceived) among the bullrushes and the weeds. 'This is how it happened', George begins, very much on the lines of the 'once upon a time' of fable. The characters themselves, though drawn from life, bear many resemblances to the archetypal figures of myth, just as the incidents and shape of the narrative conform to the 'tale types' of traditional story and song. George's mother, whom he seems not knowingly to have met before he was an adolescent, is, to begin with, an English Rose – 'a young wench eighteen years old' – 'Oh she was pretty – eyes as blue as forget-me-nots, dark hair that curled on its own'; later she is the forsaken maiden, lamenting as in the folk song, a lover's perfidy; finally she returns as a figure of death, doomed to a premature grave. Cal, the matriarchal figure who brings George up, is an earth-mother – and it was in this guise that Peggy Mount played her in the Royal Shakespeare Company dramatized version of the story.

To say that memory can be structured like myth does not mean that it can or should be reduced to it. On the contrary, the autobiographical narrative is forever breaking frame. As Natasha Burchardt remarks here, discussing the Cinderella element in stepchildren's memories: 'Reality is less tidy than myth. Time and again real personal experience breaks through, at times negating the myth, taking the story in unexpected directions and finally giving its own substance to every life story.' In other instances oral evidence can become a direct counter to negative mythical images, as with the former German maids working in the Netherlands discussed here by Barbara Henkes, for whom personal memory is 'a vital weapon against a myth they need to fight to keep the respect of others and themselves'. And more generally, myths are a way not only of structuring memory but also of exploring experience. Somebody who provides help when times are desperate really does appear in the guise of a fairy godmother or Good Samaritan. Treasure-trove stories may remind us that a sovereign or a half-sovereign, to a family who lived with the workhouse only a week away, was indeed a small fortune. Food fantasies, too, no doubt correspond to real-life perception at the time: an ice-cream or a sweet becomes a luxury if you are held to bare necessities, a modest plenty becomes a feast when famine is the spectre at the door. In such instances mythical accounts of the past can powerfully evoke the ways in which life was formerly experienced and perceived. Myth may thus take us closer to past meanings and certainly to subjectivity than thick description and the painstaking accumulation of fact.

Nor, conversely, do we imply that the invention of tradition is not an issue here. On the contrary, it is a repeated concern, from the creation of democratic ancestries in classical Greece by neat changes of side in former battles,[21] to the contemporary Algerian entrepreneur,[22] or the spurious accounts of turning points in public history so dramatically remembered by the rank-and-file Communist militants of Terni.[23] In another instance here Rosanna Basso shows us how schoolchildren created new historical myths within hours: myths which were doomed to be forgotten within weeks. The frailty and malleability of even the most longstanding traditions emerges equally clearly. The Scots national myth of Robert the Bruce is not only fading but, as Marinell Ash also shows, already changed beyond recognition. The one widely remembered story, of Bruce and the spider, was never there in the first place.

The key step, we repeat, is not the crude weighing of 'myth' against 'reality'. For when we look at these inventions, the picture is not so simple. We find that the story which the old Italian Communist falsely remembered telling to his party leader, and wrongly attributed to Lenin, about shooting thrushes, is a common folk-tale.[24] It is misleading to call this an invented tradition. It is a very old tradition, reused in a new context. Just the same could be observed of Bruce and the spider. More remarkably, Luisa Passerini argues here that the students of the New Left of 1968, who wanted to recreate everything, were acting out in their own lives two of the most ancient of all European myths, the myth of the Mother God and the Omnipotent Child. It looks as if the young people of the industrial or post-industrial West may be as prone to interpreting their own lives in terms of old myths as Julie Cruikshank's American Indian women from the Yukon, who make sense of their place in an unstable world by telling fables of the supernatural.[25] They, however, recognize what they are doing. We in the West have to pretend we are inventing, even when we are not.

This differing emphasis between the spuriousness and transience of traditions and their extraordinary continuity partly reflects what we as historians choose to seek: and we live in a society which applauds scepticism, rationality, and novelty. But the emphasis also reflects the boundaries of public and private. Most history is only able to observe myths and traditions in the public realm. Oral historians are uniquely well placed to observe connections and continuities which are otherwise invisible: the continual interaction between collective memory of recent history, whether local or national, and old symbolic fables, and archetypal images and biographical frames on the one hand, and individual lives on the other. For in order to make meaningful sense of their lives, individuals pillage the resources of tradition. They also hand on tradition, whether transformed or not. We would argue that they are its most important transmitters. There are exceptions, such as the forms of public ceremonial (although less evidently its meaning); and just because these are exceptionally documented, historians have misleadingly concentrated on examining them. But the most powerful myths are those which influence what people think and do: which are internalized, in their ways of thinking, and which they pass on consciously or subconsciously to their children and kin, their neighbours, workmates, and colleagues as part of the personal stories which are the currency of such relationships. What each of us selects and absorbs from publicly offered myth is crucially influenced through this continual mutual exchange of individual experience. Oral historians have an exceptional chance to examine this vital connection between myth in personal narrative and in public tradition. We see the papers in this volume which open this door as a major advance in our way of thinking of the relationship between myth and history.

Once private and public myth are juxtaposed it becomes abundantly clear that they are inextricably bound in a continual exchange. This two-way relationship raises a number of unsolved issues. The first is how the transmission process differs and what the implications of this are. We know that transmission everywhere is through a variety of media, oral and written: this is as true of family legends as of the contrasting images of Catholics and Protestants which generate fear and violence in Ulster. But these categories are much too crude. There are innumerable styles and contexts of oral transmission: for example oratory at the public meeting, stories at weddings, visits with relatives to the cemetery, the intimacy of the bedtime story, gossip in the powder room, boasting by the men's lockers, the lumberjacks' legends at their winter encampments, competitive joking at the saloon bar, or the televised images of family in *Dallas* or *Neighbours* .... How do these and other ways of transmission shape the message, and also its importance? How far can the form of transmission explain why we remember some myths and not others? These are questions which are only hinted at here, and need to be pursued.

The second question is whether there are recognizable differences in the themes or structures of public and private myths. The evidence we have here leads us to emphasize how much they have in common: but it may be that systematic comparison from other perspectives could identify systematic distinctions. For the moment, however, let us look at a number of thematic distinctions which both types of myth share. We can begin with positive and negative myths: idealization and demonization.

Splitting the world into images of absolute good and evil is – as the psychoanalysts know well – a classic way of handling our own fears about ourselves. As parents, for example, almost all of us carry a deep guilt at our failure to live up to the image of the ideal mother, always there, always caring, patient and loving, or the ideal father, the rock on whose steadiness the order and security of the home is built. We know that we are far from ideal parents: we are distracted by other demands, concerned at self-fulfilment as well as our children's needs, simply ordinary human beings who suffer from doubt and bad temper like those who depend on us. One way of bridging this gap between the ideal and real experience is to venerate the ideal, condoning an inadequate self through confession, like the Catholic peasant mothers who kneel before the image of the Mother of God. An alternative is to look to the opposite extreme, at a projection of our unconscious fears of what we might be, for reassurance that at least we are not so bad as that. It is perhaps in this spirit that parents who take children to pantomimes roar assuredly at a Dame more confused about being a man or a woman than either of them; and they know too that their children are safer with them than with witches or ogres or wicked stepmothers.

The same ancient demons surface in new disguises. As war and fear closed in on the homes of the Dutch middle class, their once-trusted maids were metamorphosed into traitors in the nest.[26] The British tabloids today shriek at the murderous monster stepfather convicted of child assault. But not all the former legendary fear of stepmothers has been channelled into these substitute male bogeys. The press harries the child sex abusers too: until the experts discover too many of them in apparently ordinary families. Then the tabloids turn on the women social workers as child-snatchers, or as would-be stepmothers. So old myths resurge to give new comfort to ordinary fearful parents.

Myths of idealization do not usually work so simply, simply because they are difficult to live up to. The image of the courageous egalitarian soldier who became Australia's new national hero often matched badly with the harsh real memories which ANZAC veterans kept of the fear, violence, mess, and pain of war. Some tried to adapt their memories to the legend; others suffered, and felt excluded, until the legend itself began to be modified towards their own experiences.[27] One way of avoiding this trap is to project the ideal on to another, like that archetypal workmate of miners, the Big Hewer, comrade in the danger of the pit, a man of such sheer physical strength that he could hold the roof on his own back. Another alternative is the ironic myth which intertwines self-disparagement and admiration, like John Bull or the wise fool.

We can see elements of both in the Swedish lumberjacks' tales of the quintessential 'companion' logger.[28] But rejecting or displacing positive myths is probably less common than the attempts to incorporate them through a degree of self-idealization, of which we have many instances here in personal memory. Typically this takes the form either of particular stories, or the reframing of the whole life. Thus on the one hand the disappointed Italian Communist militant invents stories of lost turning points when he was ready, with both arguments and arms, for the revolution, but the leaders would not hear him.[29] On the other hand, the rich man presents himself as 'self-made', forgetting the sacrifices of his family, wife, and workers; while the convicted criminal's confessional offers us the reverse image, a victim of cruel parents and an uncaring society, made what he became by others.[30]

We can also distinguish the idealization of contrasted masculine and feminine qualities which underlie both positive and negative myths. Memories of real lives tell us of countless women who struggle as actively as men. But the heroic myths are over-whelmingly male: partisans, soldiers and strikers carrying rifles, Fiat workers building and driving cars, Swedish loggers who can saw and drink and lift policemen off their feet as if they were giants. These male heroes are admired for their strength, their courage in dicing with violence, their willingness to risk crossing the line into forbidden behaviour, above all for their self-determination and independence. The mythic ideal of womanhood, by contrast, is the mother, home-based, self-sacrificing, acting for others rather than for herself. Against her is set the harlot, who seeks her own pleasure and makes others pay for theirs. The lumberjack is admired for his womanizing; but the forester's daughter who seduced men for her own fun would be a whore. There is, in short, an undisclosed misogyny which runs as a current through the universe of myth. When the women of Madrid took up rifles to defend their city, their heroism fitted so awkwardly with the Spanish ideal of women as mothers that their role could scarcely be recognized, even at the time, and the potential it revealed had to be forgotten as quickly as possible.[31] The migrant Puerto Rican women who came to New York had to fight in different ways, above all through throwing themselves into back-breaking, ill-rewarded work to provide the means for their children to survive. Yet despite being the mainstays of their families, they have experienced the same repressive myths of what a mother should be.[32]

We should note here an important contrast between public and private myth, for the family traditions these Puerto Rican women handed down to their daughters tell another tale – just as the direct memories of stepfamily childhoods often fit awkwardly with the image of the wicked stepmother. In the public arena the stereotypes seem much more absolute. In Athapaskan fables only the men, hunters and adventurers, can cross to the world of the supernatural and return with a glimpse of its secrets to earth. Athapaskan women live equally surrounded by spirits, but their dealing with the supernatural is through the pragmatic skills they have learnt in everyday domestic lives.[33] Similarly, in the Nazi concentration camps, the men kept up their spirits with fantasy tales of battles, while the women exchanged recipes for their dreams of home-coming feasts.[34]

Just as public or national myth can weigh heavily on private tradition and experience, it particularly threatens those of minorities. So the collective memories of minorities need continual active expression if they are to survive being absorbed or smothered by the historical traditions of the majority. Nor is this dominance a mere matter of numbers. The powerful have a breathtaking ability to stamp their own meanings on the past. Our tales of Empire are of the bravery and benign administration of a 'master race', rather than of superior military technology or back-breaking slavery in plantation or pit. And today in the English countryside memories of evictions and defiant labourers' protest through rick-burning or strikes are fading fast in the face of the heritage industry's clean image of country house paternalism, craftwork, and patrician culture.

The political career of Ronald Reagan was built on his skill as a great oral communicator, whose public speeches wove together old horror stories of government bureaucracies stifling individual initiative with epic tales of the 'countless, quiet, everyday heroes of American life', still as plentiful on the Main Streets of the land of freedom as they once were on the western frontier.[35] Here in Britain, Thatcherism has drawn constantly on its own mythical selections, finding confirmation for contemporary policy now in 'Victorian values', then in 'the success of the merchant venturers, men who sailed out into the unknown to carry our trade and bring back wealth to our people': proclaiming how 'this generation can match their fathers and grandfathers in ability, in courage and in resolution'. And when the chance of war came, it discovered in the 'spirit of the South Atlantic – the real spirit of Britain';[36] riding to the reconquest of the Falklands on a wave of popular war-fervour which was drummed up by a roll-call of imperial and national epic stories, from Churchill back to Drake's Armada. As historians, perhaps taking much of our own culture for granted, and certainly sceptical of the origins of these national myths, we risk missing their real historical significance. For such constructed myths have an extraordinary power to rally, whether at the ballot box or on the battlefield. And in exercising that power, national myths and the sense of national history which they help to build also raise fundamental questions of just who belongs and who does not. Time and again, in rallying solidarity they also exclude, and persecute the excluded.

This is why for minorities, for the less powerful, and most of all for the excluded, collective memory and myth are often still more salient: constantly resorted to both in reinforcing a sense of self and also as a source of strategies for survival. In this context it is often persecution and common grievance which define belonging. The Gaelic-speaking crofters of the Scottish Western Isles still recount being driven two centuries ago from their townships by sheep-farming landowners. In the wooded valleys of the Cévennes French Protestant families show children tree-boles where their ancestors hid from the royal troops sent by Louis XIV to suppress their religion, and in the Second World War it was these families especially who provided refuge from Nazi persecution for Jews.[37] But these myths are about the acceptance of oppression as much as its defiance. The great fund of self-mocking Jewish stories and jokes convey at the same time a real sense of vulnerability and a way of coming to terms with it.

Survival of defeat or humiliation is a common thread, not only in the myths of minorities, but more widely in other persecution myths or common horror stories. The hated schoolteacher who rapped chilblained children across the knuckles for getting the answer wrong; the flint-faced welfare official who refused relief until a family had sold their most precious heirloom, their clock; the hardhearted landlord turning out mother and infant, or the employer who sacks workmen for arriving a minute after the factory hooter blows – with different details such figures recur again and again, whether in autobiography, oral memory, humour, or song. Sometimes disaster is turned to dark humour, as with the navvies who sang of the accident in which former workmates were blown up, and their employer responds, 'You're docked for the time you were in the sky'. Sometimes the story culminates in defiance: at the price of sacking or expulsion, the servant tells her mistress what she thinks of the silver coin hidden under the carpet to test her honesty, or the grown schoolboy launches into the teacher to seize and break the cane. To call such stories myths is not to deny their roots in real incidents and real social conflicts. It is rather to indicate that, however we evaluate their literal meaning, the very fact that they recur so widely is real symbolic evidence of a collective sense of injustice and both anger and pride in having personally come through such hardships.

As Western historians trained in a rationalistic tradition of cause and effect it is not easy for us to evaluate the power of symbols, the force of illusion. Yet it is none the less real for that. The dynamic power of myth is especially clearly revealed here in Rosanna Basso's account of an Italian school strike, where the process of transmission was compressed into a few hours rather than years or centuries. We can see how myths of grievance and also of heroism, of the headmaster surrounded by heaters while the children sat shivering or daringly leapt from upper windows, were needed to generate and sustain the rebellion, to allow the children to see the authorities they took for granted as questionable and to imagine, if only briefly, a different kind of future. And that challenge to the normal everyday order is a feature of myth that recurs here. The legend of a South African country blacksmith's wartime heroism and his savage martyrdom at Boer hands, for example, an incident scarcely significant in the historical chronicle of the war itself, takes on new power with rich fantasy and even magic added to its factual core, and still survives to sustain the beleaguered small-town Cape Coloured culture; re-entering history as precious evidence of the tenuousness of a minority clinging to a shrinking ledge in a harshly racist society.[38]

The mythical elements in memory, in short, need to be seen both as evidence of the past, and as a continuing historical force in the present. This power of myth in everyday life is again and again brought home by the contributions in this volume. Stories of maternal struggle sustain the Puerto Rican immigrant garment-workers of New York; myths of revolutionary heroes, fables of ever-loyal mothers, bind Italian women terrorists to a hopeless and discredited cause; dire family omens of the price of cowardice drive the Byng-Halls to bravery on the British imperial frontier in Africa.[39] Even in the extreme situation of powerlessness, the unbelievable impotence of the concentration camp, fantasies of news, of letters home, myths of self-identity, dreams of Russian white soldiers in an apocalyptic liberation, could provide the grains of hope essential for resilience.[40]

We hope that recognizing the power of myth will open the way to a broader historical approach in future work. Identifying the mythical elements in narrative accounts, whether written or oral, and uncovering the invention of traditions, certainly remain important first steps. But such findings need to be placed in a broader context of cultural competition and choice. Traditions are as likely to be recycled in transformed contexts as to be invented. And tracing origins is only one way of viewing the evidence. We hope too that historians will respond to Luisa Passerini's call to examine individual life stories – or 'myth-biographies', as she calls them – in terms of how people choose between myths, and how they change and reinterpret them, and also how their own direct experience breaks through the mythical frame: to follow the thread in the other direction.

In the same spirit, we can re-examine just how collective myths claim and reshape the past for themselves. We need as historians to consider myth and memory, not only as special clues to the past, but equally as windows on the making and remaking of individual and collective consciousness, in which both fact and fantasy, past and present, each has its part. They admit us to a rare view of these crucial processes, which we have so far neglected: to the possibility of a better understanding of a continuing struggle over the past, which goes forward, always with uncertain outcome, into the future.

Notes

1 Geoffrey Elton (1967, 1976 edition) *The Practice of History*, London: Methuen, p.82
2 R.G. Collingwood (1946) *The Idea of History*, Oxford: Clarendon Press, p.268.
3 Passerini (1979); Grele (1979).
4 Cohen (1972); Hall (1978).
5 Lefebvre (1973).
6 Portelli (1981a), p.100.
7 Figlio (1988); more generally in the same special issue see Timothy Ashplant (1988) 'Psychoanalysis and history', *History Workshop Journal* 26: 102–19.
8 Steven Feierman (1974) *The Shambaa Kingdom*, Madison: University of Wisconsin Press, p. 15.
9 Anna Bravo and Daniele Jalla (1986) *La Vita Offesa: storia e memoria del lager nazisti nei racconti di 200 sopravissuti*, Milan: Franco Angeli, p. 63 (our translation).
10 Luisa Passerini, 'Work ideology and working class attitudes to Fascism', in Thompson (1982), p. 61.
11 Isabelle Bertaux-Wiame, 'The life history approach to the study of internal migration: how men and women came to Paris between the wars', in Thompson (1982), pp. 192–3.
12 Portelli (1981a), p. 100.
13 John Osborne (1981) *A Better Class of Person: an Autobiography 1929–1956*, London: Faber.
14 Lil Smith *The Good Old Bad Old Days*, London: Centreprise; Albert Paul *Poverty – Hardship but Happiness*, Brighton: QueenSpark Books.
15 Passerini (1987).
16 Edmund Gosse (1907) *Father and Son: a Study of Two Temperaments*, London: Heinemann; Samuel Butler (1903) *The Way of All Flesh*, London: Grant Richards.

17 Raphael Samuel (1975) 'Quarry Roughs', in *Village Life and Labour*, London: Routledge & Kegan Paul, p. 151 Jerry White, oral information.
18 Margaret Penn (1947) *Manchester Fourteen Miles*, Cambridge: Cambridge University Press.
19 Propp (1984).
20 Hewins (1982).
21 See Rosalind Thomas, Ch. 14 of this book.
22 See Jean Peneff, Ch. 2 of this book.
23 See Alessandro Portelli, Ch. 10 of this book.
24 ibid.
25 See Julie Cruikshank, Ch. 12 of this book.
26 See Barbara Henkes, Ch. 16 of this book.
27 See Alastair Thomson, Ch. 5 of this book.
28 See Ella Johansson, Ch. 9 of this book.
29 See Alessandro Portelli, Ch. 10 of this book.
30 See Jean Peneff, Ch. 2 of this book.
31 See Elena Cabezali *et al.*, Ch. 11 of this book.
32 See Rina Benmayor *et al.*, Ch. 13 of this book.
33 See Julie Cruikshank, Ch. 12 of this book.
34 Anna Bravo (1985) 'Italian women in the Nazi camps', *Oral History* 13 (1): 20–7.
35 Ellen Reid Gold, 'Politics by wordpower', *Times Higher Education Supplement*, 28 October 1988: 15–17.
36 Sarah Benton, 'Tales of Thatcher', *New Statesman and Society*, 28 April 1989: 8–11; Wendy Webster, 'First among equals', *Guardian*, 3 May 1989: 17.
37 Joutard (1977).
38 See Bill Nasson, Ch. 8 of this book.
39 See John Byng-Hall, Ch. 15 of this book.
40 See Anna Bravo *et al.*, Ch. 7 of this book.

Part I

The making of myth

1

History and the myth of realism

Elizabeth Tonkin

Many historians live by the myth of realism. This may seem a silly-sounding claim: and anyway, is it not a contradiction in terms? I want to argue that to believe in the natural veracity of any narrative form is a false faith; and also that since realism is a predominant mode of historical writing, it is too easily accepted as the opposite of myth. Myth is a representation of the past which historians recognize, but generally as an alternative to proper history. I think we should dissolve this dichotomy.

All understandings of the past affect the present. Literate or illiterate, we are our memories. We try to shape our futures in the light of past experience – or what we understand to have been past experience – and, representing how things were, we draw a social portrait, a model which is a reference list of what to follow and what to avoid. The model is part of the processes we live in and call 'groups', 'institutions', and 'society' and it helps to reproduce or modify them. Sometimes these processes and structures from the past are overturned; then there is a social revolution.

Amongst our social models are books, including history books, but the representations of the past that we shape are responses to other objects and projects as well; for we must represent to ourselves the forces of production, and other forces that we experience as external pressures on us, in order to cope with them. Here I am trying to gain an understanding of only a minute part of this complex web of life.

I shall confine my comments to oral histories, although I believe that the argument that myth and history are inextricably linked applies equally to written histories. In one sense the opposition of history to myth arose alongside the construction of a written historiography. But a little thought shows that such a distinction cannot logically be tied to 'oral' versus 'written' history, and all the experience of recent work on oral history goes against it. Nevertheless, oral historians have often retained the distinction between myth and history by treating myth as intrinsically remote. Mythic material, it has been argued, is evidence of more ancient origin in African narratives.[1] And the oral history movement itself has tended to conflate 'myth' with 'tradition', and set both firmly apart from the real history to be gathered from contemporary – and that often implies Western – working-class speakers.

An oral account of past events comes from a teller. Since people who tell a tale to others wish to be listened to, their accounts must claim to be authoritative, accounts that they have a right to give, besides offering a possible explanation of what really happened. There will be culturally accepted means of asserting these rights, and having their words accepted. It is easy to see that speakers may use their social status to validate their utterance, but a perhaps less obvious criterion is *appropriateness*. This word conveys an amalgam of perceptions and judgements, made on different grounds. I could say, for instance, that arguments were 'appropriate' even though I might not agree with them: that I *hear* them as comprehensible and reasonably coherent. And the nature of the 'I' is important, for I am arguing that oral historical accounts constitute, by definition, a form of verbal exchange. The time and the situation in which the speaker intersects with the audience can affect not just what the speaker says but also determine its appropriateness or otherwise,[2] and differently for different speakers and audiences. We can easily see this by comparing the coherence and conviction of an academic lecturer to the ears of fellow academics, or to a non-professional audience for whom an academic presentation can be heard as high-sounding gobbledy-gook.

A lecturer lecturing to fellow academics uses by right a form of discourse or *genre* which, since it is an oral mode, can be identified by its performance features as well as by its syntax and vocabulary. That is, the place, the rules of who speaks, and in which order, are all cues for the listeners: they provide a 'horizon of expectation' from which to interpret the lecture, as much as do its organizing structure and its stylistic tone. Listeners who have not learned to recognize the genre miss the speaker's intended messages, and equally, these listeners recognize resonances from other arenas, other genres appropriate to different types of message. They *register* something else, in the sense that linguists use the term for the verbal differences which mark, say, a recipe from a prayer or either from a football commentary.

Once we extend the term genre in this way, we can begin to see that people without access to authoritative voices, because they lack either status or command of the appropriate genre, are hampered in representing their accounts of the past to themselves as well as to others. They may appear incoherent and irrelevant. Organizing an account appropriately requires skill and self-assertion, and since like the readers of this book I am profoundly literate, I am ill-equipped to recognize, let alone analyse the varieties of oral performance, so neglected in comparison with those based on print.[3]

I write of 'representations of pastness' instead of 'history' because that is what all histories must be. They are chains of words, either spoken or written, ordered in patterns of discourse that represent events. Arguments and opinions too are forms of words. When we grasp a historical fact or interpretation, we have ourselves made an extremely complex set of interpretations to do so. Facts and opinions do not exist as free-standing objects, but are produced through grammar and broader conventions of discourse, which in turn are interpreted by hearer or reader in order to register as such. Meanings exist because people mean and others believe they understand what was meant.

It follows that professional historians who use the recollections of others cannot just scan them for useful facts to pick out, like currants from a cake. Any such facts are so embedded in the representation that it directs an interpretation of them, and its very ordering, its plotting, and its metaphors bear meaning too. However, if you share the author's conventions of interpretation, your own matching skills are deployed so automatically that no gap is recognized between yourself and the text. The meaning seems transparent.

Gaps are soon noticed when one encounters a discourse built upon unfamiliar conventions. Africanist historians recognize some of these: 'myth' is recognized as an unfamiliar code for representing changes and events. But the familiar, that is the apparently intelligible and rational parts of a discourse, are just as much constructed. In this sense one might say that all histories are myths. To use the word myth so broadly would be vacuous, but so is the commonplace underlying assumption that myth as against history is like truth against falsehood. Yet we can see just this distinction operating in the *Oxford English Dictionary*'s primary definition:

> *myth* 1) a purely fictitious narrative usually involving super-natural persons, actions or events and embodying some popular idea concerning natural or historical phe-nomena ... but often used vaguely to include any narrative having fictitious elements ...

This definition suggests the compiler's own views on the positivist character of history, for his earlier citations (starting in 1830 and

ε the word to suggest that myths convey truth symbolically,
ο that they naturalize as fact what might have different

ιι᷉ e I will use the *Oxford English Dictionary*'s vague, popular meaning, and argue that there is a *myth* that realistic accounts of the past are unlike mythic ones, because realism is an inherently truthful mode of representation. This belief is to me a myth. We can see it at work, for instance, in the comment of an Africanist historian, that whereas some of the accounts he got of the origins of the clans of the Lango were obviously myths, when he asked individuals about the political history of their own sections, their accounts were 'pedestrian and unadorned'.[4] These, therefore, were not myths. I arbitrarily single out this comment, from a very painstaking and perceptive account because it so succinctly makes my point. Every day, as a matter of common sense, we pay attention to the selection of events described by others, and judge if they are realistic to the degree to which they match our own understanding of how life is. If the style is conversational and the content unmythic, it seems realistic.

Of course, historians know that a realistic account is not necessarily a truthful one. The contrary argument, that a mythic account could be truthful, has been considered with more care precisely because there are obvious problems of interpretation and of 'style' involved: there is no obvious commonsensical match. But I have been told narratives which mingle 'natural' and 'supernatural' causation as one, by people who believe they are equally true, and in a commonplace, conversational mode of discourse. As Ian Watt pointed out, there are epistemological debates involved in notions of reality, and his claim that the novel arose as a specifically realistic genre was backed by demonstrations of the social conditions in which lively, detailed accounts of individual lives could be considered appropriate literary subjects.[5] In other words, realism is a point of view about the proper significance of certain events. In the context of discussion about history, perhaps *naturalism* conveys better the point of view of explicitly non-fictitious representations of the past, but I think the general arguments must be the same.

It is impossible here to do justice to all the arguments over the characteristics of realism. It has become a term of art, and we can compare realist novels to magical-realist ones, or investigate the social circumstances in which different European movements for realism arose. They have had advocates with avowedly political and scientific aims, as in social realism and surrealism (to which the founders of Mass Observation were attracted).[6] Critical analyses of literary realism have been especially directed at the novel. It has been amply demonstrated by Watt and Booth that all representations are effective illusions, so that there are conventions and rhetorics of fictitious realism, while Suleiman has made a beginning, within a different frame of analysis, at demonstrating how writers who want to persuade us of their truthfulness do so. Her examples are the 'authoritarian fictions' of French *romans à thèse* which are pointers at least to some of the means used by non-fiction writers. Hayden White has also argued that historical writing is persuasive because it is expressed through particular historical modes, and this in turn means that there are no entirely neutral styles in which a historian can write a realistic account.[7]

In everyday British life, people judge veracity by matching accounts to their own experience. Truth can be tested for, but often cannot be proved: then, as in the law, the criterion of 'reasonableness' is invoked. Of course, the term 'truth' is many-faceted, and different criteria will be used in different situations. Very often, we accept that an account must be true because its author is authoritative. Judgements include the genre in which the account seems to be made. In British 'fishermen's stories', for instance, exaggeration is allowed for, it is 'reasonable'; and politicians use the rhetoric of realism to persuade voters of their veracity, although it is not clear that voters expect politicians to tell the truth. In my terms, these are both oral genres, for even if they have no features or forms that absolutely single them out, they have contexts and themes which cue audiences to make appropriate expectations about what they hear. And of course what a historian might find informative can occur in genres that are not indigenously construed as representations of pastness. It is in such circumstances that scholars easily make the illegitimate assumption that non-mythic accounts must be claiming veracity, because they are in an apparently realistic mode.

In other words, we should be beginning to explore the structuring of historical representations, not in a knock-down spirit, but in an open one, seeking for truth, and realizing that not only does it have many faces, but equally that it must have a face; and that that face must *be* a specifically embodied argument. History may be naturalistic, but that is not the same as natural. Histories are arguments created by people in particular conditions. These conditions include the very social worlds in which they live, and which, by their telling, they model and sometimes seek to alter.

The illustration which follows of how social expectation, genre, and a hidden agenda can all be seen in an 'informal' piece of oral recall, and need to be understood in order to evaluate the recollection, is based on an example other aspects of which I have already discussed. It is therefore available for reference.[8] Here I want to suggest that the 'hidden agenda' of Jua Sieh, a Jlao Kru speaker of South-east Liberia, is an implicit autobiography, and that autobiography, as Raphael Samuel has pointed out, is complex, never artless and likely to be a genre in itself; it uses rhetoric, conventions and points morals for an audience who may be expected to recognize and respond to them.[9]

I believe that the speakers of Kru narrations I have listened to are like those of my own country in wanting to be heard when they speak, and that they try to achieve this aim by evaluating their relationship to their audience, and then formulating their message through what they take to be an appropriate style. Some of the stylistic variations I find suggest too that there are Kru rhetorics which do not use 'plainness' in ways that simply match 'English common sense'. A repertoire of styles makes historical interpretation problematic, but it also makes it possible just in so far as a patterning of narrative implies patterning of claims to authenticity, and such patterns can be 'decoded'.

To see how richly concentrated a narrator's claim to authority and his orientation gambits can be, I will look at the beginning of an account given to me in 1976 by Jua Sieh of Nrokia, Sasstown (Jlao), when I invited him to speak into my tape-recorder. I had already been living in Nrokia some months. It was then a community of about forty houses – not small in local terms – divided territorially into 'quarters' according to the clan membership of the mostly male house-owners. Jua Sieh was the oldest man of Sakrapo quarter, and therefore its 'big man' or head. My landlord, an elementary-school teacher, was allowed to build on Sakrapo land because his mother had been a Sakrapo woman. I saw Jua Sieh every day, but up till then had talked little with him. He knew I was interested in history, but I did not specify any topic for him to talk about.

Much of Jua Sieh's narrative describes phases in the Sasstown war of 1931–7 against the Liberian government. This was a far from neutral topic. The people of Nrokia fought and suffered in it, as he pointed out, but perhaps they had less to gain or lose by the public recall of such history than those with government posts in the 'seaside' towns which form the Jlao capital. The farmers of Nrokia included few who sided even passively with the government, as many of the people of the town of Jekwikpo and most of the 'civilized'[10] persons of Jlao had done at that time.

Sieh's story is opened by a brief statement which translates as:

> we [are] the Jlao, who came from the high forest, who always made Jite angry, who today occupy this land [and who] from the time when our ancestors struggled to reach the sea, never

suffered privation except in the war between Major Grant and the Sasstown people.

Clearly, Sieh's opening claims authority for the narrator, firstly by subsuming himself into 'we Jlao', and secondly by emphasizing in an allusive way, which is clear to insiders informed about their past, that Jlao's quest for the sea was sponsored by oracular spirits like Jite. The characteristically Kru positioning of the topic sentence at the end allows him to lead neatly up to, and to stress, the word which will also be his next topic – war. Jua Sieh situates contemporary Jlao as a people with a sequential, differentiated history of virtuous struggle. This claim implicitly legitimates their struggle with the government too, and gives it moreover a climatic status in Jlao history. 'Jite was angry' because – as other Kru narratives make clear – the Jlao did not always obey him. This is also a characteristic self-ascription of 'sassyness' which can be taken as a legitimating, even ironic, reference to Jlao's decision to fight back against the government.

Jua Sieh's compactly efficient opening is succeeded by an equally carefully composed and variously dramatized narrative. Here I will look at it simply in terms of authoritativeness. He continues by briefly describing how the Paramount Chief Jua Senyon Nimene summons all male Jlao to an assembly, following his first confrontation with Major Grant of the Liberian Frontier Force. When Sieh uses 'we' this time, he means the interior people, and himself as actually present, as I later learned he was. For when he tells in a later episode that some Jlao warriors literally 'tested the water' – because the government officers had forbidden them to get their water from the stream – he does not say that he was one of the boys sent to draw water, covered by Jlao guns. I only learned this when discussing some points of translation with him. Yet this was a key moment, which each side agreed was when the first shots were fired. (Of course, they disagreed on who fired first.) Here Jua Sieh's narrative is impersonal, but is made significant through its stylization. After a day in which 'we', now meaning all male Jlao, fight in the capital, Filorkli, until at last driven out, 'we' divide into groups, one for each town. Thereafter, 'we' becomes according to context, either Jlao as a whole, or the people of Nrokia, or the fighting males of either entity. Actually Jua Sieh was too young to be made a *bɔ* (the Kru adult male fighting citizenry), he was a *kafa* – a youth acting as a runner and messenger.

A burnt-earth policy finally beat Jlao, and Jua Sieh describes the scene of their capitulation, and the limping return of the Nrokia people, by then forced out of town by the Liberian Frontier Force, to stay in the church until they were permitted to build temporary houses. Gradually they got better food, but also had to act as carriers for the occupying soldiers. He then describes the so-called Peace Conference, after which it was decided that Sasstown's reparation would be to build a road – the road that was finally extended in the mid-1970s to link the towns of Sasstown to the main motorable road that spans Liberia. Finally, Sieh identifies himself. He describes how he was chief of Nrokia, instrumental in the final phase of road building; how President Tolbert parked outside his house and asked for him, but he was in Filorkli; asked for him again the next day, wrote down his name, and as chief, not overseer (the newer minor official title); but, after his departure, Jua Sieh was deprived of office. He ends by saying this is the story of how he has suffered for his land.

Jua Sieh's main narrative is implicitly autobiographical. At the beginning of most narratives I recorded, the tellers introduced themselves by name and *panton* (quarter). They often go on to give a history of their town, so that their self-introduction simply shows that they have authority as sons and, occasionally, as daughters of the soil. Jua Sieh does not do this. He focuses on events which were important for him, and claims that they are crucial to his people, too. He does not dwell on his personal sufferings and this was true of all the many participants I talked to; they described 'suffering' briefly as a general state. When asked later, he said that he had had to be a carrier for the soldiers, and joked that his head was bald still from toting the loads! He was perfectly aware of his own individual experiences, and could talk of them, but his formal narration is never individualized until he identifies his own role as chief, and his praises from the then President of Liberia.

If this was the apogee of Jua Sieh's official career, it was also succeeded by a fall, and it looks as if his narrative, with its incidents accumulated, polished, and repeated through the years, has taken on a new orientation through his chagrin at this event. Certainly he, like several others, re-evaluated the miseries of enforced road building as the new road came to be made, and felt the new motor road at least rewarded those earlier pains: it was believed that the (decayed) existence of the old road had influenced the authorities, so they decided to extend it. The new road was completed between 1972, when I first collected Kru narratives, and 1975 when I went back: it is noticeable that in the 1975–6 collections, but not before, narrators 'foregrounded' the road building with this justification.

Jua Sieh's narrative is not overtly an autobiography – a life history – but it is a history which is also a story. It is plotted. The selection of events and their ordering help to create a moral order, which redeems the sufferings of Sasstown from the senseless chaos. This ordering is also oriented by reference to his life experience, but the self which is either overtly presented, or which implicitly structures the story by the choice of events described, is less an individual personality than a social being, one of 'we Jlao'. And Jlao itself takes on a personality: tough, cocky to the point of self-destruction, but enduring in creative purpose.

This 'social personality' does not replace a sense of individual personality, as we can see from the last part of the narrative. Jua Sieh is not subsumed into some 'tribal' collective consciousness, and his narrative interestingly suggests rather how his making of history had been a means of creating a social personality for himself, a sustaining and positive identity indeed.

Jua Sieh, then, is himself a historian, for he has woven his story in complex ways, selecting and ordering by criteria with which an outsider cannot be fully familiar, but which mean that insiders will expect what they are hearing to be 'faithful to the teller's knowledge, interpretation, and imagination, a realization of his or her perceptions of what is significant and worth repeating to us at the time'.[11] In trying to grasp the ways in which his account is constructed, I am acting as a critical historian, too. I have not been attacking his veracity. In fact, other evidences and accounts support Jua Sieh's representation of what happened to him and to other Jlao people. But to treat it either as transparent narrative or a quarry for facts would be reductionist and also misleading.

Clearly, there are literate, Western historians for whom their writing has the same purpose. That does not necessarily make it untruthful, but, as I suggest here, the effect of naturalism may be superficial: the truths are presented in more complex ways, and are not self-evident as facts-in-themselves. They arise in rhetorics and structures, some unfamiliar to a Western educated, literate audience, but perfectly comparable modes can occur in oral testimonies in the West, too.

Narrative history remains a respectable sub-genre, but narratives can have different plots or modes or organization. Dale Porter has produced an interesting argument that narrative forms, operating through the expectations of known plots, are nevertheless appropriate modes of truthful representation for historians. I have investigated the structuring of very long oral narratives by another Kru historian, who used (amongst other means) the well-known plot of Manifest Destiny.[12] My example in this chapter is of a narrative which largely looks 'natural' to Western eyes because of its impersonality. Academics, like bureaucrats, often claim authority by this means, implying that there is, therefore, an absent authority, greater than themselves. It proves to be structured by much more personally directed criteria.

The importance of historiographical critics like Hayden White and Louis Mink is not that they somehow show that 'history cannot be true'.[13] Rather, they show that, as I have said, history must have a face: it cannot exist without a form and forms are cues to points of view. Form can be termed genre, which is shaped verbally but also socially – even in written history – through its necessary reliance on presupposition. All accounts depend on the experience of their tellers and hearers for both construction and interpretation – as a catchphrase of the 1920s had it, 'to the pure, all things are pointless'.

An immanent autobiography, even if it is not explicitly presented as such, we could call Jua Sieh's account a life story. But that is not a simple category of oral historical information. It is simply a label for an account which could have very different generic features. We who use life stories need to understand, and more precisely identify how, whether mythic or realistic, poetic or phlegmatic, they always have to be structured, according to known conventions, in order to convey the desire – fearful, hortatory, or ironic – of this teller to present a self to this listener, at this particular moment.

Notes

1 Miller (1980) typologizes 'traditions', and argues that the types suggest relative age, in his editorial introduction. I have looked critically at extant definitions of 'oral tradition' in Elizabeth Tonkin (1986) 'Investigating oral tradition', *Journal of African History* 27: 203–13. For our construction of remoteness, see Edwin Ardener, '"Remote areas": some theoretical considerations', in A. Jackson (ed.) (1987) *Anthropology at Home*, Association of Social Anthropologists of Great Britain and the Commonwealth (ASA) monograph 25, London: Tavistock.
2 For interesting commentaries on the temporal and social characteristics of oral accounts, see e.g. Portelli (1981a; 1981b), and Schrager (1983).
3 Suggestive studies in this field include Tedlock (1983) and Sherzer and Woodbury (1987).
4 John Tosh (1978) *Clan Leaders and Colonial Chiefs in Lango*, Oxford: Oxford University Press, p. 10.
5 Ian Watt (1957) *The Rise of the Novel*, London: Chatto & Windus.
6 Nicholas S. Stanley (1981), '"The extra dimension": a study and assessment of the methods employed by Mass Observation in its first period, 1937–1940,' PhD thesis, CNAA, Birmingham Polytechnic.
7 White (1973); Wayne C. Booth (1961) *The Rhetoric of Fiction*, Chicago: University of Chicago Press; Susan Rubin Suleiman (1983) *Authoritarian Fictions*, New York: Columbia University Press. Cf. also Beer (1983), a fascinating account of how Darwin struggled to create a convincing genre for his ideas.

8 Elizabeth Tonkin (1982) 'The boundaries of history in oral performance', *History in Africa:* 273–84.
9 Samuel (1982).
10 For historical meanings of the 'civilized'/'tribal' distinction in Liberia, see Merran Fraenkel (1964) *Tribe and Class in Monrovia*, Oxford: Oxford University Press; David Brown (1982) 'On the category "civilised" in Liberia and elsewhere', *Journal of Modern African Studies* 20: 287–303; and Elizabeth Tonkin (1981) 'Model and ideology; dimensions of being civilised in Liberia', in L. Holy and M. Stuchlik (eds) *The Structure of Folk Models*, ASA monograph 20, London: Academic Press.
11 Schrager (1983:78ff.) in an insightful discussion of veracity as it works through the social relations of talk, and of other themes in this chapter, including the representativeness of the subject and other characters: 'When [Mrs Oslund] says she was one of the children who did not get enough to eat, she may be referring to the immediate sphere of her acquaintances, but she may also be thinking of children across to the north of Sweden or even beyond ... she can be speaking about specific persons directly and about others symbolically at the same time' (p.82).
12 Porter (1981); Elizabeth Tonkin (1988) 'Historical discourse: the achievement of Sieh Jeto', *History in Africa* 15: 467–91.
13 For an argument that the shape of the text cannot free it of truth conditionally, see Pompa (1982) and Mink (1978).

2
Myths in life stories

Jean Peneff

The mythical element in life stories is the pre-established framework within which individuals explain their personal history: the mental construct which, starting from the memory of individual facts which would otherwise appear incoherent and arbitrary, goes on to arrange and interpret them and so turn them into biographical events. Such mythical frameworks are common in all societies. They are especially widespread in societies undergoing rapid development and change, where individuals tell their histories as a kind of progress or journey.

Let us begin with a classic example of one of these myths: that of the dynamic entrepreneur who started out with nothing: the self-made man. Historians of capitalism such as Fernand Braudel, Sigmund Diamond, or Louis Bergeron, see this as almost a fiction. But the transformation of businessmen into industrial worthies, who started out with nothing or owe nothing to anyone, confers a favourable label on the whole business sector of capitalism. Getting rich by exploiting the work of others becomes legitimate if those who profit by it started out poor.

> America has been carried away by the slogan of the *self-made man*, who builds up his fortune and honour by his own efforts, an example for the whole nation. Certainly such success stories do exist in America and elsewhere; but besides the fact that honesty is not always their strong point, they are not as frequent as they are said to be. Sigmund Diamond even amused himself by discovering the way in which so-called self-made men in the United States concealed the springboard which had given them family fortunes built over several generations, like the 'bourgeois' fortunes in Europe from the fifteenth century onwards.[1]

The Algerian entrepreneurs I have studied also like to appear as erstwhile members of the working class, but this situation, though certainly authentic in some cases, had typically been brief and accidental. Usually it had not lost them the right eventually to inherit their family fortune. Whenever I have been able to check the facts, I have found that those industrialists who claimed they had had an unhappy childhood omitted from this autobiographical tale their solid education and substantial privileges in colonial Algeria.[2] Equally, their claims to have led an ascetic life in their youth, or to have taken part in the national struggle, usually bore only a faint resemblance to reality.[3]

Beyond the more famous examples studied by historians, the myth of a poor childhood can be found in almost all the better-off sections of society. The sociologist meets it as soon as, for example, he asks shopkeepers, up-and-coming artisans, or rich farmers for their life story. You will find everywhere the same theme with only a few small variations. You notice three typical features.

Firstly, there is a contrast of 'before' and 'after' in each individual story, divided by an event which brought with it a new direction, a mobilization of forces starting from a memorable decision or point where a person rose above himself or herself. 'From that day onwards, I decided...', 'I declared that henceforth...', and so on.

Second, there is a tendency to cover up favourable social circumstances by removing a personal history from its context, and in particular by a forgetfulness of wider economic conditions, such as the good fortune to have been present at a time favourable to social mobility, such as an economic upheaval, war, or national independence. For example, autobiographies of small farmers never mention wealth gained by the sale of goods during the war – to armies or on the black market – or by the purchase of land at very low prices from ruined farmers.

Third, there is rarely any mention of the help given by fellow workers or by their own family. Indeed, a crucial point about these life stories is that the participation of the family in the success of their leader is forgotten. Large shopkeepers, or artisans turned industrialists, have often 'made it' thanks to the hidden, sometimes boundless, devotion of relations – a brother, cousin, spouse, or even a son or daughter; but they have a particular way of overlooking these people in their story. If their collaboration were taken into account, it would show inequalities within a family, injustice in the dividing of profits, and even an exploitation sometimes as severe as might be attributed to outsiders. There is no lack of examples of the sacrificed wife, the submissive brother, relations who have almost become servants. You get clues about these cover-ups from the narrator's relentless blackening of one part of the family or the stifling of delicate questions, like how an inheritance was divided, or the freedom of the children to make their own choice in marriage or career. These industrialists do not perhaps need to justify the exploitation of their workers; but this does not apply to unfair dealings or constraints among the members of a family – a decisive point which life stories always avoid or at least transform. The myth of success through one's own efforts tends to minimize the work of a whole group for the advantage of one individual. In the same way, by attributing to themselves an exaggeratedly modest social origin, entrepreneurs make out their rise to be more spectacular.

The autobiographies of criminal offenders, by contrast, cannot strictly be considered as mythical, although in some aspects they approach it, in that all are recorded by intermediaries: journalists, criminologists, or other intellectuals. The interest of these auto-biographies, for the reader, is not in the accumulation of material wealth as in the accounts of the self-made man, but rather in the accumulation of psychological riches gained through trials survived and difficulties overcome. The principle around which the myth is built in their accounts is of successful adaptation to a hard world, of resistance to adversity. The myth is made up of ingredients from the exotic jungle of the big cities, stories of the ways in which families and gangs manage to stick together. The consumers of this myth – sociologists, criminologists, and journalists alike – prefer people with strong personalities who develop resourcefulness and cunning, and adapt to difficult situations. Themselves individualistic intellec-tuals, with a stable way of life but with 'tortured' personalities, they are fascinated by stories of people who achieve harmony and balance in the worst situations.

This type of autobiography can help us to understand the ways in which the past is rationalized and interpreted in many incidents also related by more ordinary people. We notice, in fact, that most life stories are apologies. There is a paucity of wrongful or immoral acts, of unjust or violent practices, fraudulent behaviour of almost any kind on the part of the writer. Most life stories try to speak with one voice, without contradictions and without opponents. They easily move into the tones of speeches for the defence, of self-justification or systematic embellishment.[4] Often whole sections of life are left out, especially painful or questionable episodes which could harm the image of the speaker.

Even offenders or criminals who are asked to be interviewed or record their stories manage to recount blameworthy actions within an interpretive framework that whitewashes them. Their way of explaining themselves is relatively simple: either they were influ-enced by a harmful environment, or they blame an unfortunate string of circumstances. From the same viewpoint, the most perverse behaviour can be 'rehabilitated' by reference to laudable intentions, such as 'the desire for justice or lawful revenge', or the 'big-hearted thief'. Actions which would normally be condemned lose their negative character when situated in the context of another society, or the values of an underworld, or in wartime. The ups and downs of a person's past life are selected and arranged to fit in with this pre-existent framework which justifies them.

Most people let themselves off lightly in telling their life story, so that shameful behaviour is seldom recalled, except by accident, or – with many scruples – in confessions. Another example would be the accounts of political prisoners, or survivors of Nazi camps, who normally – although not always[5] – cover up the many small 'acts of cowardice' which people inevitably have to commit in order to survive in those circumstances. This is why in life stories hardly anyone admits to adultery or child neglect, to serious mistakes at work, or disloyal rivalry: to any of the socially reprehensible acts that we often commit, but which we delete from the official or public version of our personal history.[6] The life story can be a way of excusing ourselves in public, an effective means of building an enhanced self-image. We make up our own role by making others play the stooge or the traitor. So it is not surprising to realize the importance of the image parents are given in the favourable idea we build up of ourselves. The story of the family is always tinged with fiction, whether we run it down or embellish it, whether we judge our father and mother harshly or leniently. There are innumerable famous examples. In spite of what he said, Victor Hugo's mother was not one of the Chouans, and his portrait of his father is not at all true to life.[7] Whatever Stendhal may have said, his father was not imprisoned in the Terror. These anecdotes were told to put us on the wrong track about the childhood of the writers. When Philippe Lejeune did some research into autobiographical details about his great-grandfather, he was amazed to note the liberties taken with truth or the silence on subjects such as his birth or his marriage. 'It is a staggering mixture of accuracy and fantasy.'[8] Lejeune goes on to reveal to us by means of a meticulous enquiry how these omissions and transpositions were motivated by self-interest.

When I asked some sociology students what their father's profession was, I was struck by their hesitant replies, or by the ambiguity and half-truths they contained. Where famous writers invent a non-existent family situation, less gifted people are content to give biased or censored information. For young university students, their financial or moral dependence on their parents is experienced as a problem limiting their independence, for by their status they claim autonomy, and so it is difficult for them to show gratitude to their social origin. 'Every admission of a relationship is a shortened official autobiography which has a different value according to the individual.'[9] We all, to a greater or lesser extent, falsify our social origins for various reasons: devotion to the family, a proof of our worth and merit, the honour of the family name.

When we examine large numbers of life stories of small homogeneous groups, it is easy to pick out the constant factors, whether omissions or fantasies. These principles of transformation of reality, easily recognizable, vary in part according to the social category of the author. They form the elements of myths, mobile elements which cross over from one category to another, from one situation to another, like the facets of a kaleidoscope.

Let me give one last example of the transformation of reality: the way in which trade union militants transform their past. Let us take the case of trade unionists who are non-permanent, second-rate actors, neither leaders, notorieties, nor obscure people lost in the crowd; rather those who have organized action, without material advantage or power, without being members of a bureaucracy. We notice that a life devoted to collective action, disinterested from the standpoint of the person's career, often ends in a feeling of bitterness: what is gained at the end of a totally committed life seems little in comparison with the initial hopes, the belief that social conditions could be radically changed. Similarly it is easy to see how for the leaders of a strike the battle waged brings tensions, internal struggle, and heartbreak. So all strikes give rise to a feeling of regret, of having stopped too soon or too late, a feeling of failure compared with what had been expected or hoped for.

Let us also think about underground action in wartime: it arouses mistrust and suspicions towards very close comrades, and demands scheming, whereas upright action, open friendship, and straight talking are what we normally value. How can a person escape these difficulties and contradictions?[10] Autobiography is one of several ways of getting the better of this trap and convincing oneself that the commitment, with all the lost time and wasted energy, had a meaning, either individual – in the building of an interesting life – or collective; that history has a meaning. In the myth, the trials are reversed: lost strikes become victories, failures only temporary and meaningful for the future. If, all in all, the social relationships that the militant wanted to change remain capitalist, the life story avenges the writer on the symbolic level and consoles him or her for certain cruel aspects of a militant's life: the disagreements, the sackings, the betrayals, the awareness of mistakes. Revolutionary trade unionism, the Communist Party, and the Resistance are the three breeding-grounds of this type of autobiography, which is highly prized in France.

Another effective means, of course, is to deny everything, to forget and repress the past. A totally negative view balances the resolutely optimistic vision. But those who hold such a view don't speak, they refuse to shape their past into speech, and they avoid interviews. 'I'm ashamed now ... I don't want to discuss it any more, as far as I'm concerned, that's in the past, it's finished ... I prefer not to say anything, not to think about it any more ... Anyway, it was completely useless'.[11] At the other extreme, those who have opted for sublimation are long-winded and talkative. Sociologists don't have much trouble recording them, particularly in retirement. But whether there is denial or sublimation, in both cases the truth of the events is deformed.

So the life stories of militants have to be told in an edifying way and the stories of strikes like a catalogue of good moral reasons. That is why it is not easy to write a history of strikes or trade unions from the life stories of the actors. You can end up with complete misunderstandings. The accounts which make the greatest show of the unity of the workers, the strength of the group, the good atmosphere, may in fact relate to strikes or actions where disagreement, confrontations, rifts between close comrades have been the most violent.[12] This inversion of the story is quite a classic phenomenon. In the same way, by concentrating the story on the occupation of the factory, the celebration, or the meeting, the narrators turn away attention from what goes on behind the scenes: the shady financial deals which fill the coffers, the rigging of ballots in voting to get a favourable result. You can understand why Michelle Perrot regrets the silence which, in the autobiographies of militants, surrounds all the organizational aspects of a strike: 'Nothing penetrates, nothing remains of the secret unofficial meetings or personal conversations where a completely rule-of-thumb and purely oral management is worked out.'[13]

So no life story should be taken a priori to be an authentic account. You have to adjust the screen of what is said and portrayed; you have to judge the degree of distortion, the strength of the refraction, just as physicists calculate the angle that a prism gives to a ray of light. I have suggested some intellectual mechanisms 'reflecting' the image of the past; sublimation or blackening, exaggeration or cover-up, heightening or repressing, total inversion or partial tampering. Our knowledge about the production of oral testimony, verbal styles, or what are called narrative sources has been considerably enlarged since the work of Halbwachs – thanks especially to studies by Paul Thompson and Philippe Joutard.[14] The sociologist and historian are today in a position to exploit life stories. The ways in which individuals reconstruct and interpret their past need no longer be a matter for surprise: we should get beyond methodological speculations. Our task consists rather in studying the largest number of cases and observing the mechanisms of transformation at work in real life and no longer in artificial situations such as surveys or formal interviews.

As autobiography is a witness to oneself, the rules of internal criticism of evidence elaborated and experienced by historians have to be applied to it: searches for deceptions and mistakes, criticisms of probability or good sense. Marc Bloch showed that an *indirect* use of a piece of evidence yielded more than a direct use, because it was less liable to imposture.[15] We have additional proof in the following: if the life story of Lejeune's *Calicot* is biographically suspect, as indicated earlier, on the other hand, his description of the milieu of Parisian fur dealers is very credible. By retelling his life in fictional form Calicot, with a keen sense of observation, turns himself into 'a recorder of the lives of workers in Paris, the Saint-Simon or the Balzac of the fancy-goods shops', as his great-grandson Lejeune remarks.[16]

In collecting life stories, you have to try to distinguish what is imagination and what is observation. You have to know how to pick out by experience or intuition the spheres where the narrator will show him or herself to be a good source, and where the facts will be fudged; both dispositions can be combined in the same individual, since detachment, a sense of objectivity, and an aptitude for realism of perception can coexist with blindness to what is portrayed, a wish to pass over critical moments of existence, or a tendency to systematic misrepresentation. We can easily guess why the Algerian industrialists know practically nothing about the living conditions, the origins, or the geographic mobility of their workers. In Algeria manpower abounds: the industrialists set no limits and had no scruples about sacking their employees; they had hardly any personal or professional reason to view them otherwise than as interchangeable elements easy to find on the work market. It is also clear that, on a subject such as the accumulation of family capital, the entrepreneurs questioned were in this case not ignorant but rather that they falsified the evidence. The stakes were too high to allow a clear perception of the way capital had been accumulated.

On the other hand, the interviewees showed themselves to be good informants about the world of government officials and on the real mechanisms of the administration. Government officials in Algeria constitute an influential social class whom the employers are always trying to control, manipulate, and corrupt, with the aim of assuring the survival of their firms in the face of the power of a finicky and intrusive bureaucracy. So the industrialists had, thanks to their practical experience, perfected subtle categories of observation and judgement. They possessed an explicit or implicit knowledge – which they passed on to each other or kept secret – of how to avoid the mistakes, the blunders, and the wrong choices which would have alienated them from this social class, whose arbitrary power, if not correctly appreciated, would have made their task of management difficult.

In the same way, each individual is liable to show blindness or right perception in different spheres, which are the objects of the daily activity of reflection. When you collect life stories, you have to discover which are the spheres of maximum objectivity and which, on the other hand, are the sensitive and vulnerable areas, most favourable to fantasies, bearing in mind the particular situation and experience specific to each social group.

In the spheres with which we are familiar we are capable, either successively or simultaneously, of a propensity both to mask elements of reality and to spread myths which belong to our social group, and also, paradoxically, to put into operation quite effective powers of observation. In our self-taught way we can approximate the processes of sociology and become spontaneous sociologists (without any pejorative connotation). But the frontiers of these two practices are not fixed. They are also difficult to control, especially as a social life provides numerous exemplars which encourage easy solutions. These exemplars, these myths echoed by the professionals of the written or spoken word – narrators, orators, or novelists – suggest subtle and flexible modes upon which a satisfactory image of oneself and others can be built. The framework of nostalgia is determined by society, as Fred Davis shows.[17] Many ways of regretting, loving or hiding the past can be learned, whether in the family – through anniversaries, or photography, or genealogy – or in the professional group, association, or club where the speeches of the leaders, and conversations among members, are vehicles for many different ways of portraying the past.

Perhaps the most convincing example of a collective invention of the past, which actors persuade themselves little by little they have lived through, is the classic account in families, in veterans' associations, and public commemorations of the battles of the First World War. Jean Norton Cru shows how, at the level of an institution in historical imagery, a picture has been formed of an incident in the war which made a deep impression and which old soldiers finally subscribed to, since they started to retell it in great detail. The fiction became evidence and the invented memory became an essential element of every 'real-life' account. I am talking about the hand-to-hand fighting or the mêlée with knives, immortalized in the novel and the cinema which, according to the writer and the military technicians, were totally imaginary:

> I declare that I have never seen the bayonet used, never seen a blood-stained bayonet. I've never known a French soldier who has seen more of this than I did, a doctor who certified a bayonet wound. The practice was to attach the bayonet to the rifle barrel at the beginning of the attack: this is no reason to call it a bayonet attack rather than an attack in puttees. If you consult accounts of war, none of the best mention the use of the bayonet; but on the contrary, all the accounts which lie in other places, regale us with accounts of colourful slaughter with knives.[18]

As Norton Cru goes on to observe:

> We have all had to struggle to prevent this powerful legend taking hold; and the most lucid, the most independent of us have hardly been able to defend their reason and the reality of their experience against it. This lie on a hundred lips was in our memories, in everything we read, in all the gossip of the sector. The varied examples of this struggle and these reactions, with their result, the everchanging dose of fable and motley truth in the various testimonies, constitute the chief problem of psychological analysis which I am proposing here to specialists. The fascination exercised by the legend was so great that the majority of combatants told it in their letters and during their leave the very day after the events which they were misrepresenting. Others, refusing to betray the truth, kept silent about what they knew.[19]

We have here a fine example of the intoxication of the collective memory by the cinema, literature, and oral history. Historians have highlighted other myths of this sort. To listen to surviving Popular Front workers, you would believe they all rode off on bicycles during the paid holidays of summer 1936, whereas we know that this was the case for only a very small minority.[20]

In the capacity of researcher and interviewer, the collector of life stories can extend the narrator's capacity to stand back and can facilitate a disposition to objectivity; but by mistakes or clumsiness, he can also reduce this capacity. Let us take the case of the famous Chicago thief, *The Jack-Roller*. We notice how his powers of observation and the richness of his social judgement have become impoverished at fifty years' distance (unless it was his spirit of co-operation with a sociologist which had diminished). His life story at the age of 70 (*The Jack-Roller at Seventy*) is not a patch on the one he wrote when he was 20. What wealth of documentation, of reflections and information on himself and his times, when interviewed by Clifford Shaw![21] What banality, what poverty of information, what absence of curiosity about himself and his times are found in the painful interviews given to Jon Snodgrass![22] On the other hand, Arthur Harding, although very old, regains the liveliness, the memories, the sharpness of his social perception when he recounts his life under the critical eye and through the detailed investigation of Raphael Samuel.[23] Here, the life story takes on its whole meaning: the pretext for a description of a milieu, an era, an occasion for a portrayal of customs and manners. The documentary value of a life story can result only from the combined patient work of the narrator and the researcher. It is a work of conviction, memorization, and clarification.

We have to be alerted to the existence of this envelope of invention, of approximation or fantasy which surrounds every life story. The scholar who collects this story cannot ask us to believe the related facts word for word. The scholar must provide us with the key which transforms the crude document into a historical source, and must convince us that the mechanisms of refraction have operated here in such a way, or there in another direction. The scholar must give the reasons why plausibility is attributed to one part of the story and doubt to another, and must explain what capacity for detachment in relation to the past the speaker was liable to show. I have attempted to bring into relief some of the myths most frequently found – *the self-made man, the unhappy childhood, the modest social origin, the successful militant life;* but there are many others. They have to be elucidated before the authenticity of the life stories can be appreciated. Before they can be exploited scientifically, you have to have a good knowledge of these convenient images of society and the individual: these myths which all of us can find ready-made for adapting to our personal situation and interpreting our own pasts.

Notes

This paper was translated by Margaret Donald.

1 Fernand Braudel (1979) *Le temps du monde. Civilisation matérielle, économique et capitalisme XVème–XVIIIème siècle*, Paris: A. Colin, vol. 3, p. 542. See also Sigmund Diamond (1955) *The Reputation of the American Businessman*, Cambridge, Mass.: Harvard University Press.

2 The myth of the self-made man is often built up from a few trifling biographical events which are sometimes short-term 'proletarianizations' (a family ordeal, the heir absconding, presented later as an

attestation of character) or small accidents in the handing down of the inheritance. In fact, this handing down is not necessarily carried out in a fluid way. In periods of intense accumulation of wealth, economic upheaval, rapid transformations of all sorts, each middle-class generation has to find its own style of economic, political, and family behaviour. These problems of the transferring of the inheritance from one generation to another, worse in families with a number of male heirs, are sometimes at the origin of biographical events such as family separations, splits, and confrontations which are often discreet but sometimes glorified retrospectively in the autobiographical account of the person concerned: Jean Peneff (1981) *Industriels algeriens*, Paris: CNRS, p. 56, and (1985) 'Fieldwork in Algeria', *Qualitative Sociology* 1 (Spring).

3 ibid., pp. 158 ff.

4 We must distinguish complacent autobiographies by delinquents from real, detailed biographical research in the Chicago tradition, for example Carl B. Clockars (1974) *The Professional Fence*, New York: The Free Press, or the investigation of the East End Underworld by Samuel (1981). On the other hand, in the first category there is the self-justifying autobiography (emphasizing virile attitudes and moralizing speech) by the gangster Jacques Mesrine (1984) *L'instinct de mort*, Paris: Champ Libre.

5 Of course, there are some exceptional accounts where individuals have really researched their past life as prisoners (see the articles by Michael Pollak in *Actes de la Recherche* 41, Feb. 1982, and 62–3, June 1986).

6 In the present-day profusion of autobiographical literature, it will always be possible to find exceptions to qualify the tendency to which I am drawing attention. Thus there is a life story centred on the problem of adultery in Lise Wanderwielen (1983) *Lise du plat pays*, Lille: PUL.

7 Victor Hugo's invention of his family history in (1985) *Victor Hugo raconté par un témoin de sa vie*, Paris: Plon (indirect autobiography: Adèle Hugo writing under the direction of her husband – the original 1863 edition appeared anonymously), is prodigious. Alain Decaux shows up the process of the falsification and the results of the poet's ramblings. 'A fine story. It is *totally untrue*' (p. 30). 'Sophie Trébuchet was anything but a royalist from the Vendée. But there you are, she had to be one. First of all because antithesis is Hugo's standard reflex: a royalist mother corresponds to a republican father' (ibid.). A. Decaux, in (1984) *Victor Hugo*, Paris: Librairie Perrin, shows that the poet invents a happy childhood for himself although the reality was quite the contrary: the young Hugo was torn between two hostile parents. We should note that the opposite usually occurs: the invention of an unhappy childhood. Pious images are left for descendants or for posterity.

8 Xavier-Edouard Lejeune (1984) *Calicot*, Paris: Montalba, p. 145. The book by Michel and Philippe Lejeune is a model of biographical counter-enquiry, which brings to light some of the narrator's reasons for

distorting the facts, modifying the chronology, and transforming a person's life and destiny.

9 J. Peneff (1984) 'Statistical fabrication of the father's profession', *Sociologie du travail* 2: 205.

10 'There are two wars', wrote Alain, 'the one we make and the one we talk about: Everyone tells lies on this subject ....So, all the horror we have undergone is changed into glory, and the lie, passed down from generation to generation, takes on a mythical grandeur. Remarkable transformation ....Our memory is a liar. We want it to help us live. We have to endure, and we remember well only what we can bear. We feel sorry for ourselves. The trench becomes the place in the world where men loved each other best; war, a school for humanity'. Jean Guehenno (1968) *La mort des autres*, Paris: Grasset, p. 83.

11 Anni Borzeix, Margaret Maruani (1982) *Le temps des chemises, la grève qu'elles gardent au coeur*, Paris: Syros, p. 186. To this pessimism there is a corresponding resolute or forced optimism. Starting from the idea that 'it's the good moments above all that remain' (p. 88), this book, like the other accounts of strikes, is a sort of glorification of the collective, a reversal of the real story.

12 In these analyses, I base my findings on my experience of collection of and commentary on autobiographies. See the *Cahiers du Lersco*, University of Nantes, nos 1, 4, and 8, and the general analysis made in my (1990) *La méthode biographique: de l'école de Chicago à l'histoire orale*, Paris: Armand Colin.

13 M. Perrot (1984) *Jeunesse de la grève, France 1871–1890*, Paris: Seuil, p. 260.

14 Halbwachs (1925 and 1950); Joutard (1977); Thompson (1988).

15 Bloch, see note 20.

16 Lejeune, op. cit., p. 9.

17 Fred Davis (1979) *Yearning for Yesterday*, New York: The Free Press.

18 Jean Norton Cru (1930) *Du témoignage*, Paris: Gallimard, p. 56.

19 ibid., p. 111.

20 'There have been mythomaniac times as well as individuals': Bloch (1974), p. 86. The historian adds that the period of the First World War was fertile in invention and produced many false witnesses in spite of themselves. 'However, for the error of a witness to become the error of many men, for a bad observation to be transformed into a false rumour, it is necessary for the state of society to be favourable to the spreading of these reports. All social types are not equally propitious. The extraordinary disturbances in collective life which our generations have lived through constitute so many wonderful experiences. Those of the present moment, strictly speaking, are too near us to permit an exact analysis as yet. The 1914–18 war allows us to stand back further. Everyone knows how fertile a ground for false rumours these four years have proved to be. With the combatants particularly, it's in the very special society of the trenches that it's most interesting to study how they were formed' (p. 95).

21 Clifford Shaw (1930) *The Jack-Roller: a Delinquent Boy's Own Story*, Chicago: Chicago University Press.
22 Jon Snodgrass (1982) *The Jack-Roller at Seventy*, Lexington, Mass.: Lexington Books.
23 Samuel (1981).

3

Mythbiography in oral history

Luisa Passerini

At first sight the relationship between myth and history seems to be the most adequate to describe the complex status of oral history. Two poles, one more tilted towards the symbolic, the other towards the analytic, are implied; and oral history moves along the continuum between the two. Yet, when one tries to go further, the relationship does not appear so easily defined, and the places of the two poles not clearly set along the immediate lines of common sense. For one thing, the expression 'myth and history' points to such a huge range of meanings that it is necessary, for whoever chooses to talk within it, to indicate with some approximation which meanings are chosen in each case.

Let us remember that both terms originally shared at least one meaning in ancient Greek; *mythos* and *istoria* had in common the sense of discourse or narration, each bearing different implications: the former that of project, plot, tale; the latter that of search, interrogation, examination.

It is well known that Thucydides in his foundation of history made very clear the distinction between his science, based on careful analysis, and the *akoal*, the oral traditions, often connected with the realm of the fabulous, the *mythódes*. His position was an instance of that *scandal* which Marcel Detienne has considered a decisive component of the attitude of Western thought in the face of myths. The problem became, from then on, to cope with such a sense of scandal and to find an acceptable place for what had stirred it up. The drastic boundaries drawn by Thucydides have been challenged more than once, but have seldom been radically denied.

Scandal in what sense? Scandal of the rational mind confronting the Other, the divine, or the afterworld, the supernatural, or the preternatural. Myths, unlike history, were originally narratives trying to express all that and to do it in a pleasant form. More pleasant, according to Plato, than *logos*, the tool of philosophy. In so doing, myths had an access of their own to the knowledge of

Being, and this was so important for Plato that he was ready, if the old myths were worn out and immoral, to propose new ones, which were both beautiful and righteous, for the new ideal community of the Republic. Things already appear more complicated, even on a political plan, than in Thucydides' scheme.

It is the memory of this transcendent content that even today, after long processes of secularization, is vaguely present in the background when we talk of myths. This is reflected in at least one pale trace: myth is by definition collective, shared by many, super-individual and inter-generational, beyond the limits of space and time. Still today, decades after the death of God for Western philosophy, myth lays claims to be a discourse that does not require to be demonstrated, counting on self-evidence, a last remnant of sacredness after a long eclipse of the sacred.

There have been signs, ambiguous though they are, of some return of the sacred. But to contemporary minds, the relationships that were once expressed as between humanity and God, history and myth, search and revelation, have been reworded as relationships between levels of human understanding or consciousness: the different levels of signification and meaning studied by semiologists, and the differences between the conscious and unconscious, open and hidden, patent and latent, discovered by psychoanalysts. It is along the lines set by these disciplines that the connection and contrast between myth and history have received new definitions. At least three can be discerned that might be of use to oral history.

The first myth as an expression of alienation. For Roland Barthes, this was the essence of myth – in a double sense. There was the alienation from its own origins, the refusal of myth to recognize its historical character – of being perhaps ancient, but not eternal. For history, the claim of myth to eternity is an arrogant falsehood: and Barthes broadens the accusation. Myth steals meanings from language, transforms them into form and through form changes historical time into nature, contingent into eternal. The result is a false nature that has lost its memory: it does not want to be reminded of the labour of its own creation.

There is alienation in their content too. The myths Barthes analysed – from Greta Garbo and Brigitte Bardot to wine, milk, steak and chips – are ways of persisting in alienation, even knowingly, but making it into a tale rather than criticizing it. One could suspect that this type of myth has kept the character of being a revelation of Being, but Being has by now become the negative substance of late capitalism. Such attribution of Marxism to Barthes has in this case one justification: that when he wrote *Mythologies*, in the 1950s, he believed himself to be writing a critique of the Right, of capitalist order, and writing it from a political point of view. Twenty years later he declared that arrogance was now coming from the Left, in spite of the fact that the myths of the Left were poor and thin.

I have found Barthes' ideas interesting in trying to interpret a corpus of interviews, the product of a joint research project on the history of car workers in Coventry and Turin, co-ordinated by Paul Thompson and myself. On the Italian side testimonies often talk about what they themselves call the 'Fiat myth': the hope of a steady job, 'surer than with the state', a good career, a social as well as financial improvement.

More elements are combined in this theme (its mythemes, one might say, or mythologemes): the promise of equality and affluence symbolized by the car, from the dual point of view of producing and owning it; the sense of differentiated prestige granted to different cars – differences linked with transformations of the old skills, often still existing only in labels, cultural ones devoid of real content – like the importance given to producing a Lancia car, more refined, luxurious, technically advanced than a Fiat one; and finally the car as a symbol of progress and capacity, sometimes linked with a progressive political view of the world as with the worker–founders of Gramsci's new order, at other times incorporated in a conservative decision not to question paternalism and exploitation.

A male myth? Largely yes, and concerning mainly men of the generations born before 1950. An analysis by Edgar Morin confirms this, showing that, as far as consumption is concerned, the car may be a symbol of woman–mother–house, breeding attitudes of care, of hatred, of over-decoration as well as of neglect. But it is also interesting to find evidence of how, in certain cases, younger men and women of various ages can share parts of the myth of the car, or be influenced by, or react to it.

In trying to study all this and to compare the attitudes towards such a complex of images and feelings in two towns and two countries, some suggestions can be derived from Barthes' system. A history dealing with oral sources will in this case accept that it is dealing with expressions of alienation, and treat them as just such, mutilations of personality. History will not join myth in exalting nostalgically a world of cars and car-workers.

Yet history cannot share with political polemic the total charge against myth as if it were a present enemy. Certainly the myth worked as compensation in a certain working-class culture, had a function in rebalancing one's identity in the process of loss of skill and political role. To a certain extent the myth was shared by oppressors and oppressed, owners and workers, and gave them a common language. Oral history can help in assessing the costs, the advantages, the ambivalence of those cultural phenomena.

History may indeed be called on to give the past inaccuracies attacked by semiology in the 1950s as 'today's myths' more respect now they have become 'yesterday's myths'. We are in the position, since we live in an epoch of de-industrialization, of historicizing the myth and its impact: finding its origins, studying its trajectory, analysing the signs of its end. Oral history is particularly well situated to historicize that type of alienation, seeing its mixture of good and evil (for instance the aspects of emancipation connected with the passage from a small firm to a large industry), and the relationship between material conditions and the discourse about alienation.

The second perspective is myth as part of the history of the imaginary. Evelyne Patlagean has defined the imaginary as 'the field of representations that go beyond the limits of experience-data and of the deductive associations linked with them'. The place of myth is evident. Such a history, at its simplest, should be constructing an inventory of periods and themes; but it should also show how different types of myth relate to cultural and social contexts as well as to institutions. The most ambitious historical objective would be the study of changes over time of the very boundary between imaginary and real, as we know them today: of how generations of human beings have contributed to create our own notions of reality. This would give at the same time an understanding of our own culture, and of those of the past.

Patlagean advises us that such an enterprise involves for the historian an 'insoluble contradiction': we should be capable of drawing the boundary between imaginary and real for ourselves. But we no longer nourish the self-assuredness that led Thucydides to divide the fabulous from the scientific. We are aware that some of the problems involved in such definitions have something to do with 'a border area, between the unconscious and its emergence at the cultural level', and that altogether the question amounts to a reshuffling of cards between the sociohistorical sciences and psychoanalysis. How the game will finally end, we don't yet know. Certainly, we take part in the playing.

I have found all this to be particularly relevant to a type of oral history in which I find myself more and more involved, concerned with people of my own generation and culture. The habit of interviewing older people of the working classes to a certain extent leaves in the background – at least it did for me – a number of very relevant methodological aspects: the reaction of the narrators to their transcriptions – our contemporaries care and worry much more about the transcripts and go to great lengths to correct or rewrite them; the problems posed by talking about other people, and the continual need to change names of places and persons if the interviews are to be deposited in a public archive; and especially the difficulty of assessing the historical sense of recent events. This last point includes the question of the boundary between imaginary and real.

I shall draw my example this time from research on the oral testimonies of people who belonged to terrorist organizations in the 1970s and early 1980s in Italy. A large collective research is in progress, that includes both red and black terrorism, leftist and rightist. But I will talk here about only one seminar, including women who belong to leftist organizations like the Red Brigade and the Prima Linea (Front Line). The seminar was held every week in 1987, in two sessions, one in the Turin gaol and one at the university, for women who were out of gaol either on parole or, in a few cases, totally free, having served their time. The seminar was led by Patrizia Guerra, Bianca Guidetti Serra, and myself.

This experience originated from a request by the women themselves, who knew of our work in oral history and wrote to us suggesting a collection of their reminiscences. They had all disassociated themselves from earlier positions to the extent that they had recognized, at a certain point during their detention, their own responsibilities for violence, without involving other people by name. Some of them are serving more than one life sentence. Most were born around 1950. Some are students at our university, and the university promoted the seminar. We obtained a special permit from the Ministry of Justice to introduce our tape-recorders and cassettes into the gaol.

The uniqueness of this work has of course been in terms of relationships between human beings and especially between women. Moreover, the interviews were not produced by the usual dual relationship, but in a collective way (however, the agreement was that each woman would respond to one interviewer only and everybody else would keep quiet during the narration); the interviewed themselves discussed, modified, and analysed the interviews after we interviewers, at the end of a rather 'silent' period, put forward our observations on their narratives.

I cannot describe here all the dramatic confrontations to which this process led us. I also want to be very cautious in talking about a seminar which is not yet concluded. But one point is relevant to the present discussion: the relevance of the world of the imaginary – of dreams, images, myths, fantasy – in the experience of the ten women whose life stories we have collected. It is not only that their experiences could not have taken place without it – could not have had that form, that length or those consequences – but also that they cannot be understood today without taking it into consideration.

What do I mean by the imaginary here? Which myths am I referring to? I am thinking of a mixture of ideas and images, differentiated according to the particular individual, but characterized by the recurrence of themes such as: interpretation of the Resistance to Fascism as overwhelmingly clandestine work and armed struggle; heroic stories of revolutionaries in other countries and other times; the legend of the hero or heroine who leaves home to help the oppressed against the oppressors, even if the oppressed are as yet unaware of their oppression; the ideal of a small community united against the world, united beyond separation induced by exile and gaol, even beyond death; fables of the loyalty of mothers who do not abandon their defeated daughters, but are ready to give their lives for them, to sustain them against everything.

I am not saying that the influence of the imaginary explains why these women chose the paths of political violence and terrorism. There is no evidence of this in the interviews. What they show is how it kept them going when it was becoming increasingly clear that their goals were hopeless. Not only unattainable in general, in the sense of a realization that they were based on the shaky project of an impossible revolution, but in particular, when it became clear that for these specific women it was a question of months, sometimes of weeks, before they were arrested.

Paradoxically, the imaginary played a growing part as the enterprise became less and less real, in fact more imaginary itself. This did not mean that those involved were hallucinating or delirious, as the newspapers reported at the time. Those whose life stories we have collected described quite clearly their choice to continue in these desperate situations. Their different stories and their memories of discussions held at the time fit together to confirm this and dispel the claim that awareness is just an afterthought. I have come to believe that these people were able to persist against the principle of reality *because* they could draw on a shared imaginary.

Those of my generation who were politically involved with the New Left – and not only us – shared much of their vision and imagery. It was the reality that we did not share: we did not put it into practice. And later in the 1970s it became evident to many of us that the imaginary itself was in many ways 'wrong', in so far as it contradicted the essential connection between socialism and democracy. It was outdated, and lugubriously so.

The acceptance of myth at a certain point can become an act of complicity, conscious or unconscious. Foiled in their hopes of making history and creating an ideal future, these women seized on a common imaginary world to sustain their choice of action. Clearly the boundary between the imaginary and the real as well as that between the conscious and unconscious is a crucial problem for history, especially of recent times. These life stories help us to unravel it.

The third relationship between myth and history is that of history seen as the realization of a more general but also more archetypal myth.

I will take another area of research in which I have been involved, again about the generation of 1968. This collection consists of about sixty life story interviews with women and men who took part in the student movement in Italy.

Contemporary commentators, whether friendly or hostile, signalled one particular myth as decisive in the explosion. The conservative philosopher Del Noce accused the students in revolt, in the summer of 1968, of 'supporting the myth of the new at all costs'. One year later, in 1969, Mario Moreno, a psychotherapist, published 'a phenomenological analysis' of the student movement, which is of particular interest for our purpose. He is polemical, with the psychological reductionism that might be expected with interpretations of the kind: 'young *contestatori* are motivated by personal hostility to the father-figure'. He argues on the contrary that 'they are exposed, in the cultural situation, to the influence of one element of the collective unconscious'. From its deeper strata an archetype is activated and emerges in our contemporary culture: it is the myth of *puer aeternus*, the eternal child, that makes itself manifest in the antipatriarchal, anti-authoritarian, antitraditional attitudes of the movements of '68.

Let us follow Moreno for a while on his path. To him the emergence of the *puer* demonstrates the necessity for regression, the need to integrate elements excluded by the development of our society which has kept in the shadow essential aspects of life, like emotions, instinct, femininity, sexuality. The students' rebellion was not merely a political or social event: it was a turning point in the history of culture, the announcement of a new phase, when the oppositions between young and old, creative and conservative, child and parent, would all be redesigned.

The antecedents of this interpretation are openly stated: Erich Neumann, Marie Louise von Franz and, of course, Karoly Kerenyi and Carl Gustav Jung. Let us remember that more than half of the great work by the last two authors, *Einführung in das Wesen der Mythologie*, is dedicated to the myth or archetype of the 'divine child'. With vast and profound knowledge Jung and Kerenyi explore the universes of Western and Eastern cultures, and find the child, the principle of the new, still undifferentiated and omnipotent, in spite of its weakness, in Finnish sagas, in Indian shamanic tales, in Hungarian religious traditions, in Buddhist doctrines. It is the little orphan of the Tartars, it is the newborn Pan abandoned by mother and nurse and saved by Hermes; it is the principle that lives on in Faust.

Impressive and instructive as this book can be, the historian is likely to become dizzy in following the procedures of analysis. The method is – rightly – of association and reversal, the ways followed by language and by the unconscious. One word recalls another one, but also its contrary. Everything is liable to total change: the world suddenly appears upside down and the second after it is again on its feet. Dialectic is at its height; laughter and jokes, as well as tragedy and death. The problem of historical analysis – of every analysis – is to keep pace with such movement, trying not to freeze it into rigid concepts.

The Jungian school of thought seems to waver between a deep understanding of the dialectic of culture and a sudden rigidifying of some of its aspects. The most striking example in recent times has been in the work of James Hillman. His brilliant analysis of the polarity between old and young in the *Puer Papers* gives evidence of both tendencies. On the one hand we cannot help admiring and learning from his description of the archetype of the 'divine child':

> the Hero, the figures of Eros, the King's son, the Son of the Great Mother, the Psychopompos, Mercury-Hermes, Trickster, and the Messiah. In him we see a mercurial range of these 'personalities': narcissistic, inspired, effeminate, phallic, inquisitive, inventive, pensive, passive, fiery and capricious.

If one has some familiarity with the human types and the attitudes diffused around 1968, one will appreciate the suggestions implicit in this list.

On the other hand, however, Hillman carries to its ultimate a Jungian tendency to consider the current events of history merely as 'a reflection of an eternal mythological experience'. He proposes therefore placing 'outer history within the mythos of one's psyche', reversing the traditional relationship between the two. If this gives history the central task of dealing with the meaningful rather than with series of facts, many historians would agree. But they could not help disagreeing with another implication: that history is simply a translation of an original mythical archetype, memory a mere reminiscence of primordial ideas, imagination a priori for all epochs.

There are two ways out of the last impasse. One is theoretical, and consists in a reinterpretation of Jungism, seeing the archetypes not as a priori functions of the collective unconscious, but as cultural products forged over the *longue durée* of time. The works of Mario Trevi follow this direction, for instance his *Per uno junghismo critico*. The other, which I shall choose, follows a suggestion from the seductive Hillman: to rediscover history as recorder of the meaningful. 'For us, it would mean remembering first our individual soul history.' 'Soul history' means a history that has 'digested' events, 'moving them from case material to subtle matter', to their meaning on the psychological plane. This recommendation will have something to say particularly to oral historians.

Looking for archetypes in my body of interviews with the generation of '68, I cannot help feeling somewhat uneasy. I certainly find in these life stories the characterizing elements of, for instance, the myth of the divine child. Let me briefly state in what sense.

First, the insistence on the capacity to innovate whether in work, in politics, or in personal life, is continuous. People employ this motive in describing how they invented a new type of co-operative or a different way of travelling; how they experimented with another way of teaching and eventually produced new textbooks; how they established a more democratic relationship with the boss in the office; how they translated skills learned in the movement to the creation of new forms of work in the field of communications. One after the other, the interviewed emphasize their original contributions to changing the world, not only the world of the student movement, but their whole lives. Every type of change, from reform and integration of existing structures and values to radical innovation, is represented.

Second, the relationship with what has gone before is portrayed in a strongly ambivalent way. Most often the link with the values and attitudes of the old society – such as the anti-Fascist Resistance or, on the other side, with consumerism, the mass media, and mass culture – is presented as ambivalent, allowing for both continuity and discontinuity. The deeper values implicit in resistance are upheld, but they are opposed when officially supported by the authorities. Consumerism is welcomed as a form of emancipation from parents' habits, but is also execrated for its immorality. Moreover, in certain cases, the phases of the life course are signalled by the prevalence of one or other of the two extremes: while in one phase there was continuity, in the next all continuity was broken.

Third, and most complicated, the desire for the new is not in strict terms sexualized. Typically it preserves the character of her-maphroditism: 'effeminate and phallic', as Hillman wrote. The spirit of 1968 is not presented as virile in most cases (please note: most, not all), but rather as ambivalent, while the betrayal in favour of male chauvinism is assigned to a later period, from later 1968 onwards.

The exception to the 'most' is represented by a number of women's life stories which present traces of another myth: that of Sophia-Pistis, of gnostic origins. (There are also connections with Hebrew traditions in this.) She is the female face of God, the wise daughter who because of her excessive love of the Father falls into folly and is seduced by the demons of darkness into giving origin to the world. She is condemned to a series of incarnations, from Helen of Troy to the prostitute of Tyros redeemed by Simon the Magician, from the sublime to the abject. Suffering all sufferings, her story of the return to the Father, through solitude and despair, is the same story of the return of the world to God, with the hope of resting in final annihilation. Sophia is neither mother nor spouse; she is always the daughter, the symbol of feminine knowledge and intellectuality, eternally young and intact in spite of her vicissitudes.

There are traces of this myth in a number of life stories of women. One, who did not want to give her age, used expressions like these, to describe her childhood: 'I always felt bad. I always suffered. I felt alone'; and like these, to recall her militancy in the student movement: 'I knew from the beginning that it was violent, and against the things that I loved most, like hard study on my own. I could see where they would end; when later on terrorism appeared, I was not surprised. Yet I always went, in spite of feeling different and uneasy.' The rest of her life story tells of adventures and misadventures, during which she learns to 'recognize' what she wants. When she reads for the first time a book of oriental philosophy, she is not struck by finding something new; she recognizes it and exclaims: 'This is what I always thought!'

It should be relatively easy to show how archetypes are present in this generation of 1968. Yet I would feel unsatisfied by such an enterprise. I would feel as if I was using one of those keys that open too many doors, performing a mechanical operation, somewhat deterministic, a history devoid of self-determining actors with no choice but to translate an eternal image into present terms. History likes to proceed in the opposite way: from the concrete to the collective, rather than from the archetype to the individual. This does not contradict the deepest inspiration of Jungism, even if disavowed sometimes by Jung himself. As Mario Moreno put it 'what is really essential is the subordination to one's individual destiny'. This leads us back to the methodological reversal proposed by Hillman and introduces us to mythbiography.

The term was invented by Ernst Bernhard (1896–1965), a paediatrician born in Berlin, who underwent one Freudian analysis and a second Jungian one. Obliged to leave Berlin, he found refuge in Rome, but in 1938 the racial laws stopped him working as a psychoanalyst. In 1940 and 1941 he was in a concentration camp in Calabria. He left a book of notes published under the title of *Mythbiography*. By this word, Bernhard meant the 'mythologeme' that is at the basis of the destiny of an individual. This can use the common heritage in different ways: blindly, like the Germans who enacted the myth of Hagen, who killed the hero Siegfried ('blind loyalty, betrayal of individual spirit, envy, loyalty that becomes obedience *usque ad cadaver*'), or consciously. In his own life, Bernhard says, the legend of the Jewish people, thrown out into the desert and out again from the desert to conquer a new position, appeared, both in events and in dreams. But the change in his case was to establish with it a dialectical relationship, bringing the myth to consciousness: 'the snowball starts from this point and extends to the transformation of collective consciousness'. Suffice it to remember Bernhard's description of his attitude to his guards in the concentration camp. He worried about saving them: he was not subjected to the image of himself as the victim but promoted to that of the saviour.

How shall we go forward? I suggest that the essential need is to proceed in ways that allow the individual to prevail over the collective. The analysis has to be reversed. If we go back to our life stories of 1968 we see that the archetypes are present in each, but in different and unique ways. History is interested precisely in these *differences*. Only starting from these differences can we understand that what happened, even in the minds and in the imaginary, was *not* necessary. People could have gone in other directions, could have decided to cherish other myths or to alter them, could have interpreted a certain myth in an alternative or new way. Life stories can thus be seen as constructions of single mythbiographies, using a choice of resources, that include myths, combining the new and ancient in unique expressions.

I believe that as oral historians we have a special chance once more to reverse old procedures and no longer use the myths of the past to read the present, but use the present in order to reinterpret the myths. No universal keys exist: on the contrary, the door lock becomes the key and the key becomes the door lock. This is the principle of an interpretation that chooses to involve itself in its own genesis.

Note

For details of the relevant publications by authors cited in this paper, see the General Bibliography of this book. In addition I have drawn on G. P. Caprettini *et al.*, 'Mythos/logos', and M. Detienne, 'Mito/rito', in (1980) *Enciclopedia*, Turin: Einaudi, vol. IX, pp. 660–89 and 348–63. The Italian version of this paper has been published in my collected essays (1988) *Storia e soggettività. Le fonti orali, la memoria*, Florence: La Nuova Italia. The results of the seminar were published as 'Identità femminile e violenza politica', special issue of *Rivista di storia contemporanea* 2 (1988).

4

Myths in contemporary oral transmission

A children's strike

Rosanna Basso

We think of myths as ancient, long-lasting; but there is another kind of historical myth, which I believe also deserves attention. This type of myth is transitory, short-lived. It flickers into a brief and intense life, that can make a mark on history, share its course for a moment, but immediately disappears into the past. I am speaking of the fantasies and myths that flourish for the brief duration of a battle, a rising, or a strike. Sometimes they may be recorded as false news, as terrible scares or as prodigious expectations.[1]

The way in which the eruption of such myths can influence the course of an event has been well established, and also how the energy they generate and spread is conditioned by changes in 'crowd psychology'.[2] We know that these myths are collective images. Their vitality is connected to the expectations of a group, rather than an individual. But some myths can only be identified from the effects they produce, and it is rare for a historian to be able to trace the stages of their elaboration because the process of their production is so compact.[3]

In reconstructing through oral evidence the story of a minor local conflict, between the pupils of a middle school and their headmaster, I ran into a myth of very much this type. In the heat of the strike the pupils worked out an idea of the school and school authority which was strongly conditioned by the conflict through which they were living. At the same time this new perception proved extremely effective, as a psychological means of identifying and also directing their new situation. Thus the oral evidence allows us to go further: through it we can reconstruct the mental processes which brought this new perception, and discover how individual contributions combine and fragment to make the myth.

The school strike shows us how myth can provide us not only with clues to the deeper meaning of human existence, present and past, but also with an imaginative leap to immediate everyday life, the daily history which shapes our own lives. For this kind of myth can offer us, as it did the pupils, a way of controlling through fantasy the future we want but cannot conceive. It allows us to challenge the natural; to make the impossible seem possible.

On Wednesday, 2 March 1977, the pupils of a middle school in Carovigno, a small town near Lecce in Southern Italy, unexpectedly went on strike.[4] It was a mixed school, of boys and girls aged from 11 to 14. On that morning they gathered as usual at the main door. They were waiting to be let into the classrooms, when the news started to spread that the school's central-heating plant was still not working. The problem with the heating had already been going on for some days. So far the children's annoyance about it had been shown only within the individual classes or in remarks exchanged between schoolfriends. But that morning they decided to express their anger in a spectacular collective manner: they remained outside the school door and started to protest.

This was the beginning of a conflict which was to lead the children to challenge first, the authority of the school and also, though with less success, the council administrators. The children themselves called it a 'strike' and that is how I will refer to it; in fact, it only meant a total abandonment of school for the whole morning for a few pupils. For most, it was a short strike which lasted for little over half an hour – just time enough to convey their protest, to confront the headmaster, and then to give in and return to the classroom.

For all its apparent simplicity, this episode was far from simple: for to happen at all, even in this ephemeral way, the strike needed energy and ideas. The children had to handle a reality which they had never experienced before, had not expected to happen, and were in no way prepared for. And yet they succeeded. How did they manage it?

I collected 222 interviews about the strike – 138 with boys and 84 with girls. Most were short, usually about 30 minutes, but some were much longer. I carried out the interviews at the school, within sixty days after the event. I also asked each of those interviewed to recall their own personal story of the strike, to tell me what they themselves did, their reasons for doing it, what had inspired the protest, and I asked many other questions.

The interview thus hinges on the child as witness. First and foremost it is each pupil's particular experience and personal perception of the strike which is expressed. But this is not to say that the witness perceives and describes as a single individual, detached and distinct from the others. In fact the opposite is the case. The actions of the others are recalled very vividly, not only because the event was a collective one but also because the actions and choices made by each individual were very clearly determined by relationships between schoolfriends. Yet this inclusion of the others never has quite the same intensity. Sometimes it is just one or two friends who are mentioned – a class friend or perhaps the child he or she sat next to or travelled to school with. At other times, the account captures the behaviour and actions of a more constant group of children: a segment of a whole class, or a small group of friends of different ages from different classes. At other times again, it manages to encompass the entire class.

Each interview thus gives one child narrator's perception of himself or herself during the strike. But in combination the interviews recount the same event, from different points of view, cumulating in a stereoscopic account of the strike. Thus the collective event is dismembered, and as it changes shape, neatly reveals the intersubjective dynamics which form its basis. Relationships between both people and ideas are brought to the forefront in a dynamic manner which enables us to understand a collective action through both the individual experiences of the participants and the mutual interaction of their thoughts and behaviour.

When the pupils began their protest, they had no idea what their actions might lead to. They wanted to demonstrate forcefully their feelings of annoyance at a situation which angered them and created discomfort. That was their only clear aim.

Even when someone uttered the word 'strike' and almost every pupil echoed it, their aims were still little clearer. Although 'strike' is a word in the children's vocabulary, it has no precise meaning. It is an umbrella term which has a mass of meanings, each associated with some gesture of insubordination, of rebellion, but never distinctly defined. Most crucially, the word 'strike' acquired greater depths of meaning after 2 March than it ever had before.

During the course of the interviews, when I asked the children to define the word 'strike' I often noticed how difficult the child found it to answer the question. They would either refuse to reply or else would use a concept which reflected their own recent experience in a disguised manner which tried to impress. So for them, the strike was 'fun'[5], 'like a party'[6], 'a sort of meeting'[7], 'a complaint, a demonstration'[8], 'not going to school'[9], 'opposing an order'.[10] A further indication that 'strike' had no clear meaning for the children and did not express a definite aim, was that during the protest the word was used as a declaratory chant: 'scio-pe-ro, scio-pe-ro', and even more frequently as an appeal or desire: 'we want the strike, we want the strike'. This use of the word is especially important in showing the experimental nature of the strike of 2 March, and how its realization was the spontaneous result of something in which many, if not all, of the children had shared.

This collective element of the strike leads us to another specific feature. In order to develop and take off, the strike needed the close-knit collaboration of those who had generated it. It needed a convergence of energy and ideas, which having been created, had to be passed from child to child in the crowd as a transitory but structured and definite social group.[11] It was a social group bound together by a network of relationships as solid as it was invisible, with different natures and powers of endurance but all converging to help in the common cause: the soul of the crowd in revolt.

The fact that some children suggested there should be a strike was not enough to make it happen. Because it was a project needing the collaboration of many people to be put into effect, it required a powerful convergence of interest, although this did not have to be unanimous, uniform, or even identical. The fact that this proposal for collective action arose from a group of people sharing the discomfort that inspired the protest helped its realization, but no more than this. The situation had to appear intolerable and unjust to a large number of people; they also had to believe that they had a right to protest about this situation they thought intolerable, and that their protest might succeed. The possibility of revolt had to transform itself into the desire for revolt and subsequently into actual revolt.

In the strike all this happened in an extremely short period of time and through the single instrument of communication that the children had at their disposal: their voices. The oral expression of their ideas, thoughts, concepts, and fantasies, was sometimes articulated in showy forms and loud voices; at other times in the subdued and fragmented form of private utterances, or whispers confided to the ear of a schoolfriend.

The first form is the vibrant voice of protest, the resonant symbol of the strike. The essential collective utterance was the strong, cheerful shouting which, according to circumstance, fluctuated in intensity, but always remained the foundation of the strike. When compared with expressions found in similar adult demonstrations the children expressed themselves verbally less and whistled more. In addition they spoke in louder voices and their voices echoed each other – 'scio-pe-ro, scio-pe-ro'. They were using powerful forms of 'collective oral communication'.[12]

This was not, however, because the children were less familiar with verbal forms of communication and were using them more primitively. It was rather that the meanings and cadences of their protest seemed to be different: exhorting, inciting, or even derisory or mocking – the same shout as they used when playing games or cheering on others playing them. In adult demonstrations, by contrast, the declaratory shout is much more marked and it vindicates the cause.

The protest shout serves to bind the group together and so plays a fundamental role in establishing the collective strength of those striking. It does not allow much elaboration. Creativity is demonstrated more in its compelling and lively representation of that fragmented and submerged, but at the same time, varied and fantastic development of consciousness which is the real crux of revolt.[13]

Donato: A boy saw us – he was in the school. He opened the window and climbed out through it.[14]

Domenico: A lot came out through the window. They were from class IIID or maybe IIIC. Vincenzo came out through the window. The Religious Knowledge teacher was there.[15]

Salvatore: The children who were inside the school jumped through the windows or climbed down the water pipes.[16]

Aldo: They were being rude to the other children, I didn't see him but they told me that one of them from IIIA got down the electric cable. There's a cable that goes straight down. They told me that's how he got down. I didn't see him so I can't say if it's true or not. Others from IIIC jumped out through the windows. I know that's true because I saw them.

Angela: Like Vincenzo. He got down through the window.

Aldo: He climbed out through the window and left his books behind.

Angela: Then after a bit, he went back in through the window.[17]

On the morning of the strike, some of the children escaped from the school boldly and recklessly. This is what Donato, Domenico, Salvatore, Aldo, and Angela knew about and told me. It is easy enough to understand why this action attracted their attention and curiosity. Running away from school is not usual; it is an action which violates the norms regulating scholastic life; and it was carried out in a daring way. It drew attention because it was both strange and daring and because it was prohibited.

The children also liked other things about these 'escapes'. This was so much the case that they felt the need to recreate if not actually invent them, when they did not fully live up to their expectations. They did this by elaborating episodes that had really happened, but in far less extravagant forms.

Enzo Greco realized that one of his friends had gone into the classroom, and shouted 'Cenzino'. He recalls: 'He saw me and I told him to come down. He took his books, got out and came with us.'[18] Cenzino took the usual route to join up with his friends. Then he went down the main steps again, through the main entrance. Another boy, Vincenzo Calabretti, chose a more sensational, even though not very dangerous, route to get out – he left through the window, but his classroom was on the ground floor.[19]

When related by the protagonists, these cases are very ordinary. They are not daring enough to arouse excitement. They offer no challenge. So, when they are passed on among the crowd, they have to be 'retold': keeping quiet about which floor Vincenzo's window was on, multiplying the 'escape' routes and increasing the number of those who ran away.

The stories of 'escapes' told by Donato, Domenico, Salvatore, Aldo, and Angela are significantly different from the true 'escapes' of Cenzino and Vincenzo. If their names are repeated, it is not with the aim of recalling their exploits, but to exaggerate them. Cenzino's and Vincenzo's experiences were brief, just the duration of their reckless 'escapes'. If their actions survived it was because they were stripped of their fortuitousness, becoming fragments which could be collected and reassembled as fantasies and aspirations. They provided little more than a starting point for the stories that some children were running away from school. The rest was from over-active imagination. The children criss-crossed and brought together real truths (the first floor of Cenzino's classroom and Vincenzo's window) and inserted others which were more far-fetched but not at all incongruous. These mentioned the water pipes and the cable for the electricity supply. They were now revealed as having extraordinary qualities and unusual functions: they had become instruments of escape. They too, in their own way, were in revolt. Moreover, as previously inaccessible but now conquered routes, they were the measure of the strikers' enthusiasm and daring.

Through their imagination, the children 'retold' the escapes, using them to build up a vivid picture of themselves and their protest. They depicted an exuberant conquering crowd which, unconstrained, besieged and totally defeated a school.

The escapes were all the more important because they helped to give confidence to the strikers; they spurred on the revolt and made it seem both possible and natural. In a different and complementary way the news about the heaters was of equal importance.

Then we went to another part of the school, where the headmaster's office is, and we saw that he had his heaters on.

There were heaters in the secretary's office too. So we got even angrier.[20]

There were some children who jumped over the gate in the other part too, where the secretary's windows are, and they saw the headmaster with heaters in front of his desk. This annoyed them even more.[21]

Michele and Pasquale say that on the morning of the strike they knew that the heaters were working in both the headmaster's and secretary's offices. Both agreed that this news was not received without consequences. It generated discontent and fury as more and more of the children heard about it. It is not difficult to understand why. The fact that the heaters were on showed that the school was cold. That they were on in the headmaster's and secretary's offices show that the adults in the school had acted arbitrarily, without taking the children's needs into consideration.

As a symbol both of the cold and the injustice suffered through it, the heaters incited the protest; and helped to justify and legitimize it. They proved that if the children were protesting, it was not because they were unruly or making unfair demands, but because the cold was real. And they made their protest legitimate by showing that the children were victims of an injustice. The heaters were an intrinsically important factor which the children managed to use to their own advantage in the dispute.

Some children who went to complain saw four heaters near the headmaster's desk.[22]

They said that there were eight heaters in the headmaster's office.[23]

The strike was caused because the headmaster didn't want to turn on the central heating, giving the excuse that there wasn't any oil. So he made us stay in the cold, while he was sitting calmly reading his newspaper with a good eight heaters around him.[24]

As the news spread, it was sufficient to take the privilege of warmth away from the school secretary and to multiply the number of heaters surrounding the headmaster, to give him a new image. The headmaster with the heaters was a target for anger. He was not the only one responsible for the cold suffered by the children, but he arrogantly set himself apart from their discontent and their needs. Such a headmaster was asking to be challenged, because he excluded the possibility of any mutual dialogue.

In fact, the school headmaster that morning asked the children to believe him when he had said that he was not responsible for the cold. He had blamed the local council, and asked them to trust him when he promised to resolve the problem. When confronted with his request, the children were perplexed. But the evidence of the heaters removed their uncertainty and made the conflict much simpler and more understandable for them. It made the headmaster an enemy figure and defined the conflict in the simple terms of head-on confrontation.

How far can these transient children's stories of their escapes and the school heaters be thought of as mythical constructions? Does the idea of myth help us to understand these episodes? I think it is difficult to talk about myth if one believes that myth is distinguished by its content or by its powers of survival. It is more helpful to think, like Roland Barthes, of myth as a 'system of communication', and more particularly as 'a second semiologic system', functioning through the distortion of the meanings of the signs which it appropriates. 'Myth is a word which has been stolen and given back. Only that the word was not exactly the same when it was returned.'[25] The signs which Barthes explicitly has in mind are graphic and linguistic ones. But the case I have described here leads me to believe that 'actions' can be prey to myth too, if there is a collective action that puts them at the centre of a system of communication. This is all the more the case if that collectivity is incandescent because it is in revolt. As these flickering strike myths demonstrate, the unfamiliar action of rebellion not only fires fantasy, but feeds on it, demands it, draws life from it.

Notes

1 Bloch (1921).
2 Classic references include Le Bon (1895) and Freud (1921).
3 B. Baczko (1979) 'Immaginazione sociale', in *Enciclopedia*, vol. VIII, Turin: Einaudi.
4 Among other authors who have studied children in revolt are: D. Marson (1973) *Children's Strikes in 1911*, Oxford, History Workshop Pamphlet; B. Edwards (1974) *The Burston School Strike*, London: Lawrence Wishart; P. Thompson (1975) 'The war with adults', in *Oral History* 3 (2); S. Humphries (1981) *Hooligans or Rebels?*, Oxford: Blackwell.
5 Rosario Pinto, class IE, age 12 years 9 months, interviewed on 23 March 1977.
6 Marilisa Lanzillotti, class IIF, age 12, 2 April 1977.
7 Caterina Pepe, class IB, age 11 years 7 months, 24 March 1977.
8 Domenico Saponaro, class IIA, age 11 years 7 months, 21 March 1977.
9 Domenico Mola, class IF, age 12 years 4 months, 22 March 1977.
10 Antonio Galiandro, class IG, age 12 years 9 months, 7 March 1977.
11 Among the numerous works on the crowd, those which especially influenced me include: J. Michelet (1843–53) *Histoire de la Révolution Française*, Paris: Chamerot; G. Lefebvre (1932) *La grande peur de*

1789, Paris: Colin; L. Chevalier (1958) *Classes laborieuses, classes dangereuses*, Paris: Plon; G. Rudé (1964) *The Crowd in History 1730–1848*, New York: John Wiley; E. P. Thompson (1971) 'The moral economy of the English crowd in the XVIIIth century', *Past and Present* 50.

12 A. Portelli (1981) 'I metalmeccanici e la funzione poetica. Espressivita orale di base nella manifestazione nazionale del 2 dicembre 1977', *I giorni cantati* 2/3: 43–60.

13 On 'conversation' as an important system of communication in revolts see G. Lefebvre (1934) 'Foules historiques, les foules révolutionnaires', *Annales historiques de la Révolution française* 1: 1–26.

14 Donato Caporusso, class IB, age 11 years 11 months, 8 March 1977.

15 Domenico Galeone, class IG, age 11 years 10 months, 7 March 1977.

16 Salvatore Saracino, class ID, age 11 years 5 months, 29 March 1977.

17 Aldo Sacchi, class IIA, age 11 years 3 months; Angela Natola, class IIA, age 13 years 2 months, 22 March 1977.

18 Enzo Greco, class IF, age 13 years 7 months, 22 March 1977.

19 Vincenzo Calabretti, class IIIC, age 14 years 2 months, 17 March 1977.

20 Michele Saponaro, class IIIF, age 13 years 10 months, 14 April 1977.

21 Pasquale Carlucci, class IE, age 12 years 6 months, 23 March 1977.

22 Renato Natola, class IE, age 11 years 5 months, 23 March 1977.

23 Vito Luperti, class IF, age 11 years 11 months, 22 March 1977.

24 Franco Marino, class IF, age 10 years 11 months, 22 March 1977.

25 Barthes (1957).

Part II

Nationhood and minorities

5

The Anzac legend

Exploring national myth and memory in
Australia

Alistair Thomson

Memory is a battlefield. We fight within ourselves to make a
particular memory of our experiences, and to repress alternative
memories. We also engage in a public struggle between different
versions of the past. Since Australian soldiers first went into battle
at Gallipoli in 1915 there has been a battle for the memory of
Australians at war, to create an 'Anzac' legend.[1]

I will begin by describing two versions of the legend which have
been influential in the public struggle for the memory of the
'Anzacs' (the men of the Australian and New Zealand Army Corps,
who were also nicknamed 'diggers' – in Australia the New Zealand
role is often forgotten). Shifting from 'public' to 'private' memories,
but aware of the inadequacy of those terms, I will describe some
interviews which I conducted in 1983 with First World War
working-class diggers and will assess my traditional oral history
approach which used individual memories to debunk public myth. I
will then introduce an alternative 'popular memory' approach and
discuss how I have been using that approach in more recent
interviews.

Charles Bean, the Australian official war correspondent and
historian of the First World War, and founder of the Australian War
Memorial (the national museum and memorial for servicemen and
women), did more than anyone to create the dominant Anzac
legend. His work serves as a useful guide to the origins and nature of
the legend. Like most contemporary commentators, Bean
eulogized the first landing at Gallipoli as the true birth of the
Australian nation. The convict settlement of 1788 was still an
embarrassing memory, and the political birth of the Commonwealth of Australia in 1901 had created a nation only in name.
Gallipoli was regarded as its baptism of fire, when 'the Australian
nation came to know itself'. Thus for more than seventy years
Australians have commemorated Anzac Day – the anniversary of
the landing at Gallipoli on 25 April 1915 – as our most important

national ritual and holiday. On Australia Day, which commemorates white settlement (or invasion) we go to the beach. On Anzac
Day hundreds of thousands of people attend memorial services and
marches around the country.

Nationhood was achieved by the successful military test of
Australian manhood. For Bean, the war was 'the first revelation of
Australian character'. Bean's Australian soldier was enterprising
and independent; loyal to his mates and to his country, bold in
battle, but cheerfully undisciplined when out of the line. The
Australian army suited his egalitarian nature: relations between
officers and other ranks were friendly and respectful, and any man
with ability could rise from the ranks. These qualities, fostered in
the Australian bush, discovered and immortalized in war, were said
to typify Australians and Australian society, a frontier land of equal
opportunity in which enterprising people could make good. This
was the nation which 'came of age' at Gallipoli.

Bean was only one of many Anzac myth-makers, but his influence
was profound. His war correspondence and histories have been the
model for most subsequent writing about the war. His proudest
monument to the diggers, the Australian War Memorial in Canberra, ranks after the Sydney Opera House as the second most
popular tourist attraction in the country. And now Australian film
producers – the most powerful myth-makers of our time – have
adapted and popularized Bean's story of the Anzacs for a fresh
audience.

Inevitably, there are new features in the recent cinematic
memory of Australians at war. For example, Peter Weir's successful
film *Gallipoli*, and the *Anzacs* television series (the most expensive
mini-series ever made in Australia) attempt to portray the horrors
and disillusionment of the First World War. Yet the movie
memories still dwell on the national character of the diggers and not
enough on the degradation of war. Like soldiers in every army, the
Anzacs were frightened as well as brave, victims as much as heroes.
But as one review of *Gallipoli* noted, young Australians come out of
these films inspired by the example of Anzac heroes. Just as Bean's
eulogy for the Anzacs transcended the grim realities of the war, in
the new wave of Anzac films, war is still an adventure.

The focus on the national characteristics of the diggers also
conceals the divisions within the army and in Australian society.
Class is recognized as an issue in every Anzac film, but the wealthy
grazier's son and the working-class lad invariably find their Australian brotherhood – and to quote the poet C. J. Dennis, 'a noo
glad pride that ain't the pride o' class' – in the trenches. If there are
class enemies in Australian war films, they are the autocratic British

generals who order the soldiers to their deaths. But the films too easily use these scapegoats to acquit Australian military and political leaders.

They sustain other historical distortions. Women are always cast in secondary roles, so that the only significance of their lives is their relationship with Australian men (the legend identifies the national character as masculine). Egyptian traders, Turkish soldiers, and Australian Aborigines are usually comic caricatures. A conservative Anzac legend is perpetuated by soldier heroes who believe in nation before class, man before woman, white before black or brown, and physical bravery before moral courage. The common national identity and purpose which the legend invokes ignores the inequalities and conflicts within Australian society.

Bean's writing and recent Anzac films are only two examples of the ways in which the experience of Australians at war have been made into a potent national legend. And the jump from post-First World War official history to contemporary film neglects seventy years of struggle over the memory of the Anzacs. Contrary to today's image of national heroes, the Australian soldiers returned home in 1919 with a schizophrenic public identity. They were the loyal Anzacs who had won honour for themselves and their country. They were also the rebellious, indisciplined diggers, perceived as a threat by both military and civilian authorities. They *were* a threat, as they were throughout Europe. Working-class soldiers faced a desperate struggle when they came home. Jobs were scarce and repatriation assistance miserly. The unemployed digger became a potent symbol of the failure of the promise that the Anzacs would return to a land fit for heroes. 1919 was one of the most violent years in white Australian history, as dissatisfied and sometimes violent diggers were easily mobilized by radical or loyalist political groups.

The Australian establishment was scared, and determined to contain digger militancy and create a safe identity for ex-servicemen. Police and special constables, as well as more secretive organizations, were enlisted. They controlled soldier riots with brutal force. But in the long run it was more effective to harness the diggers' political energy. An alliance of citizen and ex-servicemen conservatives created and controlled the Returned Sailors' and Soldiers' Imperial League of Australia (now the RSL) which was granted government recognition as the official representative of ex-servicemen 'in return for defending the powers that be'.

This political struggle was intimately connected with the struggle over the memory of the war. The RSL and government committees organized memorial celebrations which offered the status of national heroes to alienated ex-servicemen. The militancy of some working-class diggers was channelled into carefully controlled Anzac Day parades. Rituals of remembrance mapped out what could be publicly recalled and silenced alternative memories. There was *some* opposition to official commemoration. For example, unemployed ex-servicemen campaigned against the creation of the Melbourne Shrine of Remembrance, arguing that it glorified war and that they wanted a more utilitarian hospital instead. But this and other challenges to the creation of the dominant Anzac legend were defeated, and are now forgotten.

Other histories are beginning to recall and explain the embattled development of the Anzac legend. That public struggle, and the eventual public dominance of some versions at the expense of others, is an essential context for understanding the tensions and changes within the memories of old soldiers. I want to shift now to the individual memories which have been entangled by the public versions of the past, and to outline two different approaches to oral history.

In 1983 I began to interview veterans of the First World War who lived in the industrial western suburbs of Melbourne. I wanted to compare their memories of the war and its aftermath with the public legend. My first impressions were not of the war. When I was invited into small weatherboard cottages or high-rise council flats, and listened to stories of battling lives, of hard work and unemployment, the myth of the land of opportunity – which I had grown up with – became a nonsense.

Early on in the project my interest was diverted by four 'radical' diggers. These were soldiers who were involved in radical politics during and after the war, organizing the men in the trenches to vote 'No' in the 1916 and 1917 conscription referenda, or joining the socialist or peace movements when they came home. These men scorned the image of the democratic army from the new world of opportunity. They had remained in the ranks to suffer the war and, at times, resist military authority. They had their own pride in the Australian army, the only army which protected its men from the death penalty, but in the postwar world they discovered that selective praise for the Anzacs too easily became a patriotic celebration of warriors, war, and nation.

When these men came home from the war they opposed the conservative takeover of ex-servicemen politics. They were suspicious of the commemorative patriotism of Anzac Day (though they did enjoy the chance to meet up with wartime mates) and opposed the shrines of remembrance that were built during the Depression. But for their radicalism they were easily labelled disloyal and they were dismissed for not being 'genuine diggers'.

They were cast out of the RSL and their version of the war was excluded from the Anzac legend.

Exclusion was a painful process. Some men threw away their medals; one used his as fishing sinkers. Others stayed at home on Anzac Day. Even now they switch off Anzac movies because 'it was not what I experienced in the war'. For many years they were unable to talk about their dissenting war memories because they did not feel that they were valued. I hope to be able to publish some of our interviews so that their version of the war will not be forgotten.

Recently my interest has shifted back to the diggers I interviewed who were not involved in radical politics, and who did not have an articulate oppositional memory. Their experiences of brutality and hardship in the war and inter-war years often contradicted Anzac Day oratory. Yet their memories had been scrambled and entangled by the legend. For sixty years they had been members of the RSL and attended Anzac Day parades. Many of them had read the official history of the war – purchased by time payments from the agents who came to their workplaces and clubs – and quoted anecdotes as if they were their own experiences. In some interviews I felt as if I was listening to the script of the film *Gallipoli*. Their use of ambiguous notions like 'mateship' (was your officer a mate?), or their understanding of who was a real 'digger', was clouded by official definitions. Memories were also reshaped by present-day situations and emotions. Lonely old men living in council bed-sits were eager to recall the camaraderie of the army, or the adventure of the war. I could not simply use memory as a pure record to challenge public myths.

The 'popular memory' approach, devised by the Popular Memory Group at the Centre for Contemporary Cultural Studies in Birmingham, is useful precisely because it rejects the notion of memory as historical record – though it does not reject the use of memory out of hand like the traditionalists who condemn oral sources for their distortion. Instead the 'distortions' produced by the effect of 'public' upon 'private' memories become the key to understanding the powerful role of the past in the present. Thus the work of the Popular Memory Group was inspired by the need for the Left to explain the rise and popularity of Conservative forms of nationalism which rely upon a particular version of the national past – exemplified by the use of a Churchillian memory of the Second World War during the Falklands war. The group explained this phenomenon in terms of the subjective resonance of public versions of the past. They have developed a complex and eclectic theory of individual memory. For the purposes of my argument here, I will sketch the bare bones of that theory.

We compose our memories to make sense of our past and present lives. 'Composure' is the aptly ambiguous term used by the Popular Memory Group to describe the process of memory-making. In one sense we compose or *construct* our memories. From the moment we experience an event we use the meanings of our culture to make sense of it. Over time we *re*-member our experiences, as those public meanings change. There is a constant negotiation between experience and sense, private and public memory.

In another sense we 'compose' memories which help us to feel relatively comfortable with our lives, to give us a feeling of composure. Some memories are contradictory, painful, and 'unsafe'. They do not easily accord with our present identity, or else their inherent traumas or contradictions have never been resolved. We may not recognize the difficulty, but we deal with these memories by repressing them, or remaking them so they are less painful, or perhaps by attempting to understand and resolve the difficulty. We seek composure, an alignment of our past, present, and future selves.

One key theoretical recognition – and the link between the two senses of composure – is that the apparently private process of composing safe memories is in fact very public. Our memories are risky and painful if they do not conform with the public norms or versions of the past. We construct and contain our memories so that they will fit with what is publicly acceptable; or we find safety in smaller 'publics' or peer groups, which may be socially or politically marginal. This is a necessary process of personal repression, as the cost of exclusion can be psychologically devastating. Witness the radical diggers of my interviews who are still traumatized by their exclusion from the Anzac legend. One old man, the last surviving digger in his town, would dearly love to attend and speak at the Anzac ceremony, but knows that the RSL will not even invite him to attend – and he is too proud to ask.

Conversely, it is not surprising that many ex-servicemen did adopt the proud public identity of the Anzacs in the postwar years. Or that in seventy years of negotiation with that legend individual memories have been reworked to become comfortable and safe. My challenge has thus been to understand the resonance of the Anzac legend in terms of its interactions with individual memory and identity. For that purpose I have devised a popular memory approach for oral history interviews.

In 1987 I interviewed again some of the old diggers with whom I had first talked in 1983. Instead of using the chronological life story approach of my initial interviews, I focused on four key inter-actions: between public and private, past and present, memory and identity, and interviewer and interviewee. This thematic approach was relatively easy because I had already developed a trusting relationship with each of the men, and had transcripts of their life stories as a basis for new questions. This allowed me to ask searching, personal questions of each man. If I had not done the original interviews I would have needed to integrate the life story and the new approach.

I tried a number of different ways of probing these four key interactions. First, I made the public myth a *starting* point for questions; what was your response to various war books and films, past and present, and to Anzac Day and war memorials? How well do they represent your own experiences; how do they make you feel? We also focused on specific features of the legend: was there a distinctive Anzac character? How true was it for your own nature and experience? Were you so very different from the soldiers of other armies? How did you respond to military authority, and did you feel that the Anzacs deserved their reputation (whatever that was)?

I asked each man to define certain key words in his own words – 'digger', 'mateship', 'the spirit of Anzac' – and discovered that some of the men who were uncritical of the legend had contrary and even contradictory understandings of its key terms. Others stuck determinedly to a conventional portrayal of the war, even though aspects of their own experience seemed to challenge it. The negotiations between public and private sense worked differently for each man, though all were framed by the dominant legend. As a follow-up to this section of the interview we also discussed contemporary (as well as past) battles over the legend, such as the recent attempts by feminists and black activists to make *their* pasts live on Anzac Day. The men who were critical of the legend's depiction of the diggers were also more likely to be critical of its exclusion of other Australians.

Another section of discussion focused on experience and personal identity: how did you feel about yourself and your actions at key moments – enlistment, battle, return? What were your anxieties and uncertainties? How did you make sense of your experiences and how did other people define you? How were you included or excluded, what was acceptable and unacceptable behaviour – what was not 'manly' – and how and why were some men ostracized? I was not surprised to discover that some men were made to feel inadequate because of their timidity in battle. I *was* surprised to find that others felt excluded by the boozing, brawling, and womanizing reputations of the digger, an aspect of the legend that has only a grudging recognition in official Anzac Day rhetoric, but which has been popular in cartoons and films.

Of course these memories, and the relative composure of memory, have shifted over time, so we discussed how postwar events – such as homecoming, the Depression and the Second World War, domestic change and even old age – affected identity and memory. For example, it became clear that many men felt that their wartime fears and sense of powerlessness were not recognized by the manly stereotype of the postwar legend. These ex-servicemen were racked by feelings of inadequacy, sometimes expressed in dreams, stuttering, and amnesia. Like the radical diggers who were alienated by the politics of the legend, they retreated into silence about the war.

Yet by the 1980s these men felt able and sufficiently esteemed to talk about the war. This is partly due to the renewed interest of old men in their youth. They are also enjoying the respect, even veneration, with which the few remaining diggers are treated, regardless of their particular experiences. But it is also because aspects of their experience which were once taboo are now publicly acceptable. They can now talk easily about the experience of 'war as hell', and of their fears and feelings of inadequacy as soldiers, because – perhaps since Vietnam altered public perceptions of war – those aspects of the war are portrayed in the history books and films of the 1980s. The new interview approach thus showed me that what it is possible to remember and articulate changes over time, and how this can be related to shifts in public perception.

Another related and difficult focus of the new interviews was upon the ways memories are affected by strategies of containment, by ways of handling frustration, failure, loss, or pain. This required a sensitive balance between potentially painful probing and reading between the lines of memory. What is possible or impossible to remember, or even to say aloud? What are the hidden meanings of silences and sudden changes of subject? Deeply repressed experiences or feelings may be discharged in less conscious forms of expression, in past and present dreams, errors and Freudian slips, body language, and even humour, which is often used to overcome or conceal embarrassment and pain. For many oral historians, psychology is an alien theoretical world, vaguely perceived in the ways that the 'unconscious' and 'repression' have entered everyday conversation. But just the barest gleaning of psychological theory can be rewarding for oral historians. For example, descriptions of war-related dreams enriched my understanding of the personal impact of the war, and of what could not be publicly expressed.

But this approach also raises ethical and political dilemmas for oral historians. Interviewing which approaches a therapeutic relationship may be damaging for the interviewee as well as rewarding for the interviewer. It requires great care and sensitivity, and a cardinal rule that the well-being of the interviewee must always come before the interests of research. At times I had to stop a line of questioning in an interview, or was asked to stop, because it was too painful. Unlike the therapist, the oral historian may not be around to put together the pieces of memories which are no longer safe.

A partial resolution is to make the interview, and the interview relationship, a more open process. I tried to discuss how my questions affected remembering, and what was difficult to say to *me*. I talked about my own interests and role, to encourage dialogue instead of monologue, even to play devil's advocate with statements which breached every oral history guideline – 'Isn't the memory of Anzac irrelevant today?'

I am less confident about the political dilemma. It is relatively easy to co-operate in the production of a history which gives public affirmation to people whose lives and memories have been made marginal, and which challenges their oppression. But how to use a memory to combat public myth when the person has already found a safe refuge within that myth? My own uneasy compromise has been to adopt different roles in different circumstances. Where possible, I like to work with people that I interview in making histories. But often that is not possible and, so long as I treat an interviewee with sensitivity and respect, it seems necessary to accept the role of the historian who makes his or her own sense of the material. It is a dilemma which as oral historians we need to consider more openly and more often.

Note

1 The classic version of the Anzac legend is C.E.W. Bean (1921, 1924) *The Story of Anzac: Official History of Australia in the War of 1914–1918*, vols 1–2, Sydney: Angus and Robertson. For the reworking of the legend in contemporary film see Bill Gammage, David Williamson, and Peter Weir (1981) *The Story of 'Gallipoli'*, Harmondsworth, Middx: Penguin. The tapes and transcripts of my own interviews are lodged in the library of the Australian War Memorial in Canberra, and I have analysed the interviews in more detail in my University of Sussex doctoral thesis 'The Great War and Australian memory' (forthcoming), and in two short essays: 'Passing shots at the Anzac legend', in Verity Burgmann and Jenny Lee (eds) (1988) *A Most Valuable Acquisition: A People's History of Australia since 1788*, Harmondsworth, Middx: McPhee Gribble/Penguin; and (1988) 'The return of a soldier', *Meanjin* 4: 709–16.

The Popular Memory Group's most recent theoretical work is still unpublished – though I'd like to thank Richard Johnson and Graham Dawson for letting me read drafts. The relatively crude initial statement of their approach is 'Popular memory: theory, politics, method', in Richard Johnson *et al.* (eds) (1982) *Making Histories*, London: Hutchinson.

6

William Wallace and Robert the Bruce

The life and death of a national myth

Marinell Ash

In 1907 that indefatigable campaigner for world peace, Andrew Carnegie, achieved one of his great ambitions: a meeting with the Emperor of Germany – which he imagined as a preliminary to the meeting he hoped to arrange between the Kaiser and Theodore Roosevelt. The emperor took the occasion to chide Carnegie about his well-known dislike of kings. In his *Autobiography* Carnegie tells us that he responded by giving the Kaiser a crash course in Scottish history:

> 'No your Majesty, I do not like kings, but I do like a man behind a king when I find him.'
> 'Ah! [the emperor replies] there is one king you like, I know, a Scottish king, Robert the Bruce. He was my hero in my youth. I was brought up on him.'
> 'Yes, Your Majesty, so was I, he lies buried in Dunfermline Abbey, in my native town ....But Bruce was much more than a king, Your Majesty, he was the leader of his people. And not the first; Wallace the man of the people comes first ...'[1]

This bizarre exchange illustrates not only the long life of the Wallace and Bruce national myth, but its power to affect human actions into the present century – often outside Scotland. In 1915, for example, there was a Black nationalist revolt in the highlands of Nyasaland, inspired in part by the Revd John Chilembwe. He, and other native church leaders had, of course, been educated in Church of Scotland schools where Wallace and Bruce were part of the daily pedagogic diet. Not surprisingly, William Wallace was cited as justification for this revolt against white oppression.[2] On the other side of the mythological coin, as late as 16 October 1946 the *Manchester Guardian* could claim, in a leader on the Nuremberg trials and executions; 'Could any Englishman doubt that justice was done, if brutally, when Wallace was executed?'

These examples of the continuing influence of Wallace and Bruce could be repeated many times and in many places over the past few centuries. Wallace and Bruce were part of the intellectual baggage of the Scottish diaspora – 'The Bible of the Scotch people', in the words of the eighteenth-century historian, David Dalrymple, Lord Hailes.[3] Both figures remained potent models of behaviour and national rallying points for Scots at home – and in alien climes. Andrew Carnegie again: 'It gave me a pang to find when I reached America that there was any other country which pretended to have anything to be proud of. What was a country without Wallace, Bruce and Burns?'[4]

And yet Scotland herself has become 'a country without Wallace, Bruce ...' in the present century. If they exist at all, it is as partisan and ideological figures rather than national ones. For example, it is the Scottish National Party who rally at Bannockburn on the anniversary of Bruce's decisive defeat of the English in midsummer 1314. William Wallace, the son of a knight (of gentle, but not aristocratic birth), has become a proletarian hero who – according to the modern reworking of the myth – was a victim of the class conflict and the conspiracy theory of historiography. In August 1985, during the run of Sidney Goodsir Smith's *The Wallace* at the Edinburgh Festival, this letter appeared in *The Scotsman:*

When I mentioned to a young friend that I was going to see the play, she enquired of me 'What is the Wallace?'...

Afterwards I began to wonder why so little accurate information about William Wallace had come down to us, while there is an abundance about the deeds of his contemporary, Robert Bruce. The conclusion I reached was that for a 'commoner' to achieve so much went against the interests of the ruling class and, therefore, the less information left behind the better. It would discourage others of similar lowly birth from emulating The Wallace.

The ruling class would appear to have achieved their aim, when Scottish children grow up in ignorance of their true heritage.[5]

As an expression of 'the Caledonian antisyzygy' (with overtones of the 'Caledonian cringe' thrown in for good measure)[6] this letter could scarcely be bettered. Yet it stands squarely in a line of development that goes back to the time of Wallace and Bruce themselves; the making and shaping of myth over the centuries, both to buttress national identity and, often, to compensate for lack of national confidence and solidarity.

The truth – what survives of it (and the materials for both Wallace and Bruce are scanty, even in medieval terms) – is well known. In 1290 the Maid of Norway, the daughter of King Alexander III, and the last direct descendant of Malcolm III and St Margaret, died in Orkney on her way to Scotland. There were thirteen claimants to the Scottish throne and the Scots requested the greatest lawyer of the age, King Edward I of England, to decide who had the best claim. He did so, but then began to push his claim to overlordship to Scotland. In 1296 there was a revolt, which was crushed by Edward. He put English civil servants in charge of Scottish castles and administration and began to treat Scotland as an integrated part of England. In 1297 William Wallace, and the aristocratic Andrew de Moravia (one of the lost heroes of the myth) rose in revolt and defeated an English army at Stirling Bridge. For a brief period Wallace became 'Guardian of Scotland' before he was defeated at Falkirk in the following year. From that time until his capture and death in 1305 Wallace never ceased to struggle for Scottish independence, both as a guerrilla fighter within Scotland, and on the continent – he is known to have gone to the French and papal courts to seek support for the Scottish cause. Aside from this one year as Guardian, Wallace's career is shrouded in obscurity; his career as an outlaw meant that within his own lifetime he was already a mythological figure. For example, in the north of England, he was an ogre used by mothers to quieten their children.

It was these stories of Wallace's exploits between 1297 and 1306, developed over nearly two centuries, that were gathered together in the late fifteenth century by the poet 'Blind Harry' in the poem, 'The Acts and Deeds of Sir William Wallace'. Far from being suppressed by the ruling class, this poem was composed with royal patronage, since Wallace like Bruce was seen by the ruling dynasty as a figure of national status. But there is little doubt that it was the stories of the deeds of 'Wallace Wight' (his size and strength and, more importantly, his relentless and bloodthirsty anti-Englishness) that spoke most directly to the common people, during the centuries of cross-border warfare that followed the death of King Robert I 'The Bruce' in 1329.

Bruce's career as a national hero – and as an individual – is altogether more complex. He was the grandson of one of the unsuccessful candidates for the throne in 1290 and, over the next sixteen years, he repeatedly changed sides – a fact that has been held against him ever since. Yet Bruce was operating not just as an important cross-border magnate – he held lands in both Scotland and England. He was also living in a period when the idea of national identity was only slowly emerging. Indeed, for the Scots, this concept was forged during the wars he led so ably. In many respects the 'Scottish War of Independence' was an early example of a war of national liberation; a prototype for a kind of conflict common in our own century.

The essence of such conflicts is either aggression by a more powerful neighbour or revolt against an occupying power. During the ensuing conflict national leaders emerge who in their character and actions become in some sense representative of the nation as a whole. All classes are brought together in defence of national integrity. In Scotland this struggle had a number of practical consequences; serfdom disappeared early, by the middle of the fourteenth century and there were no peasant revolts, such as occurred elsewhere in Europe in the second half of the fourteenth century.

Such wars of national liberation are not fought by conventional means. The defeat of a mounted army by guile and footsoldiers at Stirling Bridge sent shock waves around Europe; Bannockburn was a more conventional battle, but its results were equally threatening to the aristocratic status quo. Both Wallace and Bruce were guerrilla fighters of genius – in Bruce's case the war he fought involved the conscious abandonment of the code of aristocratic chivalrous behaviour he had grown up with.

Such wars create – or heighten – a sense of national identity. The chief agent in the growth of fourteenth-century Scottish nationalism was English imperialism. After 1314, despite centuries of warfare and periods of English occupation, the fact that Scotland was a distinct nation was never again in question.

This growth of national consciousness was, in European terms, precocious. It was forced upon the Scots by the pressures of war, and consciously reinforced in the difficult years following Bruce's death.

Another consequence of wars of national liberation is that in retrospect they appear – or are made to appear – a 'golden age'. Certainly, by the mid-fourteenth century the Scots were already looking back to the time of 'Good King Robert' for reassurance and as a consolation for the terrors of the times – the Black Death and continued warfare with England. One example of this nostalgia was the decision by Bruce's descendants, taken in the 1370s, to commission a national epic about the deeds of their ancestor.

The Brus, written by John Barbour, archdeacon of Aberdeen, is an extraordinary achievement. A long poem, altogether 13,556 lines divided into twenty books, *The Brus* is a masterpiece of Scots poetry, and is also biography and a major historical document. It covers the period from 1306 to 1329; from Bruce's final decision to claim the throne of Scotland to his death and the taking of Bruce's heart on the crusade against the Saracens in Spain by his lieutenant, Sir James Douglas, the other hero of the poem. The story ranges widely, throughout Scotland, England, and Ireland, and across the entire social spectrum of medieval Scottish society, from the king to commoners, both men and women.

The composition of *The Brus* is yet another example of the national self-consciousness of the Scots. No self-respecting medieval European nation could afford to be without a national epic – such as 'Roland' or 'El Cid' – and if one did not already exist it was necessary that one should be created. But what is unusual about this national epic is that the events it described had happened so recently. John Barbour was acting as historian as well as literary artist. In the opening passage, therefore, Barbour addresses the essential problem that faces all oral historians – the relationship between historical truth and literary art, and the limited span of human memory:

> Storys to rede ar delitabill,
> Suppos that thay be nocht bot fabill:
> Than suld storys that suthfast wer,
> And thay war said on Gud maner,
> Have doubill pleasance in herying.
> The fyrst plesance is the carpyng,
> And the tother the suthfastness
> That schawys thyngis that are likand
> Tyll mannys heryng ar plesand.
> Tharfor I wald fayne set my will,
> Giff my myt mycht suffice thartill,
> To put in wryt a suthfast story,
> That it lest ay furth in memory,
> Swa that na tyme of lenth it let,
> Na ger it haly be forget.[7]

Barbour himself was probably just a boy when Bruce died in 1329, but he is known to have interviewed contemporaries of the king. The poem is sprinkled with the phrase, 'As Ic herd say' ('As I heard say') and these are not just literary devices to help the scansion. His description of James Douglas, for example:

> Bot he wes nocht so fayr, that we
> Suld spek gretly of his beaute;
> In visage was he sumdeill gray
> And had blak har, as Ic hard say;
> Bot of lymmys he wes weill maid,
> With banys gret, and schuldrys braid.

> His body wes weyll maid and lenye,
> As thai that saw him said to me.[8]

At one or two points Barbour even names his sources, for example Sir Alan Cathcart who gives him a wondrously realistic account of a skirmish with the English in the fog in Galloway in June 1308:

> A knycht that than wes in his rout,
> Worthy and wicht, stalward and stout,
> Curtas and fair, and of gude fame,
> Schir Alane of Catkert be name,
> Tald me this taill as I sall tell ...[9]

Much of the realism of the poem must come from Barbour's interviews with survivors and eye-witnesses. This is a poem about war, but it is national freedom that is glorified, not warfare itself; the details of battles and skirmishes are painted in unrelenting detail. Here are the English and Scottish dead on the field of Bannockburn, as the battle still rages:

> And mony that wicht war and hardy
> Doune under feit lyand all deid,
> Quhar all the field of blud wes red,
> Armoris and quyntis that thay bare,
> With blud wes swa defowlit thar,
> That thay mycht nocht discrivit be.[10]

There are other oral elements in the poem. Aside from his eye-witness accounts, Barbour also collected stories of Bruce that had already been shaped into what might be called 'folk-tales' – incidents which, although based on real occurrence, had been given form and shape by the demands of storytelling. One such is the long account of the king's pursuit by the hound of his enemy, John of Lorn, in Book VI. At first the king puts the hound off the scent (and reduces the numbers of his human pursuers) by dividing his meagre group of followers into three, then shakes off the hound by walking up a stream. Finally he kills the dog, and joins the men of John of Lorn in pursuit of himself.

There is also evidence of contemporary speech patterns in the poem – many of which may have been collected from eye-witnesses – for example Bruce's speech to his followers on the eve of battle at Bannockburn. But perhaps more interesting are the figures of speech used throughout the poem, which represent modes of storytelling which must have been common amongst fourteenth-century Scots. When, for example, King Edward II flees the field of

Bannockburn he is so closely pursued by Sir James Douglas and his men that:

> He leit thame nocht haf sic laseir
> As anys wattir for to ma ...
> (He gave them no leisure even to make water)

Anyone familiar with cowboy speech will recognize that that expression has survived remarkably well!

Barbour's *Brus* is an epic, and although the impetus for its composition came from the court, it is not a courtly poem in its subject matter. The character and incident of the poem are real; so real that, for example, we are even told about the bodily functions of the king.[11] The poem is derived from an oral and folk tradition and, in turn, its stories, incidents and poetry re-entered the popular tradition.

For centuries the stories of Wallace and Bruce were traded across these lines of formal and popular culture and, after the seventeenth century, between oral and written accounts. The best known example of this process is the story of Bruce and the spider, which does not occur in Barbour. The story, in fact, was first told of Sir James Douglas and appears in Hume of Godescroft's manuscript 'History of the house of Douglas'. The first linkage of Bruce and the spider in print occurs in Sir Walter Scott's *The Tales of a Grandfather* in the 1820s. Thence it has spread around the world and become in the present day virtually the only story of the king's exploits to be generally known.[12]

By contrast, little of the blood and thunder excitement of the episodes in *The Brus* has survived in modern memory. Instead, most modern Scots (if they know anything at all of the poem) only know Barbour's apostrophe on freedom, an ambiguous passage which can be widely applied and variously understood.

> A! fredome is a noble thing!
> Fredome mays man of haiff liking,
> Fredome all solace to man giffis,
> He levys at es that frely levys.[13]

Numerous nineteenth-century autobiographies mention Wallace and Bruce as being the stuff of childhood tales and adventures – for example, Andrew Carnegie, John Muir (the American naturalist), and Hugh Miller, the Cromarty stonemason, who recalled:

> I first became thoroughly a Scot some time in my tenth year. My Uncle James had procured for me from a neighbour the loan of a common stall-edition of Blind Harry's *Wallace* ... I read 'How

Wallace killed young Selbie the Constable's son'; 'How Wallace fished in Irvine Water'; and 'How Wallace killed the Churl with his own staff in Ayr'; and then Uncle James told me, in the quiet way in which he used to make a joke tell, that the book seemed to be rather a rough sort of production, filled with accounts of quarrels and bloodshed and that I might read no more of it unless I felt inclined. But now I did feel inclined very strongly, and read on with increasing astonishment and delight. I was intoxicated with the fiery narratives of the blind minstrel, with his fierce breathings of hot, intolerant patriotism, and his stories of astonishing prowess, and, glorying in being a Scot, and the countryman of Wallace, I longed for a war with the Southron, that the wrongs and sufferings of these noble heroes might yet be avenged.

It was not until some years later, when I was fortunate enough to pick up one of the later editions of Barbour's *Bruce*, that the Hero-King of Scotland assumed his right place in my mind beside its Hero-Guardian. There are stages of development in the immature youth of individuals that seem to correspond with stages in the immature youth of nations; and the recollections of this early time enable me, in some measure, to understand how it was that, for hundreds of years, Blind Harry's *Wallace*, with its rude and naked narrative, and its exaggerated incident, should have been according to Lord Hailes, the Bible of the Scotch people.[14]

But implicit in what Miller has to say is that these stories belong to a redundant state of society, and are out of place in the complexities of nineteenth-century life. Certainly it is at about the time Miller was writing – the 1840s – that the first cracks begin to appear in the historical consensus that had bound Scots together for generations. It was not that the English threat had gone away since the Union of Scotland and England in 1707. Rather, the threat now assumed new, and less easily resisted, forms; those things, as Sir Walter Scott said, 'that make Scotland Scotland'[15] – culture, language, attitudes of mind.

Nor was the threat entirely external. Within Scotland too there were tensions that militated against a unifying national mythology. The greatest of these was the Disruption of 1843 in the Church of Scotland, which split Scottish society in half. After 1843 the two competing churches took over respective slices of the Scottish past to buttress their claims to historicity – and, at the same time, were content to leave the Middle Ages, which they regarded as a time of popery and darkness, to the Catholics and episcopalians.[16]

There were also social and political divisions. Amongst the professional and upper classes there was a growing desire to be 'British' – and in the new, hybrid identity Wallace and Bruce were not only surplus to requirements, but downright embarrassing. This trend was, however, countered by the rise of modern Scottish nationalism in the 1840s and 1850s; an early success was the raising of the Wallace Monument on Abbey Craig at Stirling. One of the leaders of the campaign for the monument was the republican and supporter of Young Ireland, John Steill, who was only too happy to use Wallace as a stick with which to beat the new 'British' classes, especially the aristocracy;

> And oh! when we try to estimate the practical benefits resulting to us from what Wallace did and from what he suffered, with what deep emotions of disgust and humiliation must we contrast the bearing of that mawkish brood of degenerate Scotchmen of these times who are to be found but in too great numbers in high places and elsewhere! ... A more contemptible order of beings than the present race of Scottish *nobles* crawls not upon the face of the globe ...: if they had a country to desert, as they had in the days of Wallace they would desert it, or a country to *sell*, as they had at the time of the union of 1706 *[sic]* they would sell it as readily as their predecessors did.... It is the peasantry, mechanics and middle classes of Scotland, who ought to take this matter into their hands. They alone fought under Wallace's banner, it was for them that he laid down his life.[17]

Another blow to the mythology of Wallace and Bruce was the reform of Scottish education. In *The Democratic Intellect*, George Elder Davie has traced the increasing Anglicization of the Scottish universities in the later nineteenth century, and how (despite attempts by such English historians as A.J. Froude to ensure a Scottish history component in the new course) Scottish history was abandoned. As Davie has said:

> There had been a failure of intellectual nerve among the Scots .... The Scottish Universities, in their anxiety to accommodate themselves to the expansive epoch of Durbars and Jubilees, had suddenly turned their backs on the long procession of characteristic personalities, whose memory had hitherto always inspired the continuing adventure of the democratic intellect ....
> Thus at the very time when other neighbouring countries were becoming increasingly 'history minded', the Scots were losing their sense of the past, their leading institutions, including the Universities, were emphatically resolved – to use a catch phrase

fashionable in Scotland of the early twentieth century – 'no longer to be prisoners of their own history'.[18]

And what came to obtain in universities determined what was provided in schools after 1872. By the last decades of the nineteenth century the historical fragmentation of the Wallace and Bruce myth was complete.

If the myth lived on in an integral and uncritical manner it was more likely to be abroad, amongst the Scottish exiles in such far-flung corners as the highlands of Nyasaland, or in the bush country of southern Texas. The Texas folklorist, J. Frank Dobie, recalled of his youth in the 1890s:

> One Christmas we got Porter's *The Scottish Chiefs*. I read it to myself, and at night as we sat by the fireplace my father read it aloud by the flickering light of a kerosene lamp. What heroes to emulate Bruce and Wallace were! My blood still stirs at mention of the mere title.[19]

Yet the myth still flickers in Scotland itself, sustained especially by the contemporary nationalist revival. As this paper was being written in the spring of 1987 a dispute broke out in Edinburgh about the purchase of a portrait of Nelson Mandela by the local council. Opinion was divided not only on the artistic merit of the painting, but on its political and symbolic value. A letter to *The Scotsman* on 13 February said:

> Edinburgh councillors who dislike the portrait of Nelson Mandela should walk up the road and vent their dislike on another man whose motivation was the freedom of his own people.
>
> The effigy of William Wallace at the entrance of the Castle commemorates a man who was dedicated to exactly the same purpose as Mandela stands for…. Today's terrorist may become tomorrow's hero.

And so the story continues. As Scotland moves into a new phase of public discussion and debate on issues of devolution and relationships with partners in the European market, it will be surprising if the figures of Wallace and Bruce are not invoked once more.

Notes

We are grateful to Margaret Mackay for supplying some of the information in these notes.

1 Andrew Carnegie (1920) *Autobiography*, Boston and New York: Houghton Mifflin, p. 367.
2 *The Scotsman*, 2 March 1968.
3 Hugh Miller (1858) *My Schools and Schoolmasters or The Story of My Education*, Edinburgh: Thomas Constable, p. 41.

4 Carnegie, op. cit., p. 18.

5 *The Scotsman*, 27 August 1985.

6 'The Caledonian antisyzygy' is a phrase coined by Professor Gregory Smith in his (1919) *Scottish Literature: Character and Influence*, London: Macmillan, to describe the combination of opposites to be found in Scottish literature: down-to-earth realism on the one hand, delight in the wild and fantastical on the other. The great Scottish poet Hugh MacDiarmid extended this concept of a zig-zag of contradictions to describe the Scottish psyche and to define the difference between the False Scot (the canny, dour, music-hall stereotype) and the True Scot (a torn, divided, questing figure).

The 'Caledonian cringe' might be defined as a negative outward expression of this divided and uncertain self, lacking confidence in the strengths of one's past, present and future.

7 The edition of Barbour's *Brus* used here is that by W.M. MacKenzie, published by A. and C. Black in 1909.

> Stories are delectable to read,
> Even if nothing but fable:
> So such stories that are true
> And told in a good manner too,
> Give double pleasure in hearing.
> The first pleasure is the speech,
> And the second is its truth
> That tells of things likeable
> And to men's hearing pleasurable.
> Therefore I have determined,
> Provided my wit suffices
> To set down a true story in writing,
> So that it remains for ever in memory,
> And no length of time erases it
> Or causes it to be wholly forgot.

8   But he was not so fair, that we
>   Should speak greatly of his beauty;
>   His face was somewhat grey
>   And he had black hair, as I've heard say;
>   But in limb he was well made,
>   With great bones, and shoulders broad
>   His body was well made and lean
>   As they that saw him said to me.

9   A knight that then was in his company,
>   Worthy and strong, stalwart and stout,
>   Courteous and fair, and of good fame,
>   Sir Alan of Catkert by name,
>   Told me this tale as I shall tell ...

10   And many that warriors were and hardy
      Down under foot lay all dead,
      Where all the field with blood was red,
      The armours and devices that they bore,
      With blood were so befouled there,
      That they could not be made out any more.

11 *Brus* Book 1, lines 225–8.

12 I am grateful to Mr A.B. Webster of the History Department of the University of Kent for discussing the origins of the spider story with me.

13   Ah! Freedom is a noble thing,
      Freedom makes men have enjoyment,
      Freedom gives man all comfort,
      He lives at ease that freely lives.

14 Miller, op.cit., pp. 40–1.

15 J.G.Lockhart (1871) *Life of Sir Walter Scott*, Edinburgh: H. & C. Black, p. 185.

16 The Disruption occurred when, following a decade of debate in which the Evangelical wing of the Church of Scotland sought in vain for government legislation and support for their position on spiritual independence from the state and opposition to patronage, its supporters walked out of the General Assembly of the Church of Scotland meeting in Edinburgh in May, 1843. It was a dramatic statement of religious and social self-determination. At tremendous sacrifice in terms of income and security, the ministers and members – 40 per cent of the church they had left in each case – created a new and influential denomination, the Free Church of Scotland, which reflected a variety of communities and concerns both urban and rural, Highland and Lowland, in a period of great social and economic change in Scotland.

For a fuller discussion of the historiographical consequences of the Disruption see M. Ash (1980) *The Strange Death of Scottish History*, Edinburgh: Ramsay Head Press, Ch. 5, esp. pp. 124–34.

17 J. Steill (1846) 'P.F. Tytler called to account for his misrepresentations of the life and character of Sir William Wallace', in a letter to the *Scottish Herald* of November 13, pp. 9, 11.

18 G.E. Davie (1964) *The Democratic Intellect: Scotland and her Universities in the 19th century*, 2nd edn, Edinburgh: University of Edinburgh Press, p. 337.

19 J. Frank Dobie (1980) *Some Part of Myself*, Austin: University of Texas Press, p. 37.

7

Myth, impotence, and survival in the concentration camps

Anna Bravo, Lilia Davite, and Daniele Jalla

Between 1943 and 1945 40–45,000 Italians were deported to the Nazi camps. They were a mixture of Jews, anti-Fascists, partisans, workers taken during the March 1944 strikes, and others who had supported and backed the Resistance movement. There were also hostages, people picked up during searches, soldiers from the army disbanded after the armistice of 8 September 1943, youngsters who refused to join when the Salò Republic called them up, people accused of working on the black market or caught by chance or turned in by anonymous informers. Men, women, young and old alike: and what is more, of them all, no more than 4–5,000 came back. Forty years later, we still do not know exactly how many left, or how many survived, nor exactly when they were transported. Little is known about their social and geographical mix, or about the main features that characterized the Italian deportation within the wider European framework.

It was in this context of general historical ignorance and indeed avoidance that we were drawn into the project on which this chapter is based. Working on it has in itself been a remarkable experience, both from what we have learnt and from the form the project took. For the initiative for it came from the survivors themselves. Work had actually begun in 1981, when ANED – the National Association of ex-Political Deportees – had suggested that all those camp survivors still living should be contacted. The association then succeeded in involving the regional council, the local historical institutes for the study of the Resistance movement, and the University of Turin.[1] We thus became the project's professional historians, working with the survivors' organization and carrying out, between 1982 and 1985, altogether 230 interviews with former concentration camp prisoners still living in Piedmont.

For all of us, the project was a challenge. It was an unusual and courageous risk for a small group of survivors to take with their

collective memory, especially considering many current misunderstandings of the past and the scant interest the academic world has
shown in the subject, including those one might have expected to be
involved, such as historians of anti-Fascism and the Resistance
movement.[2] Their decision also implied handing the job down to a
younger generation who could not have had any direct experience
of the camps. Survivors might well have feared misinterpretation of
their memories leading to an outcome inconsistent with their own
expectations and intentions. Fortunately such fears were soon
dispelled as together we developed a working relationship which
drew on an uninterrupted flow and exchange of mutual opinions.

The decision to listen to every single survivor also originally
appeared a bold one, and not just because of their numbers: for it
meant risking unforeseen revelations, excluded or not included in
the more widely known and accepted descriptions of what went on
in concentration camps. It should be emphasized that a comprehensive history of the Italian deportation has yet to be written, and that
so far only scattered fragments have been available.[3]

As we proceeded, we have been able to piece together an
increasingly detailed and full picture of the deportation. We have
learnt more from the recorded memories than from historical
accounts. Many of the stories we heard would have otherwise
remained unknown, concealed in the witnesses' minds, hidden in
families, or shared only with intimate friends. Many ex-deportees
find it difficult to put their experiences into writing, let alone write a
book or organize an adequate circulation of what they had written.
Some people wrote their memoirs[4] in the months and years
following their return to Italy, while others have done so more
recently. These texts had already given us some ideas about the
specifically Italian aspects of deportation, such as the high percentage of political deportees and the overall social and cultural mix.
They also highlighted the greater hardship suffered by those who
were deported in the later war years, and the special hostility
attached to the Italians, who were placed on the lowest rungs of the
internal camp hierarchy.

What could the recorded testimonies add to this? The 230
survivors had altogether given us over 400 hours of recordings,
roughly 10,000 typewritten pages which now make up the Archive
of Piedmontese Deportation.[5] The archive illustrates many aspects
and outcomes of deportation; but we should begin with a fundamental caution. The witnesses we interviewed cannot be considered
a representative sample, as too many voices are missing and would
have been even if the work had started long before. Time has
thinned the number of survivors down even more, depriving us of

the testimonies of the older ones. What emerges from the recordings is a significant glimpse of the Piedmontese deportation, a complex world but with a prevalence especially of young working-class and peasant males, partisans who had only a short period of actual political militancy behind them. The older camp inmates, and the Jews of any age, are drastically underrepresented among these survivors.[6]

Collectively they bear overwhelming witness to an experience so extreme, so dark, that without their testimony it would be unimaginable. Individually they reveal the many faces of Italian deportation both in the earlier personal and family histories, and in reactions and the fight for survival within the camps. No one was the same once in the camp: no one went unscathed, all were weighed down by the impact of the environment. But each resorted to those resources which their own background, experience, and personal history supplied them with.[7]

The particular camp, the time they arrived there and the conditions to which they were subjected, as well as the fellow deportees that each person came into contact with at key moments, were also essential ingredients of the mix that determined how each person experienced the camp. All these factors built up a far more complex image of the 'universe' of the camps than we had expected. Different experiences led to a variety of stories and ways of telling them, without challenge to the underlying uniqueness and specificity of the memories of the deportation.

The key to these memories is in how they relate to truth. What notion of truth develops during the passage through the hidden world of deportation? It is the hope that one day they will be able to reveal to the whole world the injury that they suffered in obscurity and utter loneliness, an injury so unbelievable that they themselves perceived it as unreal. This is why, after their liberation, survivors made up for the evidence that was missing by concentrating their efforts on a commitment to uncover and reveal falsity and deception. Their idea of justice meant telling the truth both legally and historically. Remembering deportation implied both keeping faith with the dead and unmasking the executioners. But such memories had to fight hard to win attention and counteract the indifference of a world which was reaching out towards the future and wanting to confine its past to the archives rather than face up to it.

This search, this quest produced ambivalent feelings: the need for truth and the difficulty in stating it; the personal urge to remember and also to forget; the wish to bear witness on the one hand and to remain silent on the other, as a protest. Over these forty years, memory has kept on raising new questions and trying to understand why it all happened. Both those who withdrew into silence and those who were able to speak shared the experience of their past, the recounting self still confronting the suffering self in everyone.

This is why commitment to ascertain the facts remains central in their stories, and why there is a certain tension between the spirit of the story and the conscience of the witness, the former being the life of the account, the latter the sentinel. As always with recollection, the passage of time has been important. But it has brought rewards as well as problems. For the endless toil of their memories needed time to produce the words and images to depict what had been experienced but not expressed. The testimonies also reflect the differing cultural backgrounds of those who speak.

Written memoirs proved very much more distant than oral ones: not just because oral testimony reflects clusters of memories and gives an opportunity for less formal kinds of narration, but also because the main actors change too, bringing descriptions of other situations, other ways of acting and of thinking. Thoughts, reflections, and moods are also more changeable and fuller, reacting to the description of events. And such description ceases to be the storyteller's overwhelming or exclusive objective. It was drawing out these differences between the image of concentration camps as it emerges from written literature and from our life stories which especially influenced our selection of passages from the interviews for *La vita offesa*.[8]

Here we wish to focus on one particular aspect of camp life – the forms which fantasy, imagination, and myth-producing resources take under extreme conditions. Most scientific literature uses a model of resistance based on spiritual steadfastness and ethical vigour. It has consequently reacted ambivalently to the series of mental processes taking place and has classed them as part of a pattern of passive adaptation.

Many actions could not be described as rational control strategies even if the word 'strategy' were not incompatible with the total unpredictability of camp life. We are referring to the endless talk about food and recipes; the circulation of false or exaggerated political and military news and the attention given to it – the so-called *bobards;*[9] and the daydreaming and the resort to various kinds of fortune-telling – including the interpretation of dreams and auspices, using as omens the most various elements or phenomena. There was a multiplication of mental activity connected with fantasy, imagination, and myth, echoing those familiar from stories from trenches, prison life, or natural or other disasters.[10]

It is not surprising that the judgement of the first testimonies, which were mostly by intellectuals, [11] were on the whole negative to this aspect of camp life, for even though they recognized its transient beneficial effect, this did not compensate for its regressive essence. They spoke about how it meant slipping into childish and primitive behaviour, the more humiliating because of its apparent resemblance to the state of eclipse of the mind to which the camp wanted to reduce prisoners.

Certainly this is how some of the leaders of the intellectual resistance in the camps – such as Bruno Betthelheim and Viktor Frankl – would have experienced such behaviour. This does not make it easier to appreciate the different meanings which minds with other frames of reference might have developed when dealing with deportation and captivity. It is surprising to discover that forty years later the opinions of historians remain virtually the same. This might be due to the inflexible borderline maintained between rational and irrational; and also to the fact that, in most memoirs, imagination and fantasy typically find outlets in artistic expression and literary reminiscing, a reflection of the high cultural level of the authors which was shared by some of our interviewees. More broadly, even when one does not want to classify behaviour and introduce a hierarchical order, one often has to contend with prejudices which identify imagination and fantasies as 'negative', or at the most scarcely relevant and unworthy of a second glance. [12]

Yet some of the interviews resisted this brisk dismissal of fantasy and imagination. Through them we discovered that something important was at stake. If we were to reach a full understanding of the extreme experience fantasizing could not be dismissed merely as false optimism or escapism. We started thinking about how some stories were being told and how they were judged by some of our interviewees; about how they related to environmental constraints and to attempts to face them; and also about the connections which were clearly apparent with the differing cultural backgrounds of the tellers.

Attilio Armando, who was one of the *bobard* creators in Flossenbürg, was a young partisan from a peasant family. He recalls his myth-making in detail:

> I used to draw maps on the ground of where the Americans were and where the Russians were, where the French were and where the English were; and I really knew almost nothing, thank goodness the others knew nothing at all....Because I'd say, 'They're coming from there', but it wasn't really true. I'd make a plan of the battlefield with the fronts and the armies as I thought

they might be, but rather carefully; and I'd always make it so they were coming towards us – 'just a little more, boys, we've got to hold firm, they're coming'.

It was an imaginary map. But if he didn't know how lifelike his drawings were, he did know they kept alive the will to resist. And he benefited from the comfort he gave others: 'these things to do with the armies I drew on the ground, they were already a kind of politics, I invented them to try to keep up these people's morale a bit. Because that reflected back on me too, I kept my own morale up too.'[13]

Here is matter for thought. The *bobard* is seen as fantasy, but also as useful, experienced as neither regressive nor humiliating, either by the *bobard* broadcaster or the listener. He presents his actions as a bright-minded initiative, wanting to keep his mates alert thanks to a skilled use of his imagination, keeping communication alive – an essential element for survival. The interpretation of casual chat must therefore be revised. It can no longer be considered the attribute of an anonymous mass or a fragment of individual experience, but rather a resource shared by a small group which makes use of this opportunity to generate hope.

Attilio Armando is not the only example of someone who deliberately generated false information to support a group or an individual. Others invented landings, the liberation of progressively closer areas, battles which had been won. When facts proved them wrong, they simply said they had misinterpreted them or had got the name wrong, but – 'It's nothing serious, obviously I've got the name of the place wrong, but it's certainly true because I heard it from a civilian.' There was fresh news and this time it *was* reliable. Thus, they kept their channel of communication open.[14] The *bobard* creators differed in terms of social background, culture, and personal history. Their mythical news was sometimes taken as a gift, similar to what happens when a mature intellectual receives regular visits from a young villager who is seeking comfort.[15] Sometimes it was used as merchandise: one witness remembers paying with a piece of bread for information he knew to be untrue – "'I've news to give you if you'll give me a piece of bread, give me something"; and you'd give him it, though you knew it was just a tale.'[16] Once again the *bobard* suggests a network of relationships and the existence of different roles.

Nor was this its only form of transmission: information also circulated in the camp by word of mouth, passing from one person to the next without any control. Either way its function is clearly remembered: in a situation of total isolation, monotonously repetitive, where the future has been cancelled, information, even when it was false, was healthy, because it bridged a gap with the future, manipulated time, and brought liberation nearer. In fact though they saw liberation as a certainty in historical terms, it was far from being certain on a personal level. Our interviews suggest it would be arbitrary to reduce these *bobards* to mere images reflecting a false perception of events, especially considering the prisoners' lack of direct access to information. Nor could it be reduced to an escapism from the mental and physical constraints of the camp. Quite the opposite: they appeared not to interfere with the understanding of the experience, which remains closely anchored to reality and facts even when an imaginary grid, an untrue construction, is projected on to it.

How did the mechanism work? How do anchorage and projection balance out?

The interviewees seemed fully aware of the risks underlying this kind of talk and fantasizing: though it arose from the need to distance themselves from the camp, the distance must not be allowed to grow too big, nor should it become an absolute certainty, nor generate an obsessive expectation. The boy who passed the winter sure he'd be home for the strawberry picking, died of disappointment. 'He had hope but it was an illusion, because then we weren't home for the strawberries, we were here. And he died in three days.'[17] 'Those who counted the days, like those who were expecting to be freed from each day to the next, they couldn't make it, they were the ones who died first.'[18] Escape from reality was always an impending threat.

Many authors have stressed the destructive impact that *bobards* had: they are seen as symptomatic of blind faith: but these authors do not draw out the consequences of this. Although *bobards* were a double-edged weapon, it was not one that simply corresponded with attitudes whereby prisoners could naively seize on words of hope or blunt their senses, or become a victim of an optimistic delusion. Quite the contrary: it required the ability to watch over the mechanisms of their psyche, to be able to move among the various tones and mental states, switching between excitement and disenchantment, imagination and belief. It also required flair, the knack of renovating and tailoring the story each time – unlike what happens with an obsessive fixation. Regression, if any, is limited, guided, and harnessed.

This explains why one of the interviewees, a woman, whose self-portrait and story stress her intellectual tenacity was able to make one of the most positive judgements.[19] Having experienced it herself directly, she could appreciate the complex nature of the *bobards* while others simply perceived them as a background noise. However the fact that she was a woman is immediately suggestive: a woman who held on to her belief in the pre-eminence of spirit without relinquishing the full depth of her emotional world.

The question then arises: were there other equivalent expressions of fantasy and imagination scattered in prisoners' daily lives and corresponding to the difficult balance the *bobards* represented? We found some. For instance among the younger prisoners, who met and listened to a love story told by one of them; or meeting at Christmas to write an imaginary letter to one's mother. They used irony as a filter because they did not want their thoughts about home and their beloved ones to turn into dangerous self-pity:

> There was a Frenchman who told rivetting love stories: how he had a fiancée, how it was real romantic love, wonderful, and so on....He used to confide in us, tell us these things. Certainly it was all done secretly, but it was a way of living, of resisting, of keeping a human link with life beforehand, of not being cut off from all that other reality. I remember listening to this man, who spoke very good Italian, talking of wonderful things.
>
> I remember Christmas '44 at Gusen. We had finished work, but after work we were waiting for this story-teller....And he always talked about the letters he might have written as if he had really written them, and this time he asked us if we'd all written Christmas letters. One of us was a boy, very young, and he said, 'I've written to Mama too': and his letter started by saying how he found the concentration camp, what life was like there – he said his mother always made him go out with three jerseys on, and long underpants, and here they were sent out almost naked, etcetera ... and I remember this man let him finish and then he said to him, 'That's no good like that, you don't write those kind of things to your mama, least of all for Christmas. Look, you write a letter like this and this' – it was an imaginary letter obviously, because you couldn't write any letters at all – 'you ought to say, "Dear Mama, I'm having a good time here and I'm well dressed, I've got a lot of jerseys, I'm not cold, they're treating me very well, I've got some nice friends who we call 'kapo' for a joke, but they're good chaps".'
>
> Yes it was all that sort of thing, these extraordinary things used to happen that ... made up the humanity of the concentration camp.[20]

Others interpreted dreams,[21] or daydreamed – even during roll-call, like the young girl who remembered seeing flashes of the courtyard and staircase of her home.[22] Palmistry was practised half-

heartedly, 'for the sake of encouraging one another', one interviewee said, '– even the things we said weren't true'.[23]

It appears to be difficult, even arrogant, to try to see the point at
which memories might begin to emphasize control and the damping
down of emotions. However, people who described these and other
such events do not have a history of regression in the camp. On the
contrary, they were able to mobilize resources and unpredictable
skills and to calculate the risks and benefits in the small ways that
survival required. It is also significant that they were totally at ease
in talking to us, at times ironically detached, and far from feeling
that their image was being questioned. But their sense of dignity
and the importance of preserving it even in extreme circumstances
was not any the less vital to them. In any case dignity was measured
above all in terms of still managing to relate to other human beings
in these circumstances, to suffer for other people's pains and to
offer mutual aid. Imagination and fantasy are not on trial in these
interviews.

They do however raise a fundamental issue: how did a relatively
large number of prisoners manage to achieve such a good mental
balance in these extreme conditions when it is not easily reached
even in normal life? What strength feeds the economy of this
imagination?

The answers lead us to the same difficulties we had to face when
dealing with survival. Bettelheim says that nothing that prisoners do
or avoid doing can determine events. The lawless order of the camp
randomly selects those who will live and those who will die; and they
know it. Our interviews tell the same story. However the small
impact that personal factors could have does not cancel their
existence. Although many survivors say they don't know how they
managed to survive, in their interviews they repeatedly express
positive or negative judgements about the various events they
experienced. They also gave a definition of 'the self', a self in
relation to survival, a sort of desiccated identity that seemingly
represents the subjective element; overpowered by fate, no longer
capable of action to influence events, it loses its causal but not its
existential value. This new self was like a mental identity card
required to certify the existence of an inner point of reference, a
thin thread linking people to their inner selves. Yet even this thin
thread could enable a person to keep recalling their own self and
could provide something they could count on in the daily struggle
not to be overcome.

They reacted to the coercion of disorder, to the depersonalizing
pressure of the environment by singling out one feature, one basic,
simple trait of personality to resist the continuous attacks on their

mental and physical identity, using this trait because it was precise and specific.

Thus Angelo Andreo, a former factory worker then in his thirties, kept his link alive by recognizing the 'rugged body' his youthful sporting days had left him with, even when he had become so weak he could hardly stand. 'I would say, "Yea, I'm running, I'm playing football, I'm cycling...." I'd lean up against the hut, take two steps and – pouf!: I was flat on the ground.' But 'if it hadn't been for luck and for all the sport I'd done, that my body was tough ....' This basic image he had of himself embodied all his hopes of surviving.[24] Others found it in the fact that they had been poor, and consequently had the cultural heritage and resilience of 'the poor, people had already suffered – strong, because life had tested them': a founding trait of their personality that they resorted to in moments of danger or when distressed.[25] The same sort of process led others to feel and, above all, draw strength from, their shrewdness;[26] or their optimism, their communicative ability, or spirit of initiative.[27] It was always an exclusive investment in one trait of their personality that came to symbolize all their qualities. Actions and behaviour aimed at preserving inner discipline and intellectual faculties could be interpreted in such a way that they all corresponded to the same perspective.[28] These behavioural patterns and actions could carry the essence of identity which had to be preserved as an essential weapon in self-defence.

These basic images clearly differ according to the person, their social and cultural background, and individual experience. Nor could it be otherwise, which is why it would be meaningless to list them according to some abstractly selected order of importance: they are but personal elaborations of group models, variations on a series of collective stereotypes. They shared the same underlying mental processes though this is less obvious at first glance, and these processes cannot be easily dismissed merely as childish or primitive regression. We do not feel the interviews suggest a primeval image of the self: they focus rather on a kind of primary identity, which is certainly potent, but also full of a mythical meaning closely bound to its power of salvation – its most fundamental attribute.

We are certainly no longer in the field of thought pertaining to consciously enacted and controlled rational strategies, the presence of which would surprise us in the camps. The people elaborating these images include those unaccustomed to self-reflection or thinking about themselves as well as intellectuals, militants, men and women, young and old alike. Jean Amery expresses a less common but to us more convincing opinion when he suggests that in extreme conditions and in the presence of a primeval violence, the pathways of critical thought and the habit of doubting can lead to the tragic dialectics of self-destruction.[29] If the prisoners had relied on more complex aspects of their personalities, they might have reinforced their feelings of anxiety and impotence. When the external environment becomes totally unpredictable and events appear to be dominated by the irrational anarchy of mere chance, the awareness that nothing can effectively counteract danger and the risk of abandonment can quickly lead to a collapse of mental and physical defence.[30] Some of the interviewees seem to have understood this. They avowed that the basic and mythical images they had of themselves helped them survive; they offered a way of finding a means, which had to be both extremely simple and solid, to resist the unbearably strong pressure leading to depersonalization. It allowed them to counterbalance the feeling of being totally at the mercy of fate with nothing to oppose it. Once they had something to believe in, and which they could rely on, it enabled them to reach out to their essential individual being, to back up the daily fight to hold on and to keep the hope of surviving alive.

However no mythical backing up of the self could endure without a sense of the liberation to come; it would inevitably become a delusion or fall apart. In fact all their fantasies and the world of imagination they created were aimed at the moment of liberation, for the prisoners had to admit that even the most favourable coincidence of chance and personal resilience could not be enough, and that a solution could only come from the outside.[31] Hopes and disappointments could come and go without interfering with the essential reactions, so long as salvation was perceived as something near and certain.

It is obvious that this process was neither linear nor automatic and that its roots were not solely on a rational plane. All the interviewees talked about the last months as being endless, of living in fear of physical and mental breakdown, as the workload increased and the death toll surged. Although the camp machine had become disorganized and was damaged, it worked up to the last moment, and the prisoners knew that the Nazis did not intend to leave survivors behind. They therefore needed a positive counterforce to act as a dam against this ever-present and renewed destructive force, to keep the belief that it would end.

Those were the years when throughout occupied Europe myths of Stalin and the Allies developed. At that time they were not yet conceived as opposing forces but both were thought to stem from the strong resistance and the victories over Germany, a longstanding myth. On such a myth the guarantee of the final outcome also depended. This symbolic investment is echoed very clearly in the prisoners' accounts: the myths thrived on German defeats and signs of the collapse of the organization of the camp, and myth in turn fed the notion of liberation.

The contact between different nationalities also meant sharing national epics. This is why Stalin's figure dominated. 'Joseph était là', a young French Communist said to a fellow deportee who had questioned whether or not they would be saved,[32] and a *bobard* circulating in Ravensbrück spoke about a telegram sent by Stalin – to 'The ladies of the camp', telling them to wait for his arrival.[33] Some of our interviewees, including non-Communist ones, similarly referred to Stalin as the central supportive myth and to the parallel myth of the USSR as a nation. In the camps the Russians were considered to be the most courageous and organized of the prisoners. Sometimes they were an example to follow; at others, a force to be feared, seen as a symbol of power based on large numbers and great ideals.[34] The sound of approaching cannon fire was Stalin's: 'We heard a rumble, and it was Stalin's voice, that canon'.[35] And the white-clad Russian soldiers, riding white horses into the camp seemed like figures from the Apocalypse to the few survivors of the Monowitz camp:[36] 'I remember the first patrol of Russian soldiers to come into the camp, they were all cavalrymen, all dressed in white, with all their paraphernalia in white, and their horses harnessed in white too, to match the snow. And these four soldiers were astounded, aghast at what they saw.' In the certain expectation of their arrival, red flags were sewn in great secrecy[37] – and it was *their* army that was awaited. So much so that some turned their backs on the Americans when they arrived, for that was not the liberation of which they had dreamt.[38]

Many other interviews refer to vaguer images of countless armies of soldiers from all races coming from far away, an idea that encompassed all those ideals of freedom and justice which were expected to triumph after the war was over. In both cases the border between myth and utopia is very thin, the one blending in with the other. It's the myth that shapes future expectations along with great hopes for radical change, symbolized by the end of all wars: 'But you'll see, those of you who go back, everything will change – life, society, everything will change.'[39] Here, one should in any case bear in mind that the prisoners' utopia did not really need a political model, because the dream of the new construction and rebirth echoed the recurrent millennial myth of the world turned upside down, where injustice becomes justice, loneliness solidarity, and shortage abundance.

In the same way politics was not the one and only philosophy to nourish salvation myths. Religious faith also counted, so long as it was not too undermined by camp life; and also fragments of superstition from a more distant past which could re-emerge with prescriptive ritual force like scraps of lost liturgies.

At times mixed elements which had different origins together gave rise to a more personalized belief. This happened in a way which took a course very close to the speculative and creative one of myth in the stricter meaning of the word. This is what happened to Marcello Blandino, a 21-year-old deserter from the Fascist army, from a peasant family. He first speaks of how nature is indestructible, so that hail, for instance, never destroys all the grapes in the vineyard: some always survive, however withered and damaged. This teaching came from the peasant tradition passed down to him by his mother. He then extended this philosophy to history, by remembering how, even in the worst 'robberies, acts of piracy and wars', someone survived – knowledge coming from his schooldays, with a touch of youthful adventure stories added in the reference to pirates. Then he projected the joint force of both ideas on to the camp and consequently reached the conclusion that someone would survive; and projecting his thoughts beyond survival into the future, that someone would be called as a witness too.[40] His philosophy is built on what was seemingly common sense, that 'it always has been and always will be'. Nevertheless his triple analogy goes against the reality of the camp as seen in his overall account, which denies it. Yet the story becomes a vital tool to be remembered and rehearsed so often in the mind that, when asked how he survived, he recalled it immediately after his 'I don't know': like a key to understand the common fate of the prisoners and a source of comfort that helped him resist.

Looking back on these and other ways of being, and then comparing them with material from other sources, like myths and legends about war in other contexts and descriptions of the underground life in total institutions, we think it meaningless to classify these responses on a model with a scale reaching from childish or primitive to adult and civilized – or from irrational to rational.[41] Most of all, we think it questionable merely to see them as effects of passive adaptation, even though this element is clearly present.

There is also impoverishment of thought and a narrowing down of the range of expression, but the contents and nature of *bobards*, fantasies, and mythical productions also bear the signs of active invention. In other words they are not a mere reflection of reality, but compensate for it. They tell us what the prisoners could do, as well as what they were forced to suffer,[42] how constraints were reshaped by them through myth, instead of their seeking refuge in mental escapism. The prisoners were thus able to maintain a certain psychic distance from the environment that surrounded them, instead of taking it as the only real world, and they were able to retain the tiniest fragment of what they had been, and hoped to revert to, instead of becoming 'good' prisoners.

Clearly, their scope for initiative was extremely limited and their behaviour inevitably oscillated between adapting to their environment and actively resisting it. But this was all the more reason for grasping at anything that might be made into a freedom story; or, better still, at little stories which could show how, in this or that behaviour, every and anyone could still express a fragment of the spirit of freedom.[43] At the heart of these accounts we find a resource of the human mind which, impotent in the face of overpowering force, instead drew on mythical hopes. They were hopes for actions and events which failed to happen or never could have happened. But that is not so different from so much of human hope and human thinking.

Notes

1 The Research Co-ordinating Committee members were: Anna Bravo, Anna Maria Bruzzone, Federico Cereja, and Brunello Mantelli.

2 G. Quazza (1984) 'Resistenza e deportazione', in *Il dovere di testimoniare*, Turin: Consiglio regionale del Piemonte.

3 For a comprehensive list of studies on Italian deportation see: A. Devoto (1962) *Bibliografia dell' oppressione nazista fino al 1962*, Florence: Olschky, and (1983) *L'oppressione nazista. Considerazioni e bibliografia 1963–1981*, Florence; and a study of Italian memoirs by F. Cereja (1986) 'La deportazione italiana nei campi di sterminio: letteratura, storiografia e prospettive di ricerca', in F. Cereja and B. Mantelli (eds) *La deportazione nei campi di sterminio. Studi e testimonianze*, Milan: Franco Angeli.

4 The most well-known among many by P. Levi (1948) *Se questo è un uomo* (*If this is a Man*) and (1963) *La tregua* (*The Truce*) both translated into many languages.

5 The Archive of Piedmontese Deportation (ADP) has tapes, transcripts, and other material (diaries, unpublished memoirs, documents, and photographs) collected during the research and now filed at the Turin ANED. All this will soon be available for consultation.

6 Of the first witnesses, 173 were men and 27 were women – 80 per cent at the time of deportation were under 30 and more than 50 per cent were between 18 and 24. The working-class group was the most numerous: 36 per cent workers and engineers, 15 per cent peasants and farm labourers, 10 per cent craftsmen and apprentices, 9 per cent small shopkeepers and shop-workers. The remaining 12 per cent were unemployed, housewives, professional soldiers, and one member of the clergy. Out of the 200, 13 were deported for racial reasons (all to

Auschwitz). More than 60 per cent were partisans, anti-Fascists, and workers arrested in the 1944 strikes. Sixteen per cent were members of the forces captured after the 8 September armistice and another 16 per cent had refused to go when called up or were people caught during searches, or people arrested without any definite reason.

7 All were interviewed about their lives as a whole, including the period in the camp as part of a comprehensive life story.

8 A. Bravo and D. Jalla (eds) (1986) *La vita offesa. Storia e memoria dei lager nazisti nei racconti di 200 sopravissuti*, Milan: Franco Angeli.

9 *Bobard* the word is French and means 'story', 'false rumour', and was used in the camps to indicate chat, gossip, and uncontrolled information circulating among prisoners.

10 We were helped by the following: E. J. Leed (1979) *No Man's Land. Combat and Identity in World War 1*, Cambridge: Cambridge University Press; P. Fussell (1975) *The Great War and Modern Memory*, London: Oxford University Press; and for references to total institutions E. Goffman (1961) *Asylums*, New York: Doubleday.

11 For instance see B. Bettelheim (1960) *The Informed Heart*, Glencoe: Freepress; V. E. Frankl (1947) *Ein Psycholog erlebt das KZ*, Vienna; E. Kogon (1946) *Der 'SS' Staat, Das System der deutschen Konzentrationslager*, Frankfurt: Europäische Verlagsanstalt; H. Langbein (1972) *Menschen in Auschwitz*, Vienna: Europa Verlag Gmbh.

12 See A. Devoto (1985) *Il comportamento umano in condizioni estreme, lo psicologo sociale e il lager nazista*, Milan: Franco Angeli.

13 Attilio Armando, ADP, pp. 25, 44.

14 Raffaele Maruffi, ADP, p. 24.

15 Stefano Barbera, ADP, p. 14.

16 Luigi Boghi, ADP, p. 37.

17 Afro Zanni, ADP, p. 21.

18 Davide Franco, ADP, p. 18.

19 Giuliana Fiorentino Tedeschi, ADP, pp. 19–20.

20 Raffaele Maruffi. ADP, pp. 22–3.

21 Francesco Corrado Borca, ADP, p. 42.

22 Maria Luisa Fasana, ADP, pp. 17, 36.

23 Natalina Bianco, ADP, p. 30.

24 Angelo Andreo, ADP, p. 11.

25 Francesco Corrado Borca, ADP, pp. 38, 18; Oreste Pelizzari, ADP, pp. 10–11.

26 Lorenzo Mazzei ADP, *passim*; Carlo Toniolo, ADP, pp. 18–19.

27 Giuseppina Doleati, ADP, pp. 56–7; Ignazio Depaoli, ADP, p. 68.

28 Giuliana Fiorentino Tedeschi, ADP, pp. 3–4; Bruno Vasari, ADP, *passim*.

29 J. Amery (1966) *Jenseits von Schuld und Sühne. Bewaltigungsversuche eines Überwältigten*, Munich: Sezesny Verlag. (In the Italian translation by Primo Levi (1988) *Intellettuale ad Auschwitz*, Turin: Bollati Boringhieri.)

30 H. Beuhm (1948) 'How did they survive? Mechanism of defence in Nazi concentration camps', *American Journal of Psychotherapy* 2 (1).

31 Bruno Bettelheim (1982) *Sopravvivere*, Milan: Feltrinelli, pp. 209–10 (Italian trans. of (1979) *Surviving and Other Essays*, New York: Alfred Knopf).
32 Primo Levi (1986) *I sommersi e i salvati*, Turin: Einaudi, p. 119.
33 A. Devoto and M. Martini (1981) *La violenza nei Lager*, Milan: Franco Angeli, p. 109.
34 Anna Cherchi, ADP, pp. 90–2; Biagio Benzi, ADP, p. 37.
35 Meo Bigatti, ADP, p. 14.
36 Leonardo Debenedetti, ADP, p. 14.
37 Adriano Peretto, ADP, pp. 33, 34.
38 Bruno Vasari, ADP, p. 16.
39 Mario Apruzzese, ADP, p. 44; A. Mongarli, ADP, pp. 51–2, 46–7.
40 Marcello Blandino, ADP, pp. 21–3.
41 E. J. Leed (1985) *Terra di nessuno*, Bologna: il Mulino, p. 160 (Italian trans. of *No Man's Land* (see note 10)).
42 Devoto (1985), op. cit. – but he defines them as 'basically negative activities' though he says that 'many survivors highlight the positive aspects' (p. 44).
43 Goffman, op. cit.

8

Abraham Esau's war, 1899–1901

Martyrdom, myth, and folk memory in Calvinia, South Africa

Bill Nasson

At the simplest level, this is an attempt to trace the life story of Abraham Esau, Namaqualand village carpenter and smith, through both local folk memories and conventional written sources. My purpose however is not just to reconstruct a sequence of events 'as they actually happened', but to consider how such qualities of martyrdom, myth, and legend have come to cluster around this man who became a civilian victim of a distant South African war nearly ninety years ago. For the construction and sporadic remaking of a local folk mythology of Esau, and its continuing persistence and strength in more recent times, to this day still infects social relations and political and cultural identities in the repressive and racist structure of a small rural South African town.

Abraham Esau was born in Kenhardt in the north-western Cape Colony around 1865, the eldest of several children of Adam Esau and his wife, Martha April. The family had lived for a number of years by alternating casual jobbing in small market settlements with agricultural fieldwork, but eventually settled down as living-in servants on the land of one William Seton, a wealthy stock farmer.

Oral evidence suggests that their attachment to William Seton made the Esaus culturally imitative of him. Impregnated with Anglicanism, they conversed in English and sought to provide a respectable English mission schooling for their children. Increasingly distanced from the Cape Boer social relations and practices typical of the rural north, the Esau family stood out as separate from those Coloured labouring households which were customarily bound into local Boer culture.

With English and Anglicanism important formative influences, Abraham Esau sought, as a young man, to behave as an 'Englische' or ' Engelse Kleurling'. A crucial element in Calvinia folk memory of Esau is the image of him as a 'Coloured Englishman', free of the grip of the master culture and customs of the dominant local Boer community.[1] And, as an adult, Esau developed a self-conscious and expressive 'British' social and cultural identity.[2]

For a number of years Esau worked as a carpenter, flitting from job to job in local villages. At some unknown point in the 1880s, he switched trades and settled in Calvinia as a blacksmith. The blacksmith's world was that of a late-nineteenth-century Coloured artisan class, sustained by the small market town and village economies of the rural Cape Colony.

A limited and subordinated political apprenticeship within a paternalist British colonial order had inspired this small artisan class with a passionate attachment to the liberalism of the Cape Colony's non-racial franchise, with its property and educational qualifications which excluded both a mass African proletariat and many poor whites. Petit bourgeois aspirations and ideals fed off a late-nineteenth-century tradition of Cape political liberalism which was associated with British rule. Paradoxically, at the very turn of the century when segregation in South Africa was already hardening, rooted social ideals of assimilation still persisted strongly in the Cape. What preserved this 'free' nation in the Cape was British imperial hegemony. Queen Victoria was its established local symbol.

The outbreak of the South African War (the Boer War) in October 1899 shattered social peace and threatened the continued stability of the dominant English-speaking settler political and economic bloc in the Cape. For individuals like Abraham Esau, living in the midst of large concentrations of disaffected Boers in the north, there was, from the outset, little cause to underestimate the threat from the republican guerrillas who began swarming over large parts of the countryside by 1900. Commando incursions southward from the independent Boer Orange Free State pitched Namaqualand into crisis. For vulnerable black civilians the spreading violence and disorder proved painful and traumatic.

In Calvinia and neighbouring villages like Clanwilliam, feelings smouldered during this tense and menacing period. With republican power rolling over Namaqualand, the village became gripped by a crisis atmosphere; it wintered uneasily in 1900, living in daily expectation of assault and occupation. Frightened of conquest and specific personal repression, the Coloured inhabitants of Calvinia turned massively against virtually all Boers, whether resident villagers or intruders. As a community increasingly under siege they developed a fierce, sectarian, anti-Boer identity, a militant local consciousness defining themselves as British. The force of that movement burnt itself into subsequent popular memory:

Man, our people then were born British. They did not want to go under those uncivilised Free State Boers. Here in Calvinia they were afraid. It was a common feeling to hate the Boers. Even those who lived here, most of them, they did not talk to them.[3]

Soon the Calvinia Coloured community had become a hotbed of what one might call Cape jingoism, vehemently pro-British and biliously anti-republican. A species of Cape British 'national' identity bubbled into life, visible in colourful and rowdy pro-imperial petitioning and demonstrating, and in the staging of processions in which effigies of republican leaders ('they made them out of straw with also bark and leaves')[4] were ritually pelted with dung or scattered in the wind.

Out of this turbulent atmosphere Abraham Esau suddenly emerged as a central and influential personality. His conduct crystallized the prevailing political mood. Oral tradition, backed by written sources, has him making his first major public appearance on 19 May 1900, at the head of a victory parade and rally to celebrate the relief of Mafeking on the far northern border of the colony. Characteristically in Calvinia, awareness of national struggle and crisis ran concurrently with local impulse and imagination. Some several hundred people, holding aloft flags and ribbons, massed to hear Esau denounce the enemy. An attending British army intelligence agent noted that the blacksmith possessed 'a big voice, of which he enjoys greatly the sound'.[5]

Barely four months later, Esau was pushed dramatically into the foreground of local resistance. With panic rising and rumour flying thick and fast, a large group of men, headed by Esau, clamoured for firearms outside the magistracy. The Resident Magistrate, Peter Dreyer, turned a deaf ear; he considered the issue of guns to Coloured civilians likely to lead to 'mischief'.[6]

Esau countered this official rebuff by rallying his anxious and impatient followers and readying them to resist attack with their own inadequate resources. His motley band drilled itself and posted outlying pickets with cattle horns and bells to sound warnings. Perhaps nothing speaks so eloquently of active and sustained community solidarity in the village as the involvement of children and women in flurries of defensive preparation. Women also acted as ammunition carriers, using aprons; in addition they collected wooden clubs, carried food, and 'made sharp some swords which Abraham got from skirt soldiers who were once by Middelpos'.[7] What commenced as generalized panic in the face of external force rapidly became structured into a collective resistance. But it had a distinct element of personal leadership which gave it its character.

There was only one candidate. The village blacksmith was becoming a warrior; men and women not only listened to him but were ready to stand with him against rifles, whips, and horses.

When the anticipated enemy action failed to materialize, Esau's followers stood down. Early in October, the blacksmith was out once again, hoping to capture the magistracy mind with the formal dignity of a petition for weapons with which to defend the village and surrounding area. An urgent address was signed by thirty-seven men, including two Coloured Calvinia policemen, Christian Manel, and Carolus Pretorius, and despatched to the Acting Resident Magistrate of Clanwilliam, the senior area official. A copy was also sent to Sir Alfred Milner, the British High Commissioner for South Africa. But the immediate response was again brusque rejection. 'Esau came to many houses to say that the government said that this war is a white man's business and the trouble had nothing to do with the Coloureds.'[8] One tale has him

> standing with Barend Smit and old Christian Manel, striking matches to burn the government's letter to him. It was burnt in the open, there in front of Archell's shop. He wanted the magistrate and the English whites to see it done, to see how bad it was.[9]

So began the real forging of Abraham Esau in collective memory as a kind of budding local Emiliano Zapata, and the celebration of that image in the historical commemoration of village crisis and village resistance.

At some point after the ignominy of the failed petition, Esau is known to have slipped out of Calvinia; a weekly field report by the intelligence department of the Namaqualand Field Force noted him near Williston on 25 October, riding a Basuto pony, clad in army greatcoat and hat, and accompanied by two armed 'ruffianly Cape Boys'. Evidence then suggests that with the help of local guides, this trio undertook a secret, meandering journey across hostile open countryside to Clanwilliam.[10]

There, the decisive moment for Abraham Esau was winning a confidential interview with Lieutenant James Preston, the resident British army secret agent. Several successive meetings, whose content went unrecorded, were described by the officer as 'cordial and most useful'. Indeed, the two men appear to have developed a cosy personal relationship.

Although the documentary record confirms that Esau wormed his way into Preston's confidence, direct written information on war-related activities which developed from this relationship is virtually non-existent. The picture that emerges is essentially suggestive. There are reasonable grounds for believing that the special agent's intelligence reference on 14 November to 'my new secret detective' concerned Esau. Equally, the blacksmith would in all probability have been the shadowy 'A' who prepared reports on Boer rebel meetings for the Namaqualand Field Force intelligence department.[11]

Beyond this, the trickle of written sources dries up. Further reconstruction and interpretation of Esau's conduct up to Calvinia's occupation by Boer forces in January 1901 has to draw entirely on a wealth of oral tradition still resonant in popular memory.

Esau became a provocative presence in Clanwilliam. Riding the countryside on a large black horse and brandishing a sabre, he rallied Coloured support for the imperial war effort, exhorting, encouraging, and advising at every turn. Esau's exertions brought scores of men and women to his side; their number included domestic workers, migratory labourers, road workers, and village artisans. Tradition records that he spoke of them as his 'faithful children'. After his permanent return to Calvinia some time in November, he kept a secret register of their names in his smithy. One typically apocryphal story is that he sealed the incriminating list in a metal casket at the bottom of a brick kiln. Knitted together by a sense of collective identity and a combative spirit, and sworn to secrecy by oath, Esau's followers formed a solid core of spies, snoops, and informers. Accumulating a mixture of incriminating hard information, petty gossip, and slander about the character, opinions, and actions of suspect Boer rebels, this cell poured names and details of suspicious incidents into the bulging files of British army intelligence.

To secure the passage of men and women carrying information across open country thick with guerrillas, there was a rhythmic routine of signals by cattle horn, warning stones, and marking of farm gateposts. What are popularly believed to be surviving traces of Esau's cell occasionally still come to light. In 1947 for instance, some rusted cattle horns were found underneath a pile of stones in a field alongside the road to Middelpos. 'Even though the rain was coming down, people walked out to see it. They all said it was a relic from Abraham Esau's time with the Boers. Some of them wanted a priest there so there could be a blessing.'[12]

In the very short time that it was active, the degree of discipline and organization in Esau's half-hidden force must clearly have been remarkable. Its proportions – as remembered in oral tradition – suggest that it bore many of the classic characteristics of a rural secret movement.

The blacksmith's anti-Boer adventure was both a silent, independent war against the threat of conquest and subjection, and an attempt to construct a protective form of association and allegiance directly with imperial power. As the locality's best-known British collaborator, Esau acted as a watchful external broker; the priceless asset of carefully gathered local intelligence was to be traded against British readiness to defend Calvinia against republican depredation.

Before long, Esau's known role as a British agent had made his presence in the eyes of local republican sympathizers increasingly unwelcome. Their generalized hostility soon metamorphosed into improbable fact, and thence to visions of unimaginable mayhem. It was said that the blacksmith was stockpiling an underground arsenal in readiness for an anti-settler rising on 1 January 1901. There were growing beliefs, based entirely on hearsay, that Esau was being showered with horses and krugerrands by army agents.[13] There were also stories spread by labourers intended to stimulate their masters' alarm. These celebrated Esau's capacity to penetrate settler circles in order to eavesdrop on seditious utterances against the Crown. And they built him up into a mythic individual. Several tales refer to his cunning ability to assume 'whiteness' for deception. At times he was 'covered in white clay so that farmers could not see that there was a Coloured man riding near their land.'[14] Another powerful and emotive story said that he had shaved off his moustache, grown his hair, and bundled himself up in women's clothing to snoop around farmers' kitchens.[15] By the end of 1900, according to British intelligence in Namaqualand, Abraham Esau had provoked 'great suspicion and hostility' and was regarded as 'abominable' by guerrilla commandants riding up to 250 miles away.[16]

It was just before six on the evening of 7 January 1901 that Calvinia fell suddenly to a light force of some fifty Orange Free State Boer commandos. With its position secured, the Orange Free State force set to work to establish a new layer of power. Commandos began flooding in and by 13 January there were almost 600 men billeted in the village. With the arrival of a senior officer, Judge J.B.M. Hertzog, and Commandant Charles Niewoudt, martial law was declared; buildings, bedding, food, horses, and personal valuables were requisitioned at gunpoint from sullen inhabitants. Niewoudt in particular trod swiftly. On 12 January, a day after his entry into Calvinia, he launched a manhunt of those specially marked down for retribution, and for whom an arrest warrant had been issued prior to the occupation. Chief among them was, predictably, Abraham Esau, believed to have been ferreted out of a hiding place 'which was in a cellar underneath the shop of the English Jew Cohen'.[17]

With this sweep complete, Niewoudt proceeded to proclaim himself *Landdrost* of Calvinia and thereby symbolically to take possession of the village as Orange Free State land. The story is told that he 'stood in front of the magistrate's office. With him he had four *sjamboks* which he turned around and around above his head and he threw them in different directions. "Look you people", he shouted, "this is now our land."'[18]

Oral sources paint a picture of this new authority quite as harrowing as those to be found in contemporary newspaper reports. Niewoudt is remembered as an invader who 'had no real law, no rules, only the *sjambok*'.[19] The Coloured inhabitants of Calvinia found themselves confronting an alien and abrasive political culture which brusquely overrode their sense of natural justice, seemingly turning them into chattels without civic rights. Their lives were being forcibly reconstructed, their British colonial status and common self-definition stifled.

The most immediate and direct embodiment of the 'British' and 'free' identity to which the conquered community clung was naturally Abraham Esau. The tale which probably best commemorates Esau's heroic qualities of truculence and obstinacy came from an old woman informant who, shrieking with laughter, claimed that 'you know Abraham carried in his pocket a dead Boer's ear which he showed to the Free Staters and said that he was as deaf as that ear'.[20] With Esau drenched in the spittle of republican venom, the question of his execution had never really been more than one of timing. His last days were especially wretched. At dawn on 15 January he was dragged before Veldkornet Van der Merwe and sentenced, according to Dreyer's well-informed eye-witness account, 'to 25 lashes for having spoken against the Boers and for having attempted to arm the natives.'[21]

On 5 February the end came. Presumably acting under instructions from Van der Merwe, one Stephanus Strydom had Esau clapped in leg-irons, strapped between two horses and bumped and scraped along at a brisk canter before being dumped about five miles east of the Calvinia municipal boundary. There, after another beating, he was shot dead by Strydom. Just one day later, the republican occupation of Calvinia suddenly ended with the arrival of a British column under Lieutenant-Colonel Herbert de Lisle.

Echoes of the affair actually bounced high enough to catch the attention of the Cape Colonial Secretary (who ordered an investigation) and also that of the British Colonial Secretary, Joseph

Chamberlain, as well as Milner. The High Commissioner immediately seized upon the atrocity story as a suitable decent stick with
which to beat the Boer Republics as bloody and barbarous.[22]

In the decade of postwar reconstruction some shrewd English-
language settler politicians also chose to remember Abraham Esau.
Several candidates of the pro-imperialist Progressive Party made
the most of the Esau story in bidding for the votes of Coloured
electors in the northern and north-western Cape in the colony's
1904 general election. A bitter and vituperative political contest was
a good moment for the creation of martyrdom, and for this brief
moment Esau became visibly the Coloured martyr of a Cape liberal
political culture.

The harnessing of citizenship 'rights' and 'liberties' to the
imperial interest could scarcely have been more explicit – nor more
electorally successful for the Progressives. Significantly, this reconstruction of Esau's historic British identity was also how many of
Calvinia's Coloured populace chose to see it. As one woman
remembers of her family's political traditions,

> you see, we Andersons were Jingoes. Also Abraham Esau's
> people, the Esaus, they were Jingoes. Abraham Esau, he was
> also educated, his English was full. He knew what it was to be a
> British citizen. The Free Staters hated his kind of 'kleurling
> mense.'[23]

It was Esau's personal stirring up of a British populism to confront
alien conquest that gave his dramatic experience and martyrdom
much of its popular meaning.

In the making and remaking of the Esau tradition, an obvious
question to consider is what manner of martyr was Abraham Esau
at the turn of the century? With his execution, he became and has
remained the first martyr of a poor and subordinated rural
community. Martyrdom was related to leadership: the war certainly
made Esau a leader. But it was not exclusively leadership that made
Esau a martyr. Bereaved and enraged Coloured men and women in
Calvinia needed a symbol of injustice and persecution and they
made a martyr out of Abraham Esau.

In the years following the South African War, the martyrdom of
Abraham Esau served a recognizable function. It met a psychological need in a bruised community adjusting to postwar restabilization
and readjustment and offered an integrating element at this
particular historical moment. Esau became the mythic symbol of a
revivified British patriotism in Calvinia village life. Thus, craftsmen
who constructed an annexe to the – racially segregated – Anglican

mission church which became the Abraham Esau Memorial Chapel
and the Abraham Esau Memorial Hall were

> Jingoes, you see. I remember old Jan Nortjie with us, he had an
> old Black Watch kilt, he used to work in this kilt ....Yes, old Jan,
> he said he got the kilt from Abraham Esau who had it as a present
> from the Queen when he met her in Cape Town. He was terribly
> proud of himself. He made the stone plaque for Esau ... when it
> was put down I remember how we all sang 'God Save the King'.[24]

An outbreak of Esau fever accompanying the erection of the
memorial building in the 1910s saw a folklorish scramble after
artefacts with which to adorn a living and renewed tradition:

> There are those little hills around the town, 'koppies', and a bit of
> a big hill that we call 'Revunie'. That's a Hottentot word. It was a
> Hottentot secret place. Everybody knew that Esau used to go up
> there with his spies. That's where those Boers couldn't find them.
> Many days as children we used to go up there to see what we
> could find. In manure one time we found Esau's bullet. I took it
> down to the chapel where they kept it in a box. The wood for
> Esau's altar they also brought down from 'Revunie'.[25]

A crucial dimension in the long march of an Esau folk mythology
has been its interaction with the subsequent growth and consolida-
tion of an increasingly segregationist South African state more and
more dominated by Boer Afrikaner politics. Calvinia villagers have
seen a relationship between the individual life story of Abraham
Esau and historical events such as the formation of Union in 1910,
the emergence of Afrikaner Nationalist *apartheid* rule in 1948, and
the establishment of South Africa as a Republic in 1961. For Esau
and his story have been assimilated as a means of registering an
historical identity, and perhaps equally, against losing it. 'Myth-
making,' as Gwen Davies has put it, 'can be perceived as a means to
survival'.[26]

That survival has been the inward continuity of a peculiarly
British thread in the lives of Coloured villagers in and around
Calvinia. One Anglican priest remembers being told 'the Esau
story' at his first meeting with his congregation after his arrival at the
mission church in 1937. He learned how

> the Afrikaners sewed him up in an ox-skin until he was stretched
> and suffocated to death in the sun. There was lots of bitter feeling
> towards Afrikaners. They did have an extraordinarily strong
> British connection ....Oh yes, there was a very strong jingoistic
> element, among even the common labourers.[27]

Both at outdoor services 'behind the Loeriesfontein Hotel' as well as at

> the Esau Memorial Chapel, the people wouldn't allow me to take mass in Afrikaans, even though I was fluent. They were an overwhelmingly Afrikaans-speaking congregation, but they insisted on conducting business in English. They didn't mind the Coloured Catechist doing it in Afrikaans now and again, but they demanded that the *Engelse Predikant* always take them in English. I soon learnt that it was part of their feeling of protest, over all those years, for Abraham Esau. *His* chapel had to be an *English* chapel.[28]

A rich and amazing folklore persisted alongside these rituals. Towards the end of the 1940s the resident Anglican priest recalls being told

> a quite fantastic yarn by Martha Baartman, one of the oldest women in Loeriesfontein. Her story was about how two old and well-known Afrikaner farm women who were completely dumb came to lose their voices. It so happened that as children they were out at night on the Clanwilliam Road when the Free Staters were about, when they saw Abraham Esau and his spies galloping past in the dark. When he turned his eyes upon them they were so overcome with fright that they could no longer speak. I was also regaled with another peculiar story about how Esau used to drive sheep into the deep waters at Brandvlei. As they floated, their bodies rotted and turned into Afrikaners. These stories were told to me in pretty ropey English ....These Basters were all terribly proud of the fact that they had these connections with Abraham Esau.[29]

Here an Esau folklore is expressed directly as myth, in the sense of a fantasy told in an especially powerful and vivid way. The accumulated working of myth is not to diminish its content nor to constrict its telling, but to expand upon them. It is to unharness the implausible or fantastic and to project it into the world as an enactment of power.

National events also played their part in sharpening local bitterness and enmities. When the old Boer republics were incorporated as provinces alongside the established British colonies of the Cape and Natal in the new Union of South Africa in 1910, there was strain in relations between some Coloured and white villagers. At the Anglican mission church people drew the memory of their martyr around them like some rough blanket against the winds of a new centralized state. For across the Union fell the ominous shadow of 'Freestater' and 'Transvaler' Afrikaner leadership. A teacher remembers learning from his family that:

> It just wasn't right to have the Union. Our people were bitter then about the situation as it was turning out after the war. My father spoke at a special service for Abraham Esau that year, he was a Catechist. He said the Union would help the Boers, that it was an insult to the memory of those who had died for the British. He said that we in the Cape, we who were Esau's people, would find life hard.[30]

Simmering hostilities around 1910 were as nothing compared to the disturbance centred on the election of 1948 and the subsequent Nationalist victory. At this time a special element in Calvinia's social life was the presence of an unusually energetic and abrasive Dutch Reformed mission church pastor, Eerwaarde Uys. In Calvinia the Afrikaner nationalist class alliance turned upon vestiges of 'Britishness' which had long affronted them. Uys, for instance,

> went to the Esau Memorial Chapel where the Union Jack always flew, and tore it down and tore it in half. He said Esau had committed treason against the *volk*, and that respectable Coloured people would not honour murderers. What followed was a forceful appeal to 'so-called Coloured' members of his congregation, that the National Party was the party that really cared about the 'kleurling mense' and that old memories and grievances should be buried ... now they were part of them and therefore they must vote for them. In those days some had the vote ....it was common knowledge that Uys was up to no good standing at the polling booth, next to the police, without saying a word.[31]

Uys' attempts to form a new paternalist consensus between an ascendant *volk* in 1948 and a subservient group of Coloured retainers foundered on the back of a young schoolteacher named Lesley Carelse. With his moralistic radicalism of rights and freedoms, Carelse seemed to be renewing old traditions and aspirations; a shop-worker, then in her twenties, thought 'he was a fighter for our people, another Abraham Esau in Calvinia'. In this perception she was neither alone nor unrepresentative. In popular imagination the Carelse drama caught echoes of the Esau episode, bouncing off a popular tradition which had hardened into memory. Among those who bore witness, what characterizes accounts of Carelse's clash with Uys is an historical awareness of the Esau inheritance in Calvinia. As a local doctor remembers:

Mr. Carelse said that he had been accused of being a communist by the *Sendingkerk* missionary, Uys ....He was supposed to have said something out loud, at a meeting somewhere, which Uys interpreted as communism, and as an attack on the Church of the Afrikaner people. So he got a group of his elders to waylay Mr. Carelse and they took him out – this was the first time – and assaulted him very badly. He said he was going to sue Uys. Then, things began to build up ... Afrikaans-speaking people in the town came together to take action. ... They said they'd given cheeky boys like Abraham Esau many a hiding in their time, so Carelse should expect one now.

Finally, in the night, while Carelse was asleep, a group of whites went and got him out of his bed. They took him by car, right out into the veldt, they took all his clothes off and they *sjambokked* him within an inch of his life and left him there. He was found, naked and bleeding, trying to crawl his way back to Calvinia. Of course there was a sort of token search for his attackers, 'token' being the operative word. It was a tough sort of area. I had the sad experience of being taken to where Carelse had been whipped, it was near to the spot where Abraham Esau was said to have been murdered ....People said they did that *deliberately*.

The case really caused terrible upheaval at that time, opening up old wounds. Many people felt the connection with the events of the Boer War ....Some of my older patients wanted a plaque for Lesley Carelse put up in the Esau Chapel. He had a bad mental breakdown, you see, and then died.[32]

Twelve years later came the white referendum on the Nationalist government proposal to reconstitute South Africa as a Republic, breaking with the British Commonwealth. In Calvinia, as elsewhere, Afrikaner Nationalists poised to write *finis* to the tradition of constitutional connection with the British Crown.

In opposition to the orgy of white republicanism, Calvinia's dominated classes turned once more to their own form of patriotism. Drawing on the ghost of Abraham Esau, introspectively local, it also reached out to a wider historical consciousness and a sense of imperial political culture never completely eroded by a dominating Afrikaner nationalism:

Well, Daantjie Scholtz, he was the chief of the National Party there in 1960, he came to the school to brag that 'we've got our new Republic, we shall be a new proud nation'. And he was actually shouted down by the teachers and some of the pupils. One of them got up to say that he had a murderers' Republic,

which was stained with the British blood of Abraham Esau. He
was very brave. He hissed at Scholtz that the Boers were making
slaves of people, that they had been robbed of their rights left to
them by the British.

As you'll imagine, Scholtz was absolutely furious. He said 'If I
hear that man's name again, there'll be trouble for you people.
You are traitors, just as he was. You and the English-speakers,
those Cape liberal types.'[33]

We can see the Esau story as an active, self-conscious historical
legacy in Calvinian life, shown up by episodes such as the simmering
tension over republicanism in 1960–1. And their long confrontation
has given Coloured and Afrikaner people two different histories
and two different memories. The power with which the Esau legend
has worked through the phases of that struggle has helped to make
those histories and memories almost hallucinatory. Indeed, oral
history provides one vivid example of a hallucinatory spasm, a case
of a literally fevered memory. One informant remembers moving to
Calvinia as a nurse a month after South Africa became a Republic:

> I went there in June 1961 and was introduced to the patients as
> the *rooinek* sister. An elderly woman muttered something about
> the damn British. Well, when I was next on night duty she flew at
> me about the Boer War, about the British sending that Coloured
> Esau to spy on them and poison their children. She screamed that
> it was right that he was shot, they should have burned his body.
>
> Well, I can tell you I was totally dumbfounded by this woman's
> hysterics. After a doctor came in to sedate her because she was so
> uncontrollable, I learned that she was having hysterics about an
> incident that related to sixty years before ....It was just as if it was
> happening right there, there and then.[34]

Here historical emotion was a spring from which it was impossible
to break free; folk legend was a nightmare into which one awoke.

And remembrance continues to be enacted at other levels. On
Calvinia sheep farms, herders and shearers still talk animatedly of
the events and atmosphere of the South African War, with a relish
for adding to the inventions of the Esau folklore. Oral tradition
carries the mirrors of their own past, the yoke of Free State Boer
conquest and the settled paternalistic rule of a Victorian Cape
liberalism. We can still glimpse some of them as the bearers of a
half-hidden identity ultimately derived from an old and dead British
order, reliving that moment when conquest seemed about to
remake their lives and historical future:

> Coloured chaps on the colonial side called themselves 'Rooi
> Esaus', that name is still heard today. There's also a dance called

'Rooi-rooi' which the older workers do on the farms. One old man I know does this party piece for his fellow shearers when he's tight, as his father taught him. Kind of folk dance I suppose, about Abraham Esau driving off the Boers and then being captured by them, and then having to dig his own grave. When he's finished he stands up to salute and sing to Queen Victoria before they shoot him.[35]

Within Calvinia, the folkloric presence of Abraham Esau has lodged deep within popular memory and feeling. It does not represent a classic mythic story cycle which reverberates across all imagined time. For in both oral tradition and the conventional historical record the Esau story is datable, rooted in a specific historical context and playing a clear ideological role in remembering that past. However much oral invention has come to cluster around it, its character in human memory is structured by what Isidore Okpewho terms 'an historical faith'.[36] Abraham Esau lives as much in history as in folk mythology.

The invocation of an Esau 'tradition' of a Cape British 'patriotism' in oral remembrance and storytelling is the projection of an alternative identity which continues to reside in the – often muted – consciousness of Calvinia's inhabitants. It marks off a collective popular memory of resistance and oppression from the ways in which memory is officially mythologized, and celebrated through ruling white political forces in the state. Indeed, an undeclared contest to establish a heroic Esau legend over a dark and demonic memory can be seen as itself integral to local political, cultural, and moral distances between Black and white. In this sense the nourishing of an Esau mythology provides a social form through which memory and a lingering older identity are established and renewed.

The power of the orally circulated narratives and interpretations of the Esau story thus lies in its particular illumination of a community's view of its own past and historical fate. And the oral making and remaking of its mythic qualities shapes a consciousness of history as a morally dramatic and episodic force. As threads from 1948 or 1960 loop back to the conflicts of 1899–1901, popular historical consciousness in Calvinia becomes, to use Ron Grele's reflection, 'a dramatic view of eternally contending binary oppositions'.[3] And, as significantly, the place of Abraham Esau's martyrology in oral history reflects upon the nature of oral history itself as well as upon the role of myth. It admirably exemplifies Luisa Passerini's and Alessandro Portelli's conception of the special quality of oral sources, namely that they are not just about factual content but about the representation of cultural modes and meanings.[38] For in the final analysis, the character of Esau remembrance has meaning in terms not only of empirical accuracy but above all of ideological content. In the ignition of the Esau folk tradition we can glimpse a mediation between the predicament of a brutal South African past and the predicament of a brutal South African present. In this country the long march of white domination 'has indeed produced some highly instrumental myths. But struggles against oppression produce their own historical myths, symbols of resistance and interpretations of the past....It is important that they too be explored and understood'.[39] For the Black subordinate classes of Calvinia, the mythology of Abraham Esau has actively helped to shape their social identities and ideological standpoints. And it survives today as one of those symbols of resistance and interpretations of the past.

Notes

1 Interviews, Mrs Florence Malan, teacher (b. 1903); Wilhemina Isaacs, domestic worker (b. 1900); Nettie Daniels, dressmaker (b. 1889).
2 W.R. Nasson and J.M.M. John (1985) 'Abraham Esau: a Calvin martyr in the Anglo-Boer war', *Social Dynamics*: 65; K. Schoeman (1985) 'Die Dood van Abraham Esau: Ooggetuieberigte uit die besette Calvinia, 1901', *Quarterly Bulletin of the South African Library* 40 (2): 62.
3 Nettie Daniels.
4 ibid.
5 National Army Museum, London, NAM 6807/190, 1st Cavalry Division, Intelligence Papers, District Military Intelligence Reports 1900–2: Section E, 21 May 1900.
6 Cape Archives, Cape Town (CA), Archive of the Resident Magistrate, Clanwilliam, 1/CWM/4/1/2/1, RM Calvinia to Special Justice of the Peace (*secret*) 23 September 1900.
7 Nettie Daniels. 'Skirt soldiers' probably refers to a battalion of Scottish Fusiliers which was stationed in Namaqualand.
8 Interview, Mr Willem Peters, stonemason (b. 1894).
9 Florence Malan.
10 Nasson and John, op. cit., p. 67.
11 NAM 6112/190/15/4, Namaqualand Field Force Papers, 1900–2, Summaries of Intelligence, June 1900–January 1901, Confidential Report, 31 November 1900.
12 Interview, Mr Samuel Anderson, warehouseman (b. 1923).
13 W.R. Nasson (1983) 'Black Society in the Cape Colony and the South African War of 1899–1902: a social history', Ph.D. thesis, University of Cambridge, p. 171.
14 Nettie Daniels.
15 ibid.; Willem Peters; Florence Malan.

16 NAM 6807/190, Military Intelligence Reports, 1900–1, Section C. Summaries, 22 December 1900.
17 Florence Malan.
18 Interview, Mr John Esau, carpenter (b. 1911). *Sjambok*: a leather whip.
19 University of Cape Town, Kaplan Centre for Jewish Studies, Oral Life Histories Collection, Testimony of Mr Jacob Zurne (b. 1887).
20 Nettie Daniels.
21 CA, Attorney General's Department, Anglo-Boer War Files, AG 2070, Papers relating to the occupation of Calvinia by the enemy, R.M. Calvinia to Secretary, Law Department, 29 January 1902; *Graaff-Reinet Advertiser*, 6 February 1901; *Midland News*, 19 February 1901.
22 Public Records Office, London, CO 48 Cape Colony despatches and correspondence 1899–1902, CO 48/551/5078, *encl.* in W. Hely-Hutchinson to J. Chamberlain (*conf.*), 20 February 1901, *Memorandum* from G.V. Fiddes, Imperial Secretary, 18 February 1901; *Telegram from Sir A. Milner to the Secretary of State for War, relating to the Reported Outrage on Esau at Calvinia, Cd. 464, 1901*; Milner to Lyttelton Gell, 19 February 1901, in C. Headlam (ed.) (1933) *The Milner Papers, South Africa, 1899–1905*, vol. 2, London: Cassell, pp. 233–4.
23 Samuel Anderson. 'Kleurling mense': Coloured people.
24 Florence Malan.
25 Wilhemina Isaacs.
26 G. Davies (1986) 'The art of self-defence', *Planet* 57: 107.
27 Interview, Revd Alastair McGregor (b. 1910).
28 Interview, Revd Reginald Pearce (b. 1915).
29 ibid. 'Basters' or, more colloquially, 'Bastards': descendants of migrant communities of mixed African or Asian slave and Dutch culture who emerged in eighteenth-century South Africa.
30 Interview, Mr Leslie Newman, teacher (b. 1913).
31 Reginald Pearce.
32 Dr Alfred Liddle (b. 1919).
33 Reginald Pearce.
34 Interview, Mrs Taffy Shearing, nurse (b. 1925). 'Rooinek': redneck, a derogatory Boer and Afrikaner term for English-speakers, made popular in the South African War.
35 Taffy Shearing. 'Rooi': literally red, as in redneck or red tunic, a common Boer identification of British soldiers.
36 Okpewho (1983), p. 89.
37 Grele (1979), p. 40.
38 Passerini (1979), p. 84; Portelli (1981a), p. 99.
39 W. Beinart (1986) 'History of the African people', *South African Historical Journal* 18: 228.

Manhood and images of women

9

Free sons of the forest
Storytelling and the construction of identity among Swedish lumberjacks

Ella Johansson

Lumberjacks played a very important part in the rapid transformation of Sweden from a peasant society to a modern industrial state. For most of the period between 1860 and 1940 which I am studying there were more loggers than factory-workers.[1] Central to their ideology was an emphasis on *freedom*, which to them differentiated their work from other jobs, and a strong sense of *individualism*. These factors suggest a class identity with features distinct from that of urban workers, which has tended to dominate and, to some extent, to stereotype notions of the working class. Here I shall concentrate on the loggers' storytelling about a heroic type of lumberjack and attempt to show how this type of hero was relevant to a certain kind of class conflict and construction of identity.

Swedish logging started in the 1860s at the time when Britain ceased to impose protective duties on wood products. Logging was an activity of the winter season and usually migrant work, with the workers living away from home, isolated for months in the northern Swedish forests and living in very poor housing conditions.[2] It was a very tough existence with a competitive work ethos and ruthless self-exploitation. Work was organized on the basis of piecework contracts. Farmers sold the right to fell their forests to companies. The companies contracted horse-owning men to deliver the timber from a certain area. These contractors did the work of transport and in their turn paid other men to fell the timber. Although working for wages paid by employers, loggers saw themselves as individual entrepreneurs, who handled and transported logs for a price. Demarcation lines between workers and employers were thus blurred, while the relation between the amount of work and its result in money terms was very clear.

Before the logging period northern Swedish peasant culture was relatively egalitarian. Most men stood a chance of becoming head of a middle-sized farm or smallholding. Shortages of resources could be supplemented by exploiting the forests (in those days communally owned) through grazing, hunting, or slash and burn cultivation. The possession of land, kinship, luck, or fertility were not seen as very important or necessary to the production of wealth. Hard work was the real source of successful survival, and to be a 'workman' or 'workperson' gave a clear status open to any assiduous man or woman:

> The difference between the wealthy and the very poor was not that great. The wealthy certainly always had food, while the poor sometimes did not. But they both wore patched clothes and they were both used to a hard day's work. A proper workman was respected and judgment of any who had a tendency to be lazy was hard. Nobody took their own work more seriously than the richest family in the village.

Although the rapid population growth of these decades meant that many descendants of freeholders were disinherited, the landless clung to their belief that basically they were equals of the farmers. But for farmers, possession of inherited homesteads – rarely bigger than 5 to 7 hectares – became an important social factor and work became less important than status acquired by inheritance. In the *bygd* – the cultivated land and old settlements of the river valleys – young or landless people were either unemployed or exploited in summer by the farmers. Farmwork in the *bygd* was characterized by arbitrariness in payment, poor lodging, and harsh treatment and working conditions. Logging with its autonomous work situation and fixed prices was perceived as a just and liberating alternative.

The egalitarian, individualistic, and competitive life in the forests in winter formed a sharp contrast to the increasing hierarchization of the *bygd* areas which the men went back to in the summers. It was striking that the loggers consistently avoided anything that could contribute to the formation of a hierarchy among them. Both their meals and their processes of work were extremely individualized and isolated. The lifestyle lacked most of the elements that for an anthropologist would constitute cultural unity: sharing of food, ritual, initiations, rules of order, and cleanliness. I am not claiming that these things were not culturally organized, but rather that they were organized in such a way as to deny the existence of cultural uniformities. Loggers differed from many other egalitarian cultures in that they avoided sharing and co-operation.

At an abstract level, northern Sweden might be said to be socially divided into landed farmers and landless lumberjacks. This was how the people themselves saw it. But when one comes to look at the intimate details of life stories, this dichotomy is no longer clearly apparent. People's actual beliefs and strategies did not correspond unambiguously with their class position. It was more of a continuum between two poles with those in the middle of this continuum holding complicated, even contradictory values, between these two opposing class positions. The picture is even more blurred, since lumberjacks – understood as men working in the forest – consisted both of farmers and 'real' lumberjacks – that is, the landless, who preferred to identify themselves as lumberjacks.[3] During the winter, a *bygd* was almost empty of its male population, including children and old men. But in spite of this social mix as we shall see, the value system of the forest was controlled by the landless.

During my fieldwork and the reading of life stories I was struck by the emphasis on story telling. It was a favourite way of passing time during long winter evenings in the isolated camps. The predominant theme was 'the quintessential lumberjack', depicting a certain type of cultural hero. Before discussing the stories of the 'ultimate' logger, let us look at their stereotype of the other extreme of the continuum: the rich farmer. Farmers, unlike the landless loggers, were not represented by any set of stories about individuals. The farmers' way of being sometimes came into the stories, but they were not folklorized like the 'essential' lumberjacks.

The Swedish word for farmer, *bonde*, has a somewhat old-fashioned connotation, because it refers to peasants. For twentieth-century cash-croppers the term was seen as stigmatizing and was replaced with the modern *lantbrukare*. I believe that the successfully articulated 'farmer hate' of the landless working class was to a large extent the cause of this stigmatization. A significant feature of the Swedish working class was their strong rural connection. It was not only to lumberjacks but also, for example, to sailors and fishermen that a *bonde* was synonymous with a pitiful landlubber, an ignorant and provincial yokel. The landless in the north developed a similar way of representing the farmers. Here, access to agricultural land was not the dominant source of wealth as it is in most peasant economies. But in terms of prestige there was an important distinction between owning a proper homestead in an old cultivated area, a *bygd*, and living on a small, new farm, which was often leased, in the woodlands. The latter group were more likely to identify themselves as lumberjacks, although they might spend their year divided in exactly the same way, between farmwork and logging, as the proper farmers.

The livelihood of farmers was based on a guaranteed subsistence, although they often lacked cash, while the loggers' way of living was based on the flow of money and the purchase of commodities of industrial, and often foreign origin. For the lumberjacks, this was a major factor which allowed them to deride the farmers for being old-fashioned and tardy.

> From the wealthy agricultural districts around Storsjon and Nackten the 'Grey Homespun-peasants' came travelling with crispbreads and butterkegs in their foodbuckets and with sourmilk in wooden tubs buried in the hay. The people of the woodlands had no love for them. They were stuck up and self-important and buttered their peabread thickly even if their income was lean. Their work always gave them some cash to pay their taxes.

This peasant food is often contrasted to the 'exotic' imported food that the landless so proudly consumed; wheatflour, salt pork, sugar and coffee. In the farmers' value system, these expensive imported goods were offensively luxurious, and everyday consumption of them was an intemperate sin. The farmers' access to their own food meant they had less need for cash and that they could make the lowest offers on contracts with the companies. They were ridiculed for not working as hard as the landless who really needed the money. In some areas there was a very definite split between landed and landless, because during food crises and periods of famine, the farmers had ignored the moral economy and refused to help their landless relatives and neighbours. This departure from their previously paternalistic position might be seen as a modern rationalization but the lumberjacks saw it as another sign of the farmers' stupidity and narrowmindedness, which offended their own openness and generosity. The intellectual trade union activists especially stressed how ironic it was that they should find themselves dependent on such uneducated men.

> they had no other thought in their heads than sowing and harvesting. Socially they were illiterate. They couldn't imagine that there were people who were worse off than themselves, who had nothing to eat, nowhere to sleep and so on. No they were illiterate, socially illiterate.

The stereotype of the most 'genuine' kind of lumberjack has its roots in a mobile type of logger, the *bolockare*. The term is rather strange: basically it meant somebody who arrived with the companies, and was thus a stranger. The word however also implies somebody one shares house with. I have chosen to use the English word 'companion' to translate it. The companions were the ideal woodsmen of the lumberjacks' stories. I will use the terms *companion*, *character* (in Swedish *original*), and *hero* to mean the same thing, all suggesting the culture hero of the loggers' folklore.

The companion was a man without family or home. The central, most regular part of his life was the winter logging. At other seasons he might also take part in floating logs or felling them for charcoal making. A man on the move, somewhat of a tramp or vagabond, he made short forays into other casual work. Companions always did the felling, while the transport of logs to the rivers was the job of resident people who owned horses. The number of logs a 'hero' could saw in a day was often said to be a hundred, that is two or three times a normal good day's work, and he was always said to be an excellent worker. Heroes had three main attributes: they were very good workers, they were gifted and entertaining, and they flouted social conventions. Here is an example of a typical way of talking about a companion, chosen from many similar stories:

> And Johan Volker, who was the greatest character we have had here, he lived that way. He wanted to go to get some shopping as he didn't have enough clothes. He went to Bollnas and got his payment for floating-logs, or some money that they owed him. So he went down to buy a summer outfit. But no, he didn't get his suit. He kept drinking all his money away. He never got any new clothes. But he was happy just the same, as if nothing untoward had happened. He recovered and got a hold on things again. And he travelled the Earth: not just in Sweden for he went to Norway too. Got a child there I believe. Yes, he was so clever, he was so shrewd. He could draw and paint, he could do anything. And Vikman, the manager at the Vastana sawmill, came to work as the accountant at first, but couldn't manage it. Then they called in Volker. So Volker was a great person. He would have been the manager if he had stayed there. But he wandered, wandered all around Sweden. He came home in time for floating the logs and sometimes for the felling. An incredible man!

Another account from the same storyteller:

> One of them stayed up in Nysjon. He worked there for several years. He had that way of living, felling for nine months and almost starving himself during that time. These people didn't even have it in them to spend money on food. Then he took his money and left. He was gone for two or three months. When he came back he hardly had any clothes. But he paid his bills at the grocers. Yes, they were absolutely honest. And good workers. The ones who wanted them the most were the companies.

The ordinary loggers worked so as to get money for the summer and their minds were filled with dreams of future wealth, calculations about how to get rid of debts and make investments for their homes and families. As the companions always spent their money on travelling about and drinking, their hard work and supposedly 'big' incomes were never measured against the actual situation of the respectable loggers. The work and money of the companion were easy come and easy gone, untouched by the problems of the complex everyday life of summer that made money scarce and problematic. As the motto of the wild character 'Mad Sievert' said, 'the price [per log] is unimportant as long as there are enough trees'. Thus the ideal winners of work competitions were never rewarded financially or socially outside the forest. Their only reward was their standing in the tales of the camps.

The stories often stressed the bad clothing of the companions. For the common logger, a new suit every year was a minimum mark of respectability – the proof that the winter had not been a total economic failure – and much time was spent mending work clothes. But a companion would wear his clothes till they fell off his body, eventually keeping them in place with string from sugarloaf wrappings. Tools, on the other hand, were bought new every season. A real companion always sold his tools in spring which left him with less to carry around, and more money to drink with.

Many stories concentrate on the physical strength of the hero and tales of fights during his summer sprees in town. Fighting is perhaps not the right word, as usually the hero simply grabs and lifts the policemen who are coming to get him, and then throws them into the cell. When he is just about to knock somebody out he regains self-control and hits out at a building instead, knocking off the corner with his fist. The hero has supernatural strength and is capable of great anger, but he is in full control, and only uses his strength to save his integrity and to rid himself of people who are irritating or nagging him.

Although companions were ideally good workers and comrades, the stories do not always depict them as such. Some tell of tramps arriving at a camp but only staying to get credit for new clothes, tools, and food, to delouse themselves, then escaping, with stolen tools, leaving behind their lice and shortage of manpower. These stories however are, like the others, told in an approving way. The runaways are seen as part of the colour and adventure of forest life. Though it seems likely not to have been such good fun when it happened, the folklore expresses the tolerant and open atmosphere that ideally should have prevailed in the camps. In this way, men unfit for camp life – the senile, insane, dirty, or those unable to work properly – are also described as if they just added a touch of colour:

An old Finn lived with us in the cabin. His name was Isak Sjoblom. At night he slept under his worn out fur in a corner and during the day he lived in the same spot, with bread, saltpork, tobacco and other necessities keeping him company in a regular muddle. There was also this piece of sugarloaf, which during the week shrunk a bit but darkened even more and got lost among the other things. He welcomed people to have coffee with him, and if we wanted sugar we took his Finnish knife, which was stuck in the foot end of the bunk, and chopped a piece from the loaf. There was no difference if, say, the superintendent of woodproducts was visiting us and accepted Isak's hospitality. The superintendent put on a good face and helped himself to what was offered.

The appreciation of such characters cannot simply be explained as the admiration of an ideal worthy of imitation. Rather it is a moral statement of tolerance and of the ideal of individual autonomy, representing the character's independence of every- thing and the storyteller's independence of the character's actions. Some characters were mainly intended to be laughed *at*, not *with*, just as even the most admired characters were to some extent laughed *at*. Here I have emphasized the admired, trickster-like side of the character, but there is no doubt there was also sometimes an element of ridicule, where the respectable lumberjacks drew the line between the outsider and their own normality.

The 'physical' character type was, however, overshadowed by another with more emphasis on inner qualities. The intelligence of such a character was revealed in his way of expressing himself, which established an identity between a good storyteller and the hero. Characteristically he pitted himself against those who tried to bully him; company representatives, cocky farmers, or foresters who tried to catch him out in illegal hunting. Sometimes he had a sharp tongue, sometimes he used crude and direct language: he swears and curses at a clerk as he lifts him from the ground, breaking his chair. But the most subtle way of getting the better of a superior, the way which caused the most mirth, was through the use of a sense of humour that was almost unintelligible to educated middle-class people – and that was indeed also the point of it:

> It was that same Sjoberg who came walking on the railroad tracks in Bracke carrying his backbasket, gun and axe. A railroadman told him that he was not allowed to walk on the tracks. Sjoberg answered: 'Oh thank you, thank you for telling me. It is so tiring to walk on them, you know.'

The technique of this fine irony is to agree and act the fool and then continue to do whatever was intended in the first place. The skill lies in the balance between abusing superiors and keeping one's own integrity, so that they cannot control the speaker or accuse him of being stuck up. All claims of positive recognition by the superiors are sacrificed, although it is better if they are left in a state of suspicious confusion than treated with absolute contempt. One logger managed to make logs of incorrect, but to him financially advantageous, dimensions for a whole winter by consistently answering the forester, 'Oh yes. I know you are a clever man, Eklid. You know these things better than I do. But I'm sure I will learn and improve.' These are unusually wordy examples. The fewer words spoken the better: for instance, one enigmatic man always answered merely by repeating twice a keyword of the complaint directed against him.

Another side of the companions' speech styles was related to their involvement in political agitation and the building of trade unions. The syndicalist union had its greatest success in the forest region. Mainstream Swedish history tends to emphasize the labour movement's self-discipline and respectability. Some scholars have however pointed out that the early movement had another side which was more adventurous and rebellious, and sustained by the mass of unmarried, mobile workers of the early twentieth century.[4]

The cleverness and special personalities of the characters were inner qualities, which would not be noticed by anybody prejudiced by external and conventional standards. The characters' clothing, drinking habits, and other signs of lack of respectability indicated that they belonged to the bottom rung of society. This image is countered by the unequivocal view that most of them, under the shabby surface, were real gentlemen: talented, interesting, distinguished, and honourable. They were often described in terms of aristocracy and nobility. The freeholding peasants of northern Sweden had not experienced feudalism or the presence of an aristocracy, so the conceptualization of 'nobility' was poetic and symbolic in origin, basically conceived through history learnt at school.

What did we talk about? ... Some people have got the idea that the lumberjacks' thoughts circulated around food, booze, juicy affairs with women and coarseness. This was not true: at least not for us Jamtar [people from Jamtland county] and the people I have met. On my honour, I can say that Jamtar very rarely get coarse. There is nothing refined about being coarse. No, the psyche of the Jamtar is more like that of – how can I put it – that of the author of the Nick Carter books. Not coarse, but thrilling, or exciting, rather. If I may boast a bit, there is often a kind of delicacy of the soul in the workers of the forests. It is as if, after peeling off the rough crust, there is a fresh core underneath. Yes, somewhat like a sea mussel – rough on the outside, but gleaming on the inside.

There was clearly a very warm and affectionate atmosphere in the cabins. At night the men would sit mending their tools, playing music or cards, reading or, above all, storytelling. Stories were the chief currency of common exchange and sharing in their individualized culture. The winters are remembered as unique and heartwarming experiences. In 'Holiday Night in the Log Cabin', a song which is highly symbolic for Swedes, the sensuous praising of beauty and radiant masculinity is so much in evidence that someone less familiar with the context would probably interpret it as homosexual love poetry. The song tells the story of every man in one camp, each portrayed in turn with some characteristics picked out for praise. Many life stories are organized in the same way. The longest recollection consists of 500 pages dominated by short descriptions of colleagues, one after the other. Even if everyone could not be a special character, the intention was for every man to be mentioned with approval. But because the most colourful were emphasized, most stories about personally remembered characters and companions became transformed into tales of archetypal lumberjacks.

The way colleagues are praised, one by one, one after the other and not as a group, stresses again the individualism of the way of life of the loggers. But these stories about more and less colourful loggers also formed a cultural charter of the group. When – rarely – they speak for the group they tend to use semi-literary, romantic, or somewhat ironic terms like 'the free sons of the forests', 'children of the forest', 'men of the log cabins' and even 'the knights of the American salt pork'. When generalizing about themselves, they talk about 'the Lumberjack' rather than 'a lumberjack' or 'lumberjacks'.

If 'we' was absent in their speech, then 'I' was even more controversial. Despite the individualism of their culture, self-praise was regarded as a serious fault. Although a character had to be entertaining and expressive, to show off by talking too much was seen as effeminate. In Sweden, the stereotypical image of the man of the north is of a secretive man who allows others to do the talking and encourages them with short and ambiguous comments. This was as a way of avoiding giving oneself away to strangers, and was due more to artfulness than to the shyness often attributed to it.

The conflict revolved round the wish to assert the self through words and the risk of being regarded as ridiculously talkative and boastful. It was possible to allude very subtly to one's own achievements and income but never to speak of them directly. One simple device was to tell the story of a man who managed to fell 100 logs in a day, admiringly commenting, 'as for myself, I have never managed more than 85' – which was of course itself an extremely large number. A migrant lumberjack who thought that his achievements had escaped the attention of the other villagers sent his pay cheque back just to ensure that it passed through his home post office a second time. But this ruse was discovered and backfired on him – his standing fell. Heaping generous praises on other heroes was a surer way of bypassing the self-praise taboo, indicating, without mentioning oneself, that one shared something with them.

Some storytellers were of course more skilful than others – that is those who were 'characters' themselves. They stood above the convention of the self-praise taboo. Their performances were expressive and theatrical, in sharp contrast to the demure behaviour of a more typical respectable man. The word 'colourful' was often used when describing such characters. One of them used to walk round the fire with a sausage in one hand and a piece of bread in the other, gesticulating, eating, and talking at the same time. Another walked to and fro, totally poker-faced talking to his hat and vest; and a third produced genuine tears while doing an imitation.

This chain of stories, telling of and praising the personalities of other men, transcends the peasant society's perception of the individual. In a study of one local community in the north, B-E. Borgstrom shows that in conversations on the *bygd*, stories about events or people are always brought together into a sequence on the basis of genealogy, or the locality of the people involved.[5] They always connect with each other because the people involved are either relatives or neighbours, and never because the people or the events are inherently similar or through some other thematic connection. An individual's personality or actions are in themselves insufficient to form the subject of the stories, the purpose of which is primarily to sort out and map genealogies.

In the log cabins, on the other hand, linking of genealogies was not possible, as the social network was of a different kind. The content of the stories was important. A sequence of stories was linked by similarities between them, or rather between the personalities and actions of the characters involved. Through storytelling, both the competitiveness and the individualism of the work itself was continued, but now as a process involving the judgement of the listeners as to whether a new hero or story was better – or, as they put it, worse – than a previous one. In order for a new story to be superior to a previous one, the special qualities of the new hero had to be elaborated and distinguished. Although in many ways the treatment of hard work, fights, drinking, and witty talk was stereotyped, exaggeration could end up in absurdity. This process of elaborating stories was quite different from the way that stories linked by genealogy were told.

A similar difference between the *bygd* and the loggers' culture appears in the way people were named. In peasant Sweden people were known by a first name and patronym. There were only a very small number in a given locality, no more than those present in an average group of siblings. The oldest son was named after his father's father, so the heads of a farm might be named, for example, Jonas Persson and Per Jonsson, every second generation for hundreds of years. I discovered a line of descent named Erik Eriksson for 300 years and a village where the majority of the farmers were called Jonas Jonsson for about a hundred years. It was the name of the farm, put before the first name, that served to identify a person in daily speech in northern Sweden. People were spoken of as Erkpers Eris, or Jonerkes Kristin, but spoken to by just their first name. Farmers and their wives were called Jonerks-father and -mother. There was nothing individual in these names. They localized people into a pattern of relationships and land. An entirely different manner of naming people prevailed among the loggers. Nicknames and invented names were common, especially among those associates who were the subject of heroic stories. Some of the nicknames retained one of the proper names, like Chimney-sweeper-Lindgren, Sorcerer-Johansson, Stingy-Karlsson and Kalle (Charlie)-Applecheek. Others totally left out the name, like Evil Boy, Beautiful Child, White Racoon, The Blackcutter, Yellow Hook, Black Elk and Little Nippersweet. Many referred to elitist or aristocratic titles such as The Duke, Little Gent, The Philosopher, Emperor or King of the Forests.

These new names, which fully or partially replaced the old ones, disguised some aspects of the person. It took him out of his local and social context and made it impossible to know whether he came from a farming or landless background, or whether he was from northern or southern Sweden. On the other hand, the new name revealed a man's individuality by pointing out his personal qualities. It made him distinct from all the other Jonas Olssons and Gustav Johanssons who shared his trade.[6]

Nicknames were connected with characters and it was colourful vagabonds who had the most prestigious and poetic names. A nickname was very desirable, showing that its carrier was one of the 'free men of the forest', the wilful, strong, and quick-witted men of the stories. In a later, less 'adventurous' period, nicknames were distributed very widely in youth groups where every member had to share a name: but this sequel might be seen as a devaluation of a currency which in the northern forests had a rare value.

Logging as a way of earning money was seen as a means of liberation from the patronage of the farm owners. The isolated and egalitarian life which they led in winter gave a breathing space and temporal refuge from the social pressures and increasing hierarchization of the *bygd*. But it is not simply a case of the forest standing for equality and the *bygd* standing for hierarchy. In the storytelling we find a generosity, a will to share, to communicate, and to exchange among equals; but the stories also convey the message that some lumberjacks were 'better' than others, both as workers and also as more authentic people with superior inner qualities. Furthermore, the relationship between the storytellers was competitive, just as in practice the work was competitive.

The culture in the forests can be seen as shaped in contrast to the traditional, oppressive culture of the *bygd*. It was a basic rule of the culture to avoid anything that could make people suspect that one had pretensions to superior social standing. The farmers identified with traditional values. The landless loggers also made this identification when they characterized the farmers as narrow-minded and old-fashioned country bumpkins. But at the same time the lumberjacks used important parts of the old values for their own ends, when stressing the status they had achieved and justifying how they had attained respectability and a decent life through their own hard work. It was the old 'workperson' ideology that they used, an ideology whose legitimacy was hard for the farmers to ignore.

The breakup of kinship and family is often presented as a process in industrialization, leading to atomization, disintegration and with that, to individualism. The extent of this loss of belonging has often been exaggerated. Most loggers remained integrated with their own kin and community. But their storytelling illustrates how contacts with other loggers and life experience during their migrant youth were significant in the development of modern individuality and also in the form in which class conflict was expressed. An important element in this was the new type of relationship between people in the camps; the more abstract and open relations which developed between strangers.

The stories articulated this experience of meeting strangers. A logger had not usually come from a society greatly different from that of the respectable workers; his background was similar to theirs. Becoming the 'essential' lumberjack resulted more from his new position as a stranger, never integrated into the *bygd*, neither seasonally nor through the life cycle. Both in the stories and in his real life the companion revealed this stage of disintegration to others, both by simply being a stranger, and also through the lifestyle he developed as a stranger among other strangers. The men who shared a camp could not relate to each other like those in the community of the *bygd*. They were individuals on their own, uprooted from the complex structure of life, at least for the winter. The lack of a fixed social designation helped the workers to confront their comrades' 'inner' qualities. The low level of social interaction in the camps allowed a 'pure' sociability where the self could be presented or expressed as a role acted.[7]

The stories of characters were statements that emphasized inner qualities hidden under a coarse surface, a surface repelling the prejudiced who judge by the outside alone. The farmer by contrast was presented as an illustration of the superficiality of formal social status and mere money wealth. The stressing of equality, autonomy, and tolerance in the stories carried a serious political message. Perhaps this was what was most important about the praise of the freedom of the forests and which made the landless see work for wages as liberating. The stories were part of a class struggle which aimed to create legitimacy around new values; and their success was linked to the loyalty of the listeners. In the camp situation, a farmer not only had to give way to those who were better workers than he was himself. When stories were told, he had to put on a good face and had to participate in praising people who, from his *bygd* point of view, were of the lowest kind. The central values of modernity are usually traced to the opinions of the classic liberal philosophers of the urban middle classes; but in the forest, the farmers heard them in the myths of the landless poor, the free labourers of the forest.

Notes

1 The main sources of my work are the 'Loggers' Memories' of the Nordic Museum, Stockholm. These consist of about 200 autobiographies or recorded life stories of lumberjacks, written on the basis of a list of questions in the late 1940s. This material is combined with life story interviews that I have made, various other kinds of autobiographical material and state records.

2 The sizes of northern Swedish parishes are comparable with English counties, so even if a logger worked in his home parish it usually meant that he stayed in a camp, away from his family.

3 Another distinction between the old homestead farmers and the tenants, colonists, and smallholders was that the former had been given vast areas of forest land, when these were divided up during the first half of the nineteenth century, previously having been communally owned.

When logging started, these forests were usually sold or leased out on long-term contracts to the companies and their economic significance was ignored.

4 M. Lindqvist (1987) *Klasskamrater. Om industriellt arbete och kulturell formation 1880–1920* (*Class-mates. On industrial work and cultural formation 1880–1920*), Lund: Liber; B. Ostling (1980) *Den 'andra' arbetarrorelsen och reformismens framvaxt*, Stockholm: Federativs.

5 B-E. Borgstrom (1982) 'Historia som kulturell komponent', unpublished paper, Department of Social Anthropology, University of Stockholm. The paper deals with the present time.

6 Independence of place has been singled out as one of the most important dimensions of modern individuality: J. Asplung (1985) *Tid, rum, individ och kollektiv*, Stockholm: Liber.

7 ibid., Ch. 13.

10

Uchronic dreams

Working-class memory and possible worlds

Alessandro Portelli

> If it had been me, if I'd been the father, I wouldn't have allowed
> him to die, up there hanging on that cross.
>
> Maddalena, textile worker, Terni, Italy

Oral testimony has been amply discussed as a source of information
on the events of history. It may, however, also be viewed as an event
in itself and, as such, subjected to independent analysis in order to
recover not only the material surface of what happened, but also the
narrator's attitude toward events, the subjectivity, imagination,
and desire that each individual invests in the relationship with
history. I shall discuss here an 'imaginary', 'wrong', 'hypothetical'
motif which is found in working-class narratives in several different
parts of Italy but focusing mostly on its occurrences in a specific
group, the old-time Communist working-class activists and cadre of
the naval steelworks town of Terni, the oldest industrial town in
central Italy. Most of the field research on which this analysis is
based was carried out in the mid- and late 1970s, when Communist
Party policy hinged on the 'historical compromise' and 'national
unity'. The working-class imagination embodied in the testimony
must therefore be placed in the context of the party's policies and of
the official explanations of their historical background and
precedents.

I will consider first a story which contains the motif in its fullest
form. The narrator is Alfredo Filipponi, a former factory-worker,
tramway driver, coal merchant – as well as secretary of the
Communist underground during Fascism and military commander
of the partisan brigade 'Antonio Gramsci' in 1943–4. The interview
was carried out in 1973; at the time, Filipponi was already seriously
ill, and he died shortly afterwards.[1] He was speaking in response to
my question: 'During the resistance, did you have in mind only
national liberation, or were you also hoping for something more?'

Well, we thought of national liberation from Fascism, and after that there was the hope of achieving socialism, which we haven't achieved yet. At that time, with the partisan struggle, we should almost have made it. After the partisan war was over – Terni was liberated eleven months earlier than the rest of the country – comrade Togliatti spoke to us. He called a meeting of all the partisan commanders and party leaders from every province and region of Italy. He made a speech, he said there was going to be an election. 'You have prestige, Omega (that was my party name: Gramsci himself had named me that way. My partisan name, instead, was Pasquale); the reason I asked you to come is, you must get to work for us to win the election.' Four or five others spoke, and they agreed. I raised my hand: 'Comrade Togliatti, I disagree.' 'Why Omega?' 'I disagree because, as Lenin said, when the thrush flies by, then it's the time to shoot it. If you don't shoot when it flies by, you may never get another chance. Today the thrush is flying by: all the Fascist chiefs are in hiding and running away, in Terni as well as everywhere else. All the others said it was the same in their parts, too. So, this is the moment: weapons, no need to talk about it, we know where they are (we had hidden them). This is the time: we strike, and make socialism.' He put his motion and mine up for a vote, and his got four votes more than mine, and was passed. But they got the warning; they had to admit I was right later.

This confrontation between Filipponi and Palmiro Togliatti, postwar Communist Party secretary, never took place. Filipponi was giving here his imaginary version of a crucial event in the history of the Italian Communist movement: the so-called 'svolta di Salerno'. This was the political 'U-turn' when Togliatti (just returned from his exile in Russia) announced to the party cadre at a meeting in Salerno that socialism was not on the agenda, and that the party should co-operate with anti-Fascist forces toward the creation of a Western-style democratic (and 'progressive') republic.[2] Reactions to this announcement ranged from opposition to incredulity, and old-time activists still debate whether Togliatti's line was correct. In this story, Filipponi suggests that history might have been different if another road had been taken.

The shape of the tale depends on personal and collective factors. Filipponi was old and ill when he was interviewed; he had long been removed from active party leadership, against his will and following a dramatic confrontation. As the conversation went on, the epic and detailed (though factually inaccurate) style he had used in the beginning to describe his partisan experience gradually broke down, and he slipped deeper and deeper into fantasy and fabulosity. First, he claimed a central role in the founding convention of the Communist Party (at Livorno, in 1921), which he actually did not even attend; then he told a detailed story of how he escaped from prison with the party's founder, Antonio Gramsci, and hid with him for months in the mountains (which also never happened); finally he ended his story with the imaginary confrontation with Togliatti.[3]

It was as though, as the weariness of age, illness, and the fatigue of the long interview eroded his conscious controls, the censorship of rationality gave way to dreams and desires long buried in the unconscious, in a process greatly reminiscent of a daydream. This dream gave vent to the personal desires and frustrations of the narrator. Although he had devoted most of his life to the party, Filipponi felt he had never been sufficiently rewarded and recognized. Thus, he placed himself in imagination at the very centre of the party's history and at the side of its 'founding father', from whom he claimed to have received, in a sort of baptismal investiture, his party name and his political identity.[4]

But there is more than a personal frustration to this story: Filipponi also voices a collective sense of disappointment in the shape history took after the great hopes aroused by liberation from Fascism. A 1947 report of the Terni Communist federation says:

> Among the rank and file, there is a widespread disappointment for the way democracy has evolved so far. It must be recognized that we have relied too much on institutional and legal action, awaiting solutions from above, and have not given the workers enough responsibility in the solution of their own problems.[5]

Stories of disappointed expectations caused by the restoration of class relationships in the factories and in the state are common in the generation of the 1940s. As the desire and hope for revolution and socialism were removed from the party's agenda and eliminated from open discussion, they were gradually buried deeper and deeper in the activists' memories and imagination, to re-emerge in fantasy, dream, and folklore. Filipponi's 'wrong' tale is the result less of imperfect recollection than, ironically, of a creative imagination; it is the narrative shape of the dream of a different personal life and a different collective history.

Such stories do crop up occasionally in different parts of the country. A construction worker from Subiaco (Latium) used to tell a story about himself very much like Filipponi's; an artisan from the San Lorenzo neighbourhood in Rome also described a confrontation between himself and Togliatti (or Togliatti's 'representative', as he sometimes put it); relatives of the Terni anti-Fascist exile Giovanni Mattioli also talk about a 'quarrel' between him and Togliatti about the Salerno line: 'Had Togliatti followed Giovanni's advice, things would have been different', says his niece.[6] Such conflicts did not happen only in memory and imagination: in Calabria, the local party cadre refused to believe the party documents describing the new line, and thought they must have been forged by 'provocateurs'.[7]

Two other aspects enhance the meaning of Filipponi's story. One is the structural relationship of the episodes about Togliatti and Gramsci. Stories about Gramsci are even more common than stories about Togliatti, which is understandable given the former's 'founder' status. Most of these stories mythically associate the speaker and the place where the story is told with the founding hero's presence; as such, they have much in common with stories about the other national founding hero, Garibaldi. On the other hand, most stories about Togliatti tend to differentiate the speaker from him. As founder, Gramsci represents the ideal reasons at the roots of the party's identity; Togliatti, on the other hand, is remembered most as a shrewd tactician and politician. Therefore, Gramsci's role in folk versions of history is to reinforce identification with the party's origins; Togliatti's, sometimes, is to express disappointment with its historical action. Filipponi's testimony is a perfect example of this process.

The second aspect of his tale is the presence of a material correlative to the post-liberation stories: the practice – mentioned by Filipponi and widespread in the 1940s – of hiding away the weapons used in the resistance, expecting to take them out again sooner or later for the revolution (or, as some speakers say, to defend democracy against expected attacks of reaction). Arms were found hidden in the factories of Terni until 1949; one informant told me he had kept his until as recently as the late 1970s. The preservation of arms meant that the job begun with the anti-Fascist resistance had been left unfinished and would have to be completed some day. In a way, the revolutionary desire buried in the subconscious of activists like Filipponi is another hidden weapon, left to rust unused.

This feeling was bound, on the other hand, to come to terms with the personal and collective need to survive, to rebuild, to defend and expand the limited but concrete gains of the postwar years, within the existing framework. Revolution or not, life must go on. As the party leadership declared that revolution and socialism were out of the question and in the 'historical compromise' increasingly identified itself and the class it represented with the values and the machinery of Italian democracy, it became increasingly difficult to express, or even to entertain, the frustrated hopes and desires. The result was a deep-seated conflict between the rationality of the world as given, and the dream of another possible world.

Filipponi manages to voice this conflict in a recognizable form, because his personal disappointment coincided with his view of history, and most of all because in many ways he embodied the relationship between political vanguard consciousness and the folk roots of working-class culture. Born in Valnerina, the mountainous backyard of Terni's steelworks, he was always more at ease with dialect than with the standard Italian of political parlance (although his sixth-grade education made him one of the best-schooled party activists in the underground generation). When the Fascists raided his home searching for subversive literature, one object they found and destroyed was an *organetto*, the small accordion which dominates folk music and folk dancing in his region.[8] Even when he described the way he was fired from the tramways, the story took the shape of a folk-tale;[9] and the need to 'seize the time' in the post-liberation period was couched in a proverb about hunting, a very popular sport in Umbria: 'when the thrush flies by, then is the time to shoot it'. Like other working-class activists who justify their politics with proverbs and folk-songs, Filipponi attributes his proverb to Lenin, in an attempt to reconcile his class-conscious folk wisdom with the theoretical prestige of the founding heroes of the Communist movement.[10]

The cluster of stories about the missing revolution of the 1940s are not an isolated instance. The motif of 'history that could have gone differently' is found in narratives dealing with all the major crises of working-class history, both local and national. Many stories concern the period between the end of the First World War and the advent of Fascism. Describing the cost-of-living strikes of 1919, another Terni informant says:

> The leaders of those struggles had no authority over the working class; we didn't have the true class that the Communist party created later, in spite of all its shortcomings. If there had been a Communist party then, there would have been a revolution.

The 1921 sit-ins in the factories are one of the most commonly cited missed opportunities:

> We should have gone on to the insurrection, I mean, because this was what we had in mind – we're going to make a revolution, we used to say then. But the union leaders had other ideas in mind, they weren't going to make any revolution.

> The Socialist party had 157 members of Parliament; power should have been in the Socialists' hands. But [Socialist secretary Filippo] Turati wouldn't take the responsibility. He should have taken power, but wasn't man enough.[11]

When Giacomo Matteotti, a Socialist MP, was murdered by Fascist killers in 1925, the regime suffered its first (and last) serious crisis:

> the Fascists were scared. But we had no leaders, the Communist party was still weak, and the leaders who had a following among the people, [Claudio] Treves, Turati, were all in exile abroad; ours were all in jail. If we had had the right leaders then, maybe Fascism wouldn't have lasted twenty years.[12]

The last quote is factually all wrong: during the Matteotti crisis, Socialist leaders Turati and Treves were still in Italy, and Gramsci had not yet been arrested. But the political analysis is serious: at that all-important moment, the working-class had no leadership.

Stories about the 1920s explain the missing revolution by lack of leadership, thus blaming the Socialists, from whom the Communist Party split in 1921. But the history of the 1940s cannot be 'justified' by the lack of a legitimate Communist leadership. Therefore they focus on specific, individual decisions, reiterating one motif – 'they told us to keep calm' – to describe the implicit contrast between the 'political', tactical approach of the leadership and the state of mind of the rank and file. But the meaning is the same: at one point, which varies with each narrator, history needlessly went wrong.

> I still can't believe September 8 [1943 when Italy made its separate peace with the Allies]: that day, we could have picked hairs from the Germans' asses one by one; there was nothing we couldn't have done. Instead – be calm, calm, calm.... Just the same as when they tried to kill Togliatti [in 1948]: calm, calm, calm.... And the cops at the arms depot had already handed their guns over to us...[13]

The construction worker and folk singer Amerigo Matteucci, mayor of a hill village near Terni, improvised *stornelli* to sing on the national reconciliation and amnesty to the Fascists, promoted by Togliatti, which thirty years later he still saw as a mistake which prevented the revolution:

> Caro compagno te lo voglio dire
> l'errore fu la gente perdonare
> l'errore fu la gente perdonare
>
> E condannato sia il traditore
> se bene voi ave'all'umanitane

se bene voi ave'all'umanitane

Scusate amici mia se sto a sbagliare
io sono sempre alla rivoluzione
io sono sempre alla rivoluzione.[14]

The theme of the missed chance which could have launched an alternative history occurs in stories about several postwar events: the workers' reaction to the pistol wounding of Palmiro Togliatti by a young Christian Democrat in 1948; the police killing of the Terni steel-worker Luigi Trastulli in 1949; the firing of 3,000 steel-workers in 1952–3 and the street-fighting that followed. After Togliatti was shot,

> The next day, he began to speak, to say a few words, and he always recommended the same thing – calm down, calm down, calm down.... But I think it was a moment when...I may be wrong, but at the moment I think all our problems could have been solved.

After Trastulli's death,

> again – the people, the workers, might have been willing to do something, but were held back by – by the leaders, because... it was like after Togliatti was shot. If it had been up to the rank and file, it looked like revolution would break out any moment.

Similarly after the 1953 layoffs:

> On the third night of street-fighting all the people were ready, with gasoline tanks and other stuff, to strike down the cops. But they promised they would hire two hundred men back, and things calmed down after those promises. But the workers didn't want to give up the fight; the workers said, all our jobs back or we fight; all our jobs back, or we fight. When things ended that way, the working class lost faith, and never gained it back, because they were disappointed. Why did we have to give up? Because the other (non-left) unions would have come along only up to a certain point and then they would leave us to fight alone.[15]

> The night after the layoffs were announced, we took a stand: tomorrow morning, we said, 'Let's do an action in the factory. Let's kill fifty of the bosses': it was all established, all minds made up and everything. We had filed iron bars to a point, real sharp. But the unions called us in: 'look,' they said, 'things are looking good and the struggle is won, you're ruining everything, don't do anything rash...'. So we had to give it up. I mean, fifteen of us would still be in jail today, but I still believe that if that morning we had cut down... I mean, we didn't have to stop at fifty, we'd

make it a hundred, once we got going, it wouldn't make any difference. And once you had a hundred dead bosses in there – I guess things would have been different. Perhaps after they'd buried those fifty, sixty bosses, they would have gone on and fired the workers anyway. But at least there would have been fifty vacant jobs. I admit it might have been the wrong thing to do; but I am still convinced that they would have re-opened the gates to all the two thousand.[16]

All these stories are not about how history went, but about how it could have gone: their realm is not reality, but possibility. We gain a better understanding of them if we connect them to the great literary form of the refusal of existing history: uchronia. Uchronia is 'that amazing theme in which the author imagines what would have happened if a certain historical event had not taken place'; the representation of 'an alternative present, a sort of parallel universe in which the different unfolding of an historical event had not taken place'.[17] The stories we are discussing offer us a glimpse of the possible alternative worlds which might have existed if appropriate leadership had given a different turn to specific events between 1919 and 1925, and again between 1943 and 1953. By contrasting a desirable world to the existing one, and by claiming that it is only by accident that it did not come into being, the uchronic hypothesis allows the narrator to 'transcend' reality as given and to refuse to identify himself and be satisfied with the existing order.[18] Through uchronia, these speakers say that the most desirable of possible worlds – which to them was still identified with Communism – could be created some day, if the right chances are seized. And the old textile worker with the appropriate name of Maddalena carries uchronia to a further and more radical point when she says that, had she been God – had God been a woman – the most crucial event in our history might also have gone differently. And who knows what the world would be.

We could dismiss these stories by saying that there are at least ten times as many stories that go in the opposite direction: stories that deny that history ever went wrong and claim that not only did it go the only possible way it could have gone, but that this was also a just and satisfactory one. But the relevance of an imaginary motif cannot be measured on statistical grounds alone. For one thing, we must consider the quality of the narrators. Among the sources of the quotes in the preceding paragraph are a disproportionate number of activists who held places of responsibility and prestige in the party, unions, and local administrations. These stories are not the mumblings of isolated and disgruntled old men, but a rationalization of their past by individuals who were the backbone of the working-class and Communist movement in the town for three generations. Also, we must consider the place of the motif within each individual life story. In almost every case, the uchronic turn is placed so as to coincide with the peak of the narrator's personal life, with the moment where each played the most important role or was, at least, most actively involved as a participant. Paradoxically, the 'inaccurate' motif tends to be linked with the best-remembered historical episode: as though the 'wrongness' of history became most evident when seen at the closest range.

Finally, we may take a hint from the autobiography of Frederick Douglass.

> I have been frequently asked, when a slave, if I had a kind master, and do not remember ever to have given a negative answer; nor did I, in pursuing this course, consider myself as uttering what was absolutely false; for I always measured the kindness of my master by the standard of kindness set up among slaveholders around us.[19]

A negative judgement on the slave's condition was not only dangerous to express, but also difficult to conceive: the slave would have had to evaluate the master on a scale other than that of the existing order, a scale which not all were strong and imaginative enough to envision. Also in less dramatic situations, the voicing of a critical view of one's own experience against the prevailing interpretations of history runs against outer and inner sanctions. It takes a much higher emotional investment to admit to oneself that things are wrong than it takes to consent to conventional truths. Doubt and dissent can only surface when they possess a high degree of intensity; and then those who express them are often also partly speaking for the majority who dare not admit their doubts even to themselves.

Yet, the common sense of history does say that this is the only possible and the only desirable world. Against hypothetical, conflictual stories like Filipponi's stands the running argument: there could have been no revolution in Italy in the 1940s, because the Allies would not have allowed it – look what happened to Greece. 'They would have blown us like bagpipes', says a narrator (who – in another context – also relates his own uchronic episode):[20] the same speakers who say that history went wrong at the crucial moment of *their* lives, accept the common sense of the inevitability – and justness – of history in other respects. The conflict, in fact, is not between irreducible rebels and passive conformists, but runs within each individual, in ever-changing shapes and terms.

The inner, personal nature of the conflict is shown by the frequent narrative contrast between the party – bearer of reason and knowledge – and the instinctive, angry rebelliousness of the masses. 'We were nothing but fighters, we were not armed with the politics of knowledge; we wanted a fight, which the party knew we couldn't sustain, being too few':[21] there is a distinction between *us* and *the party*, and the party, not us, is right. Though the speaker meant to underline his allegiance to the party, somehow the subjectivity of desire smoulders under the objectivity of reason and clamours for recognition. How do we reconcile the fact that we know that the party was right with the fact that we irrepressively feel that history has been wrong?

In order to deal with this contradiction, rank-and-file narrators must deal with the image of history which they have absorbed in school and which the party itself has reinforced: a linear process of growth and progress toward some desirable end. 'History, don't you see, marches toward liberty', says a song by a Communist farm-worker from Genzano near Rome.[22] This vision was articulated by the elites in order to legitimize their role and strategy; it was subscribed to by the Socialist and then by the Communist leadership in order to raise hope in the rank and file, and again to legitimize their own leadership. If history is directed either by providential guidance or by the lights of reason and objective socioeconomic forces, then the existing state of things is only a necessary stage in a process both inevitable and desirable. While uchronia claims that history has gone wrong – and has been *made* to go wrong – the commonsense view of history amounts to claiming that history *cannot* go wrong – and implicitly, that what is real is also good. History tailors the desirable to the given: as Russell Kirk once said (apropos the conservative mind) a true statesman is distinguished by the 'cognizance of the real tendency of Providential social forces'.[23]

Togliatti's 'svolta di Salerno' is a case in point. Though it may very well have been in itself quite wise, this choice retains legendary overtones in the party's memory because it is described as *both* a free choice and an enforced one, the result at the same time of Togliatti's subjective wisdom, his concept of the 'mass party' and the intuition of the 'Italian road to Socialism', and of objective circumstances – the Allies – which allowed no other course. The historian Claudio Pavone has noted that 'Togliatti often presented as victorious initiatives what were in fact defensive actions', and 'this was to be among his more lasting contributions to the party's mentality'.[24] This heritage was reinforced during the 'historical compromise' and 'national unity' phase of the 1970s, when the Communist Party seemed to be approaching state power in partnership with the conservative Christian Democrat party. The practice of presenting defeats as if they were victories was very much in use in those years. When workers' rights that had been hailed as historical conquests a few years earlier were jeopardized, Luciano Lama, national union secretary, described them as undesirable 'barrels of ashes', to be left behind on the road of power and modernization. Enrico Berlinguer, Communist Party secretary, skilfully tailored the desirable to the possible when he said that 'a Left government would not be a good solution for Italian democracy at this time', because it might tempt conservative forces to a coup. Both Lama and Berlinguer would, clearly, have been glad to keep the union rights and to achieve a Left government; but since they felt it was not *possible*, rather than admit to impotence they declared that it was *undesirable*. And as the Communist Party increasingly tried to identify itself as a 'responsible', 'acceptable' political force, it began to take responsibility not only for the future but also for the past: all the historical events preceding – and, implicitly, leading up to – the imminent accession to power were now to be seen as positively good even if the Communist Party had originally opposed them. Thus Berlinguer described NATO – once fiercely opposed by the party – no longer as a vehicle of imperialistic hegemony but as a 'guarantee' of Italian national independence.[25] In retrospect we know that the Communist Party was never allowed access to state power; but the ideological price paid in the attempt remained.

This approach was reproduced at the local level. While all Terni workers describe the 1953 layoffs as a major and lasting defeat, the local historian and Communist senator Raffaele Rossi described them as an almost unadulterated good:

> The great layoffs of 1952–53, and the struggles that followed (in various forms, including grave street-fights, a state of siege, the use of firearms, barricades, many wounded and hurt) preserved and increased the unity of social and political forces (the all-party Terni Committee), promoted research and ideas on the relationship of state-owned industries to regional economy, hastened a deep reorganization of the factory which prevented its closure and changed it, for the first time, from war to peace production.[26]

This description, which literally puts what happened to the workers in parenthesis, and accredits the layoffs with a sequel of positive verbs – 'preserved', 'increased', 'hastened', 'promoted' – has hardly more factual credibility than Filipponi's uchronic dream.[27] But it squares with the need to imagine a progressive history leading up to the progressive 'historical compromise' anticipated by instances of co-operation between what used to be described as antagonistic forces: the 'all-party' committee. This version of history is so far from the direct experience of the majority of the population that it takes no hold on rank-and-file imagination; but the process functions more effectively when it deals with distant events on a national scale which individual narrators have little opportunity to verify against their own first-hand experience. The encounter between the imagination of the historical compromise and the folk imagination of the rank and file creates utopian visions of a triumphant present. As Alfeo Paganelli, factory worker says:

> All our struggles did serve a purpose, because the working class has prevailed, and they [the ruling class] have been forced to give in. They may rule in the House or in the Senate, up there; but down here, inside Italy, they don't. If they want to rule, they must apologize to Berlinguer and place him on the chair, the first one, where the crown used to be once. Now it's gone. There's a hammer and sickle in its place now, and nothing else.[28]

This vision has much in common with Filipponi's stories about Gramsci. The speaker establishes a relationship between himself and the hero by pointing out that 'our' struggles helped enthrone him; he thus manages to give meaning not only to party history but to his personal history as well. If the past serves to justify the present, a life of struggle must be seen as a success in order to give a sense of self-esteem and personal identity. In fact, the need to claim something for oneself, to defend one's own dignity and historical presence, is often at the root of a 'consensus' version of history: by saying that history was 'good' we claim that we have made something out of ourselves.

On the other hand, however, each time I asked old activists whether their present lives correspond to what they struggled for, the answers were reluctant and dubious. 'No, it doesn't; because all of our leaders own their own houses, and I'm still renting', said one old man; 'we might still lose everything we have', said another – who was living very scantily though he had held positions of power in the city administration for twenty years: 'today, I have a small pension, just enough to buy me and my old woman a piece of bread, so we don't have to beg. But it could happen yet', because the ruling classes are always trying to take back what they were forced to give.[29]

Personal experience, then, both reinforces and limits the affirmative view of history. On the one hand it prompts narrators to insist on the usefulness and success of their lives, by stressing the positive aspects of reality; on the other it forces them to come to terms with the deferral or cancellation of their ultimate goals, with the limited and precarious nature of actual gains, with the personal sense of discontent and loss of meaning. The affirmative discourse, however, is sanctioned by the leadership; it is available, ready-made, articulated. The discourse of negation, on the other hand, must piece itself together from scratch every time, and is burdened by the fear of disapproval and isolation. 'I'm sorry comrades, if I'm talking wrong', apologizes, defiant and timid, Amerigo Matteucci, 'but I'm still for the revolution'.

So the conflict between the affirmative and negative impulse often results in silence, passivity, assent without participation: 'a passive, often merely formal agreement with the party line, a tendency to delegate to others, which prevents dissent from coming to the fore', as a panel of national leaders put it in 1977.[30] The discourse of negation is distorted, buried, deviated, and allowed to emerge only between the lines, as dream, metaphor, lapsus, digression, error, denigration, uchronia – all forms which give vent to the narrator's feelings and yet control the tension by means of the formal organization of discourse.

The means of control embedded in the narrative correspond to two major motifs: the wrong turn of history is traced to a single event; or the blame is laid on errors or failures of the leadership. The latter motif is frequently found also in New Left historiography, where it is used to support a – largely imaginary – image of a revolutionary working class regularly betrayed by reformist and 'revisionist' leaders.[31] Uchronic tales, while apparently similar to this rhetoric, in fact perform an opposite function. Blaming the 'wrongness' of history on 'our' side means, for one thing, that it is still our side that makes history. It is the same frame of mind that inspired the Pueblo myth which attributes the creation of white men to Indian black magic, or the Black Nationalist myth in which the white race is invented by the mad Black scientist Yacub.[32] These myths reinforce the group's sense of its central role in history, and suggest that if the group had power to generate the evil powers it also has power to eliminate them: 'if Indian magic has created white people, an Indian ceremony will control them'.[33] Similarly Matt Witt says about a Navajo Indian,

> Maybe he had violated a taboo, such as talking about certain legends at improper times. If so, if natural disasters were caused by something he had done, then there was hope: perhaps he

could prevent future calamities by not making those mistakes again.[34]

Likewise, the function of the uchronic motif is to keep up hope: if our past leaders missed their chance to 'shoot when the thrush was flying by', better leaders in the future will not. The world of our desires is possible: we needn't even change the magic, but only work it more correctly, and perhaps replace a few people at the top.

In uchronic tales the leadership plays a role similar to that of mediators in Lévi-Strauss' structural interpretation of myths: two-faced creatures that hold together conflicting but equally necessary presuppositions. In this case, the contradiction – we, the makers of history, must be right, and yet history is wrong – is explained by the agency of individuals who are both *with* us (in the party, which actually they represent) and not *of* us (not members of the working class, in terms of status, power, education, sometimes income). The ambivalent, internal/external position of the leadership keeps it all in the family, and yet saves the family from guilt and blame. Allegiance to the party is not based, as outside critics have often claimed, on a mythic faith in its infallibility, but rather on the ability to shift its failures to the sphere of myth.

This is where the factual inaccuracy of most uchronic tales becomes relevant again. Italy did not become socialist after the Second World War for reasons quite removed from the fact that Togliatti's line overcame Filipponi's imaginary opposition; the triumph of Fascism after the First World War was not caused by Turati's hesitancy in seizing power.[35] The uchronic motif removes the presence of social and political adversaries; reduces complex historical processes to single events, complex situations to yes-or-no dilemmas. Thus it saves the narrators' self-esteem and their sense of their own past, but makes it much more difficult to evaluate the party's actual role in those crises and its long-term identity, culture, and strategy. Everything is brought back to the merely tactical plane.

The consequences can be seen both at the level of everyday politics and at the level of political imagination. On the one hand, most rank-and-file reactions to the historical compromise policy tended to be couched in tactical terms: 'we gave them too much leeway, and paid for it in the elections'; 'Berlinguer proposed an alliance because he knew the Christian Democrats would refuse, and then the blame would be on them'; 'Look, Berlinguer is no liar. He did it to reach our goals more rapidly'.[36] The historical compromise, in fact, was much more: it was a symptom and cause of deep changes in the identity, class composition, and political role of the Communist Party. This process marginalized many old-time activists, whose identity was so tightly knitted to the party that, while they were hurt, yet they recoiled from recognizing what it really meant. Tactical criticism allowed them to voice their discontent, and yet to remove its deeper and most disturbing sources.

The primacy of tactics goes hand in hand with an image of history as a series of discreet 'turning points', crises, crucial moments, which envisages the revolution as a single, traumatic, violent confrontation, rather than as a slow and deep process of social change. Though all these narrators dreamed of a new world, they were all but incapable of imagining it: they concentrated on the revolutionary seizure of power, but were extremely vague when asked to describe what kind of society they expected afterwards. The closest they would come was by referring to the Soviet Union – that is, to another *existing* world.

The uchronic imagination thus reveals the inability of a significant part of the traditional Communist rank and file to consider that basic characteristics in the structure and theory of the Communist Party – and thus of their own identity – may have been at the root of the 'wrongness' of history. It also reveals that for many of these activists it was too painful and difficult to admit, and even to imagine, that the party was becoming something quite other from what they had known and lived for. On the other hand, the uchronic imagination also reveals the failure of official history to explain the existential experience of a majority of the rank and file. Uchronia thus saves the precious awareness of the injustice of the existing world, but supplies the means of resignation and reconciliation. While it fans the flames of discontent by uncovering the contradiction of reality and desire, it helps keep this contradiction from breaking out as an open conflict.

Notes

1 Alfredo Filipponi was born in 1897 at Ferentillo, a village in the Nera river valley (Valnerina), 10 miles from Terni. The interview was recorded at his house in Terni on 7 June 1973.

His story needs to be understood in its historical context. After the Allied landings in Sicily in July 1943 Mussolini was forced to resign and the new Italian government made peace, but the German army fought on and for a while re-established Mussolini in the northern regions. Behind the German lines partisan brigades, in which Communists were in the forefront, waged a war of liberation against both the Nazis and their Fascist allies. Many of the fighters saw the war as leading directly to socialism. They were astonished when Togliatti returned from exile in Russia in March 1944 to announce in the 'svolta' (U-turn) at Salerno that the Communists would work with other democratic parties to create a 'progressive democracy'. The Italian Communist Party was subsequently transformed into a national mass party with a membership of over 2 million, and for forty years the largest electoral force on the Left, peaking at 36 per cent and still 22 per cent in 1988. But although locally in power in many cities, after their ejection from the coalition government in 1947 the Communists have been permanently excluded nationally.

2 Palmiro Togliatti (1984) *Opere*, vol. 5 (1944–55), ed. Luciano Gruppi, Rome: Riuniti.

3 Cf. A. Portelli (1979) '"Gramsci evase con me dal carcere, ci nascondemmo per sei mesi sui monti...." Tutti i paradossi della "storia orale"', *Il Manifesto*, 11 May; Collettivo di ricerca del Circolo Gianni Bosio (1981) 'Observazioni del folklore su Gramsci', *I Giorni Cantati* 1: 32–45.

4 Filipponi had actually been expelled from the party in 1949, after a conflict with the Terni secretary, Carlo Farini. Most witnesses say that Filipponi's frustrated ambition played a part in that episode, as well as the fact that his fighting partisan mentality was unfit for the postwar political climate. He was later quietly readmitted, but never given any responsibility. An activist says that when Filipponi was expelled 'there was a sense of loss, like at the death of an important person' (Mario Filipponi, b. 1924, no relation, 9 March 1982). The name 'Omega' was in use in the 1920s not by Filipponi, but by Filippo Innamorati, a typographer from nearby Foligno, who was regional secretary after the advent of Fascism. Filipponi (who worked directly under him) appropriates, with his name, Innamorati's leadership role. Filipponi's connection to Gramsci is reinforced also by the fact that the partisan brigade he commanded bore Antonio Gramsci's name.

5 APC (National Archive of the Communist Party, Rome), 1945–8, folder no. 142.

6 The Subiaco story was communicated by Mirella Serri at a 1978 seminar of the Instituto Storico Romano della Resistenza; the San Lorenzo episode is a personal communication from Lidia Piccioni and Alfredo Martini, based on their own fieldwork in the 1970s; the interview with Mattioli's niece Diname Colesanti (b. 1903) took place in Terni, 4 August 1980.

7 Cf. Renzo Del Carria (1970) *Proletari senza rivoluzione*, Milan: Oriente, vol. II, p. 337, n. 214.

8 Interview with Ambrogio Filipponi, Alfredo's son (b. 1930), 11 May 1979.

9 'After I had been working [at the tramways] for several years, Mussolini wrote a letter to the manager and told him: "Within five days you must fire the famous Communist chief Filipponi Alfredo and send word to me about it." The manager sent for me, read the letter, and said: "I don't have the heart to fire you." After ten days or less, there comes another letter from Mussolini: "I have heard that Filipponi is still at work. If you don't fire him within three days, I'll fire him myself and you'll be fired too." He sent for me, and said: "What must I do?" "What can you do ,"

said I: "go ahead and fire me."' The archetype is the story about Snow White, the evil stepmother queen, and the hunter who is charged with killing the princess.

10 See A. Portelli (1980) 'La storia non lo vedi marcia verso la libertà', in Circolo Gianni Bosio, *I Giorni Cantati. Cultura operaia e contadina a Roma e nel Lazio*, Milan: Mazzotta, p. 150. The article describes an interview with a traditional singer of Genzano, near Rome, who believed that the 'Internationale' and 'La Marseillaise' were written by Karl Marx ('The Marseillaise, you see, was called this way because it was made by Marx at Marseilles.')

11 Arnaldo Lippi (b. 1899), 15 November 1978 (interview by Agostino Marcucci); Remo Righetti (b. 1902), 9 December 1979; Gildo Bartoletti (b. 1896), 17 February 1974 (interview by Valentino Paparelli).

12 Arnaldo Lippi (see n. 11).

13 Settimio Piemonti (b. 1903), 7 September 1980.

14 Dear comrade, I want to tell you
    it was a mistake to forgive those people:
    traitors must be condemned,
    for the good of mankind.
    Forgive me friends, if I'm wrong;
    but I am still for the revolution.

Improvised by Amerigo Matteucci (b. 1919), 28 December 1973; the original field recording is on the album *La Valnerina ternana. Un'esperienza di ricerca/intervento*, ed. Valentino Paparelli and Alessandro Portelli, Dischi del Sole DS 523/34.

15 Amerigo Matteucci (b. 1919), 14 December 1974; Calfiero Canali (b. 1916), 30 April 1979; Antonio Antonelli (b. 1923), 7 July 1973.

16 This story is part of an interview recorded in Valnerina in the spring of 1973; to protect the speaker, I do not indicate his name here. The facts were independently confirmed by other informants.

17 Pierre Versins, comments in Jean Tortel (ed.) (1970) *Entretiens sur la paralittérature*, Paris: Plon, p. 275; Collettivo Un'Ambigua Utopia (1979) *Nei labirinti della fantascienza*, Milan: Feltrinelli, p. 75.

18 Some of the many science fiction novels based on uchronia are Philip K. Dick (1965) *The Man in the High Castle*, Harmondsworth: Penguin Books; Norman Spinrad (1974) *The Iron Dream*, St Albans: Panther (both of which describe an alternative history created by a Nazi victory in the Second World War), and Keith Robert (1970) *Pavane*, London: Panther (in which the Spanish Armada defeats Queen Elizabeth's England).

19 Frederick Douglass (1962) *Life and Times*, New York: Collier Books, p. 64. Reprinted from the revised edn (1892).

20 Calfiero Canali (see n. 15).

21 Arnaldo Lippi (see n. 11).

22 Silvano Spinetti (see n. 10).

23 Russell Kirk (1953) *The Conservative Mind*, Chicago: Henry Regnery, p. 48.

24 Claudio Pavone (1985) 'Un Togliatti mal trattato', *Indice* 11 (1) (January–February): 13–14.
25 Luciano Lama, interview in *La Repubblica*, Enrico Berlinguer, interviews in *Stern* 34 (August 1979) and *Corriere della Sera*.
26 Raffaele Rossi (1977) 'La storia dell'ultimo trentennio in Umbria. Gli anni difficili. 1947–1953', *Cronache Umbre* 11 (1)(January): 63–76.
27 The reorganization which followed the layoffs was much less 'deep' than Rossi seems to believe: a competent historian says 'the company was unable to seize the opportunity to create a new company identity' (Franco Bonelli (1975) *Lo sviluppo di una grande impresa in Italia. La Terni dal 1884 al 1962*, Turin: Einaudi, p. 288). The all-party committee (which included even the Fascists) achieved very little.
28 Alfeo Paganelli (b. 1908), 4 January 1980.
29 Agamante Androsciani (b. 1902), 21 June 1982; Arnaldo Lippi (see n. 11).
30 *Rinascita*, 6 January 1978.
31 The typical example is Del Carria's *Proletari senza rivoluzione*, op. cit., which was very popular in the late 1960s, and claims that 'the absence of revolutionary intellectuals is, in the last analysis, the cause of the missing Italian revolution' (vol. I, p. 21). Jeremy Brecher (*Strike*, San Francisco: Straight Arrow Books, 1972) also says that, far from fomenting strikes and revolts, unions and their leaders have always done their best to contain them, while the impulse for agitation always originated within the rank and file. What these theories fail to explain is why the revolutionary rank and file always manages to generate reformist or sell-out leadership.
32 Leslie Marmon Silko (1977) *Ceremony*, New York: Viking, pp. 139–45; (1968) *The Autobiography of Malcolm X*, with the assistance of Alex Heley, Harmondsworth, Middx: Penguin Books, pp. 258 ff.
33 Paola Ludovici (1980) 'Narrativa indiana contemporanea', in Elemire Zolla (ed.) *I contemporanei. Novecento americano*, Rome: Lucarini.
34 Matt Witt (1979) 'God's country', in *In Our Blood, Four Coal Mining Families*, Washington, DC: Highlander Research and Education Center, p. 76.
35 There is one event to which, however, 'uchronic' history might be applicable: the Fascist march on Rome of 28 October 1922 might easily have been stopped if the king and the government had used the army against them; perhaps history *would* have been different. No narrator, however, deals with this event in uchronic terms: it is of the essence, in fact, that the failure be on 'our' side, not the ruling classes'. Incidentally, uchronic versions of history are also found among the Fascists: Mario Sassi (b. 1906, 12 January 1983) says that Italy would have won the Second World War had not Enrico Fermi and other nuclear scientists defected to the other side.
36 Veniero Maroli (b. 1931), 29 January 1980; Amedeo Matteucci, conversation, 30 April 1982. Dante Bartolini (b. 1916), 28 December 1973 (in response to Amerigo Matteucci's verse about the revolution: see n. 14).

11

Myth as suppression

Motherhood and the historical consciousness
of the women of Madrid, 1936–9

Elena Cabezali, Matilde Cuevas, and Maria Teresa Chicote

The elements which contribute to 'being a woman' are phenomena
of an ideological superstructure built over centuries. To this entity
has been attributed not only qualities and attitudes, but also feelings
and perceptions, and even different forms of consciousness. Within
these ideological constructs, myth has a pre-eminent place in
processes of socialization and indoctrination through the internalization by individuals of a model of behaviour. Here we wish to
explore how the centuries-old, enduring myth of woman-as-mother
continued to fulfil its role of socialization during the tragic period of
the Spanish Civil War. At the same time cracks in this ideological
construction became more evident because of the circumstances of
the war.

The nature of our subject meant that we had to design a suitable
methodology, which we based on a comparative analysis of
ideological social discourse, as reflected in the press; and the
awareness of women themselves of their activities during three
years of war. We have extracted from the Madrid press of the time
everything referring to discussions of women. The sample was very
broad, covering all shades of political opinion, except for the far
Right, which was not published in the Republican zone.[1] The
information we obtained was chronologically analysed, to establish
the relation between the different stages of the war in Madrid and
the changes in the messages aimed at women.

We have juxtaposed this with oral evidence to reveal how social
discourse operated in women's consciousness. In spite of the
difficulties involved in the use of such sources for analysis (reli-
ability, present influences upon the past, failures of memory...), we
think there is no better alternative for elucidating how women
internalize their social role. We have also sought to minimize the
difficulties by using a wide sample, covering the entire political
spectrum of wartime Madrid, and by comparing oral evidence with
written sources.[2]

Myth is a system of communication, a message with a characteristic structure which fulfils a specific social function: it offers a model of behaviour. As an atemporal construct defining a partial reality, myth alienates the individual, taking him, or her, into a false reality, at the same time as giving meaning to his or her existence, separating what is essential from what is accidental. The 'Myth of Woman' as we discovered it in these newspapers of the 1930s has characteristics proper to all mythical discourse – reiteration, contrasting stereotypes, interaction.... It is formed round a central concept: that a woman's essential being is in her motherhood,[3] which is the supreme purpose justifying her existence. The myth may take a direct form, or be transferred to images of wife or sister. It is always linked to characteristics such as abnegation, sacrifice, and protection. In general, it is a passive role, fundamentally governed by the needs of men.

> [Women] are conservers of life, health and dignity. They are revolutionary in preserving liberty, in fighting for the Republic, in preserving the integrity of their own offspring... since they wish, passionately, to preserve the lives which they bore within them with long and painful effort.[4]

The image projected on to young women who are not yet mothers is different: it includes sex appeal, though this is never portrayed directly as such but rather in images of beauty, grace, and charm; and has characteristics which show a good potential for motherhood, such as enthusiasm, sensitivity, understanding, delicacy, and modesty. There are behavioural guidelines aimed at those who will become mothers:

> but, hand in hand with the pain there are always the open and hopeful smiles, of the sweet, youthful faces of the nurses. These good girls, humble, generous, dressed in white, like brides or like youngsters in their First Communion dresses....[5]

There is an astounding uniformity in the images presented by the press of that time: all the political trends reflected in Madrid's newspapers agree, and the message is repeated to saturation point in all of them.[6]

Because of the conflict, however, the war years were to see changes in these images. From October 1936 onwards, Madrid was a key objective for the rebels, and all recent studies show that the city did not have the capacity to resist the attack. It was essential to incorporate ever-wider groups – including women – into the city's defences in order to take up arms against the enemy, maintain production, and reinforce battle morale. As Madrid continued under siege until April 1939, these conditions prevailed throughout the war.

In this situation, the discourse of all the political sections of the Popular Front show women being used as a group, through the manipulation of the traditional woman-as-mother myth. A series of variations of the image appear so as to transmit a dual message in which new values directly connect with the changing needs of war. While generally women are bound to protect life in these new conditions, this function sometimes becomes exactly its opposite: the grandeur of motherhood consists in sending a son to his death because it is necessary, and this must be internalized as an act of heroism. Two examples illustrate this: 'the farewell was very brief, a long embrace, kiss and a few words: "my son, I would rather see you dead than defeated". It was the mother who spoke.'[7]

Or the famous words of 'La Pasionaria': 'We would rather be the widows of heroes than the wives of cowards.' Social acceptance of this variant of the myth is ensured as this is a very old construction, deeply rooted in popular belief: 'You who, although not believing evoke inevitably the image of the mother of God with the lifeless body of her Son in her lap...'[8]

For others, the qualities which shape the traditional wife-as-mother myth were sufficient to ensure that they met the new tasks thrown up by the war – evacuation, provision of supplies, and the care of the wounded.

Throughout the war, Madrid was chronically short of supplies. People were hungry, evacuation was never completed, and yet groups of refugees arrived constantly. Supplying basic needs for families and replacing services which had disappeared because of the war were vital to the resistance. In addition to undertaking this exhausting work, mothers proved essential in sustaining the will to fight and preventing the demoralization of the civilian population. The constant praises aimed at mothers in the press served to reinforce their abnegation and sacrifice:

Nothing could lay them low, nor make them vacillate. They were like heroic sentinels, firm at their posts, custodians of the home, zealous ants, the people's flesh and blood in dramatic tension. Silent fighters, fertile collaborators, they have had their martyrs and their victims. How many will have fallen, murdered by the daggers of the cold, or wounded by the pains of illness?... In these last dramatic months, the anonymous woman of the people has found us bread and soothed our spirit.[9]

The course of the war in the city was also marked by variations in behavioural guidelines addressed to young women. Until April

1936, the most urgent task was to defend Madrid. A new image appears, in open contradiction to the traditional one: the fighting woman with a pistol, the woman at the front, keeping watch and defending trenches, becomes a central subject of calls to arms in posters and photographs. This image reinforces myths rooted in collective memory, like that of Agustina of Aragon, Mariana Pineda, or Manuela Malasana.[10] The new images do not contradict habitual behaviour: 'grace in grasping the pistol', 'beautiful girls on the tanks', 'women soldiers who have not lost their femininity'.

> They have exchanged the shawl for the blue or red jersey, and are valiant, serious-minded and aware of their patriotic duties. They pass proudly through the city streets with firm step and vigilant gaze, carrying a burnished pistol which they handle with the same ease as a fan during warm summer nights... these are our courageous womenfolk, still sweet, with a mother's sacrifice, loving wives, affectionate sisters, brides with passionate hearts and, also, guerrillas.[11]

From summer 1937 on, following the order to withdraw women from the fronts, the image of the woman fighter becomes a negative one, in conflict with feminine qualities:

> Woe to humankind if the enlistment of females were ever to become a constant rule. Gone for ever would be the source of love and consolation in great misfortune and affliction; ideal love would have become confused with mere animal attraction which, once satisfied, would cause dejection. 'Animalia post coitum tristia'. Future mothers, masculinized and devoid of tenderness, would not be able to fulfil their role.[12]

Women in the militia as a central theme of the press is replaced by that of women carrying out all the tasks required to back the struggle of the men at the front. Now women were needed to cover services and production behind the lines, in a war which it was no longer thought would be short.

At this stage, calls to work and for political participation were directed at young women with the aim of changing their image – to that of the active working girl beside a lathe, or a machine, or tending the wounded or holding meetings. The image represented them as able to do what men did, but remaining women. A workshop report reads as follows:

> A new prospect opens up for young women. Girls! We must show that women are not flowerpots servicing men, but life companions and workmates who will collaborate with them in all tasks....

instinctively through girls' inevitable flirtatiousness, hands go delicately to heads. The hairdo, carefully done, always has something else that needs putting in place. And the house echoes in the workshop, filled with a youthful racket and contagious joy.[13]

Women had to be convinced of their capacity to do work to which they were not accustomed, and articles begin to appear affirming and illustrating the capacity of both sexes for any work.[14] The example of the working woman was embodied in the Stakhanovite.[15]

On the other hand, the identification of victory over Fascism and women's liberation is also a constant theme. One of many examples appears in the programme of the Union de Muchachas (Girls' Union): 'our liberation will be effected by the Popular Front and the people's army. Fascism is our oppressor and enemy, because it seeks to keep women in ignorance and to degrade them.'[16]

This promise of the liberation of women proves to have been without firm foundation if we analyse the political discourse of the period of the Republic. It is easy to see that only small minorities in the political parties took up the problem of women, and these certainly did not include the party leaders. In the excitement of the freedoms granted by the Republic, women's groups arose which began to claim their rights: but it is fairly clear that society's view of the role of women had not changed substantially and, in fact, only one practical consequence had resulted – the granting of the vote, an achievement which, it should be pointed out, was won in spite of the opposition of the most progressive groups. However, it was during the war that it was just these progressive sections which raised the question of women's liberation and rights, together with other characteristics of the regime which they sought to defend.

There can be no doubt that, in the rebel zone, a traditional model was advocated for women, which in principle denied them any change in their social role. It is equally certain that sections of the Popular Front in the pre-war period threw up different images to meet the needs of the moment, with a clearly instrumental purpose. Owing to these contradictory factors, a particularly confused image arises which does not make clear what 'liberation' was thought to mean. It was rather a faulty construct without solidity, perhaps including the following irreconcilable characteristics: that of a woman with full civil rights, better educated, having the right to work, but basically dedicated to housework, basically a mother, basically beautiful, feminine, in other words the same as ever. The resulting image was used as a recruiting banner for many young women who began to perceive, albeit intuitively, that in a free system they would have to achieve their own liberation.

We should not fail to mention an aspect which, in our opinion, is important and was introduced as a further element in motivating all women to join the battle. As in any conflict, the elaboration of the myth of the 'enemy' plays an important part in the political strategy of the two sides. Exaltation of the warring spirit for defence is much more effective if what you are fighting against is 'Evil' in the full extent of its meaning. The enemy embodies all negative aspects, to the point of becoming monstrous. Fascism in itself had enough traits, which were not invented, to ensure the negative reaction of the working masses. However, to the facts, sufficiently expressive in themselves, are added wild tales which exacerbate the imagination to truly fanciful heights:

> the fighting men at the fronts must remember their mothers, sisters, fiancées, wives and daughters. Franco, Mola and their cohorts have offered them as the most precious of war booty to the Moors and Legionnaires. If they surrender or flee, not only will they fail to save their lives: they will be handing their womenfolk, the very beings who are the joy of their existence, to the *awful* lust of the savages of Africa and international thugs.[17]

The Fascist regime is portrayed not only as the oppressor of society but also specifically of women, and a parallel is created between the victory over Fascism and the liberation of women: 'We wish to live, to be responsible beings, we wish for freedom, and Fascism cannot give us this: for Fascism means death, destruction, annihilation, oppression, ignorance.'[18]

On the other hand, there was never any suggestion either from the political parties or from the most representative of the women's organizations, that the core of the old attitudes to women should be destroyed. The myth of the wife–mother–spouse–sister, with virtues accepted as being proper to them and essentially feminine, persisted and the new images were constructed on the same foundations. The qualities of mothers, on the one hand, and of fighting women and workers on the other, are tirelessly transmitted through messages containing reverse stereotypes. The attributes change, but the negative stereotype is always the same:

Groups	*Positive Attributes*	*Negative Stereotype*
	abnegation	selfish
	sacrifice	bad mother
	sister	ignorant
Mothers	wife	cowardly

	indefatigability	irresponsible
	role-fulfilling	
	pretty	frivolous
	beautiful	irresponsible
Young women	smiling	cowardly
	gracious	indolent
	vivacious	selfish
	valiant	frivolous
	heroic	irresponsible
Fighting women and	dignified	cowardly
politicians	serious	selfish
	zealous	disputatious
		aggressive

The negative image in all the groups is identical and reveals the nature of the message which it is intended to transmit to all women: work, abnegation, and sacrifice. The negative stereotype thus conveys the image at the same time as disguising it. Internalization of the myth, through identification with the images, fixes the person's identity as recognized by themselves and by others, and ensures they are unaware of other potentials not defined by such an image.

This mechanism of identification and capture at the unconscious level explains the difference between what the women of Madrid did during those three years and what they had internalized, what they remember. The selective nature of their memory is remarkable, for they retain only those features which identify them with the essential nature of women as transmitted to them through the myth. The analysis of the interviews has shown us that the process of internalization operated differently, depending on the type of activity and where it was carried out. We have selected four groups for analysis – wives, militiawomen, workers, and political activists – to examine how these two variables operated.

In wartime Madrid, housework was an economic activity fundamental to the survival of the population. It is apparent that the operation of the war industry and supplies to the front depended on the survival of the population. Domestic work had to replace the disrupted channels of marketing and distribution in order to keep the city alive. To fulfil this role, these women spent exhausting days, walking long distances through the city looking for places where goods were being sold, waiting for whole days and nights in queues, or at home made scarce products for barter, looking for and carrying fuel, obtaining food for the ill and for children through health centres, and so on. This exhausting work, though essential to the resistance of a city without community services, has been lodged in these women's memories as their wartime family life, as the effort they put into feeding their offspring.

The need to identify with the wife-and-mother myth has meant that the women did the work but lack the awareness that they did so, or they have forgotten, or they do not think it relevant, nor connected with victory or defeat in the war. Thus Conrada Martin, after declaring that she did not work hard during the war, tells us:

> we did a little of everything – I exchanged things – I used to make soap and exchange it for cigarettes, and would take 100 grams of tobacco to a town seven kilometres away – walking mark you, and as for children, well there were so many, they just kept on coming and coming ... my life was like a slave's. One way or another, always on the go, because to bring up 9 children ... [It was] a life of constant work and suffering.[19]

The conservative function of myth in the social order is palpable: these women have no awareness of what they have done, because they internalize it as 'natural' in such circumstances, 'what any mother must do', 'what must not change'. This explains why the majority of women, housewives, whatever their politics, did not experience the onset of Francoism as a specific oppression of them. They were certainly forced back into the domestic sphere, but the attack was not directly on what was most important to them, their family, except when the repression touched them, through their children, husbands, fathers, and brothers:

> Good heavens! Look, I don't want to hear anything about the right-wingers – I don't like them, don't understand why they made me suffer so much, they made us suffer a great deal .... What I went through nobody knows, I buried two of my own flesh and blood and I went through hell as a result, during the war and after.[20]

The wartime variations in the myth also allowed adjustment to new situations. It does not seem that even the militiawomen who went to the front saw themselves as 'valiant woman'. Their recruitment seems to have been a response to a strong immediate need – everybody had to help to halt the offensive against Madrid – rather than to their identification with a new self-image. The duration of this mobilization (nine months) was too short for it to be fully internalized. Thus the image is diluted in their memory and all that remains is the recollection of additional tasks of the domestic type to help soldiers – sewing, washing, and so on. The women at the front did watches, defended trenches, yet when asked what they did they spontaneously recount the following types of activity: 'We washed the fighting men, we washed them, we got rid of a lot of their wretchedness.'[21]

It is only when asked specifically about the military actions which they had undertaken that they say that they handled rifles, show their war wounds or tell of the heroic deaths of many of their companions at the front.

One of the cases where the effect of myth on the collective consciousness is seen most clearly is in the withdrawal of women from the army, under a decree of the summer of 1937, which required women to leave the fronts. It is clear that there were objective reasons which led the government to enact this rule. On the one hand, there was the conversion of the army from voluntary to full-time, with little tolerance of the presence of women and, on the other, the realization that, contrary to what had been thought at first, the war was going to last a long time, so that it was necessary to provide a stable back-up from the rear: with the young men called up, women's help behind the front was essential. Nevertheless, the basic argument which recurs in the testimony of the women interviewed was that venereal disease had been spread through the presence of women in the army itself. This view of the matter is surprising when it is remembered that the soldiers from the Madrid front spent their leave in the city, where prostitution flourished. Yet this version of the facts is shown in the responses of those we interviewed:

> The withdrawal of the militiawomen seemed right to me because there was a lot of scandal, wasn't there? To be sure, they brought the men out of their shells ... the militiawomen .... No doubt some went for the right reasons, to defend the republic and to help their companions ... but others went to have a good time ....[22]

There is something which gives particular force to 'the proliferation of venereal disease' argument – the head-on confrontation of 'good' and 'bad' women, the latter being regarded as the source of misfortune and destroyers of homes. Prostitutes in Madrid during the war were suspected of being fifth columnists. The power of the image endured and led to the loss of other less direct arguments so that the collective memory only retains the negative image. But, by opposition, this also reinforces the identification of women with the traditional positive stereotype.

The newer and more positive image propagated through calls to work and to political participation was taken up in different ways by the various women's groups at which it was aimed. As far as working women are concerned, there were many in Madrid who worked for nothing to supplement services which were now lacking. We cannot count the number of hours of unpaid work that were undertaken but there can be no doubt that these were extensive and included jobs fundamental to the war economy, for example making garments in the workshops, working in factories outside normal working hours, and work at home. Women also attended to all types of social service, such as community dining-rooms, crèches, nurseries, or mothers' refuges. The women who did this work experienced it as 'aid' for the war effort, and it has remained as such in their memories: 'aid' to their husbands, sons, and brothers in the trenches. As the journalist Natacha said, 'It was the least we could do to be useful to those who were defending us with their blood and, hour-by-hour, shaping the Spain of the future.'[23]

Those working for wages were almost all working-class women, doing so for two reasons: financial need and the political will to win the war. The latter meant that the work day was extended and production intensified, with formation of shock and Stakhanovist brigades:

> The sound of the motors in the plants is a victory tune. I am going to get ready to be the best 'shock' worker in the workshops. We had to work, we thought of nothing else, we had to work, we had to work to win the war.[24]

The Soviet model of the Stakhanovist woman volunteering for unpaid extra work hours dominated the factories. It was necessary to replace the men and not only to equal but even to beat previous production levels: 'Well, you know that when the men were in the factory they said they made 40 while the women had only made 20'. 'So what? Men are better workers than women?'[25]

Large-scale inclusion of women in the labour force was seen only as a transitory phenomenon: as Suceso Portales puts it, significantly, 'we shall return the factories to the men proud that they were never closed'.[26]

The political activists, by contrast, remember the war years as the best of their lives despite the physical hardship and the uncertainty of ever-present death: 'There are those who, often, have cursed the war.... I tell you it was a happy period for me.'[27] They felt exhilarated to be part of a new social project, and also by the destruction of the old order. Their passive, receptive role had become active. Their sense of social usefulness was internalized and remembered as the time of their real fulfilment as people. But their awareness is not altered in respect of 'being a woman': maternity remained even for them the sacred pillar of female being. It was as a class, not as women, that they joined the revolutionary movements:

> Our training is not to separate men from women, but to integrate women into society; I must say that the brain has no sex.
> I was not aware of the feminist movement at that time, since the feminists' claims then were not for me.... I did not think that there were many people who did in fact go along with them.
> Feminism? Never! But humanism for ever.[28]

Politically active women not only received but also transmitted the image which they themselves internalized. The political task of mobilization meant that they had to present themselves as a new type of woman and, at the same time, as possessing the traditional virtues of exemplary mothers, decent and morally impeccable. Women as influential as Federica Montseny provide many examples of this idea: 'Women without children are like a tree without fruit, a rosebush without roses.'[29]

The Ahora factory girls dreamt of their lovers at the battle front:

> Your hand cannot give way, nor your eyes turn back: the barrel of your gun is always at the ready. I am waiting for you, happy and confident, so that together we may harvest the mature fruits of the liberty we sow.
> My life-companion, my darling, the tips of my fingers ache like yours as do my heartstrings. But we must endure, smiling, until the sun appears on the horizon.
> For the future is beautiful for us. Our home will be joyful with bunches of flowers, and books everywhere. I have always dreamed of a grown-up boy, brought up in happiness; now his time has come.
> You say: 'If only everyone worked for the war....' I too am working now. Sure, I didn't use to do much; now I will do more, from today; all I am sorry for is that I do not have a hundred hands to stretch out to enclose our ancient Spain.
> The sound of the motors in the factories is a victory tune. I am going to prepare myself to be the best shock worker in the workshops. And if I find my head too weak for hospital work, yet will I bind the bleeding wounds of our fighters, with care and tenderness. And should my heart shrink, trembling, with the pain day and night, I will ply my needle to make clothes to keep you warm. Should my eyelids droop down, weary from sewing, I shall shout out to the girls and to the women, 'Our time of happiness has come. Work, work for it.' And so on until I am worn out.

That's the way it is. There is no more room for faith or more joy in such a small body. Do not loosen your grip, may your rifle and gun be ever ready to fire.[30]

Despite the dramatic historical changes they experienced directly in the Civil War years, for the women of Madrid the timeless mythical core image of woman as wife and mother remained as central to their consciousness as ever. The myth limited the social being of women to a single aspect – motherhood, hiding the remainder of women's functions from social awareness and from the women themselves. Through the operation of this mythical scheme the contradiction between what woman is and what she has now to do is enshrined, turning it into 'something natural in the circumstances'. This made it possible, for example, to develop mobilization campaigns for work but to ensure that women would only do what was asked of them and no more and that they would not subvert the role society required of them. As a system for the organization of experience, the myth exercized a hypnotic effect so that women forgot what they did and neither disclosed it nor passed it on to future generations. The language of myth, covering a wide social field, can itself cause a suppression of the collective memory. Thus, on a subject such as the Spanish Civil War, on which so much has been written, *nothing* is known of what women did even though if their actions are left out, the course of the war cannot be explained.

Myth thus maintained the status quo, based on power relations where women are dominated and remain submissive. The ancient social concept emerged unscathed from a revolutionary process, carefully concealing itself behind the colours of each new image. Myth, in short, is not only a simple way to transmit history but also a selective two-sided process through which the past is handed down – or obliterated.

Notes

1 Press information is from a search of all the regular publications in Madrid during the three war years. The following yielded most information on the subject: *ABC, El Sol, Mundo Obrero, Ahora, El Socialista, La Libertad, El Liberal, Castilia Libre, CNT* and sectorial publications such as *Produccion* and *Vestido*.

2 Oral sources come from a sample made by the Oral Sources Workshop of the Complutense University of Madrid. There were forty interviews, chosen to take into account age, social standing of origin, profession, political ideology, militancy, marital status, and family situation. The interviews refer to the three years of war in Madrid.

3 On the content of the central part of the myth, the 1938 articles in *Castilia Libre* are interesting, e.g. on 31 May, speaking of women;

'vestal, mother of peoples, entrusted with keeping the home fires'. The 1 January 1938 number speaks of women as 'matrix of the world'.
4 *Informaciones*, 21 July 1936.
5 *Cronica*, 13 March 1938.
6 Of particular interest are the October, November, and December 1938 numbers of the publications listed in Note 1.
7 *La Libertad*, 29 October 1936.
8 Margarita Nelken, *Claridad*, 11 December 1936.
9 'Marriage to the unknown women of Madrid', *Mundo Grafico*, 5 May 1937.
10 Heroines of the Spanish War of Independence against Napoleon: these women are extraordinarily popular in this country's oral tradition.
11 *La Libertad*, 22 July 1936.
12 *El Liberal*, 10 November 1937.
13 *Ahora*, 10 October 1937. There are almost identical messages in *La Voz*, 23 December 1937, *Produccion*, 12 May 1937, *Ahora*, 29 April 1937, *La Libertad*, 1 August 1937, *CNT*, 30 November 1937, and *Mundo Obrero*, 17 February 1937.
14 Messages such as the following are constant: (captions to photographs of women digging trenches) 'they have also shown in all their activities that they are as efficient as men'. 'We have admired and been proud of the conduct of the women of Madrid in production. This is a great movement which destroys the reactionary conceptions which showed us the woman as an inferior being.'
15 There are many reports on Stakhanovist women in, for example, *Ahora* in 1937 and 1938.
16 'Union de Muchachas' was an anti-Fascist women's organization formed during the war.
17 *La Libertad*, 30 November 1936.
18 *Mundo Obrero*, 5 October 1936, reported these words from a speech by Julia Bea to a meeting as representative of the Spanish Communist Party: 'the entry of the Fascists to Madrid signifies the triumph of the feudal tradition and the slavery of women'.
19 Interview with Conrada Martin.
20 Interview with Josefa Lopez.
21 Interview with Leonor Benito, militiawoman.
22 Interview with Mercedes Garcia, a left-wing worker who spent the three years in Madrid.
23 *La Libertad*, 25 October 1938.
24 *Ahora*, Girls' Section, 26 December 1937, and interview with Carmen Caamano: the idea is repeated in other militiawomen's testimony, e.g. Julia Vigre, Aurora Arnaiz, Petra Cuevas and others.
25 Interview with Carmen Caamano.
26 *Castilia Libre*, 27 June 1937.
27 Interview with Petra Cuevas: backed up by a complex explanation in the interview with Maruja Cuesta.
28 Interview with Aurora Arnaiz, and Carmen Caamano and words of Federica Montseny.
29 Federica Montseny, *Revista Blanca* 1935.
30 *Ahora*, Girls' Section, 26 December 1937: Song to our Companions.

12

Myth as a framework for life stories
Athapaskan women making sense of social change in northern Canada

Julie Cruikshank

I discuss here a continuing tradition of storytelling by Athapaskan women who live in the southern Yukon Territory in north-western Canada. The stories they tell show remarkable persistence and address important questions in women's lives during a period of industrial expansion and social upheaval. Narrators who make use of apparently archaic imagery are utilizing a traditional dimension of cultural life as a resource that translates and makes sense of their life experiences. I would argue that storytelling is central to their intellectual tradition and that we should pay attention to how it *continues* to be a communicative act. Meaning in these stories is not inherent in structural relationships among narrative elements, but is related to the context in which narratives are told. Examining the 'point' made by particular stories may alert us to the role of narrative in sustaining culture faced with rapid and disruptive change.

My attention was drawn to this storytelling tradition when I recorded life histories of Yukon women of Athapaskan and Tlingit ancestry. Here I examine three aspects of the relationship between myth and life history. One issue is the persistence of traditional narratives: despite dramatic social and cultural changes in northern Canada, Athapaskan elders continue to tell the same stories recorded by ethnographers almost a century ago. A second issue is the contemporary *use* of those narratives: women who tell them in the 1980s seem to be using them to explain their personal life experiences. A third issue is the relationship of narrative themes to gender: female protagonists in these stories behave differently from male protagonists when they face crises, and when the point of the story is to dramatize appropriate behaviour, this may have real social consequences.

From the mid-1970s to the mid-1980s I lived for ten years in the Yukon Territory, carrying out ethnographic and linguistic research funded by indigenous political organizations. In 1974, at the suggestion of several Athapaskan women, I began recording the life histories of eight women born during or shortly after the Klondike gold-rush of 1896–8, preparing and compiling their accounts in booklets for the storytellers and their families.[1] My initial objective was to document perspectives on northern social history in a way that provided each narrator with tangible results of our work; in each case *their* objective was to produce their own booklet of family history.

As our work progressed, it became clear that these women were approaching our task with a different narrative model of a life history from my own. My expectation had been that these discussions would trace the impact of the Klondike gold-rush, the construction of the Alaska Highway, and other disruptive events on their lives. But very soon, several of the oldest women began shifting the focus from secular history to traditional stories. The more I persisted with my agenda, the more insistent they were about the direction our work should take. They explained that these stories were important to record *as part of* their personal history. In addition to biographical material, we therefore recorded more than one hundred stories, later published by the Council for Yukon Indians.[2] From a conventional research perspective, our work progressed in two stages, moving from autobiography to storytelling and mythology. From the perspective of the narrators, the two aspects were inseparable. The essential issue addressed here is how these women use traditional oral narrative as an explanation of their individual life experiences.

These stories can only be properly understood in their cultural context. Until recently southern Yukon Athapaskans were nomadic hunters and fishers who travelled widely. Social organization was structured around two matrilineal kinship groups, 'Crow' and 'Wolf'; clans, crests, and kinship obligations all passed through the maternal line. Compulsory exogamy reinforced obligations between those kinship groups; a man moved to his wife's camp for at least a year after marriage and was henceforth responsible for assisting her parents.

Women's accounts of their lives differentiate clearly between appropriate behaviour for men and for women, even though environmental constraints and domestic necessity meant that, when necessary, members of either sex could do tasks normally assigned to the other. Strict gender differences began at puberty when girls were secluded for several months and received intensive instruction from older kinswomen. This may actually have been the only time in a woman's life when she was physically separated from other people for an extended period. Married women spent a lot of time together sharing such tasks as child-rearing, fishing, and gathering roots and berries. Men were likely to be occupied in solitary activities like hunting. If fortunate, a young man acquired power in a solitary encounter with the spirit world, but there was no institutionalized 'vision quest' comparable to girls' puberty seclusion.

By and large, men provided and women prepared the food, clothing, and shelter necessary for smoothly functioning camp life. Relationships between men and women were perceived as complementary, and this principle of male/female balance is reflected in many of the stories.

A root metaphor in these stories portrays animals and natural phenomena as thinking beings, able to adopt human disguise. Human beings understood that each person was born into a material world suffused with and animated by power. Encounters with power were inevitable, and one's ability to survive in the secular world, both as an individual and as a social being, depended on the quality of one's interaction with such powerful beings. Resolving this issue was a major intellectual preoccupation for all adults in the western subarctic.[3]

This Athapaskan culture of the late nineteenth century was the childhood world in which each of these women grew up. But virtually every aspect of Indian economy, social organization, and style of life has changed during this century. The Klondike gold-rush brought some 40,000 would-be prospectors into the region for a brief but turbulent period between 1896 and 1900. Early in this century, Anglican and Roman Catholic churches launched their competition for souls, establishing residential schools for the care and instruction of Athapaskan children. The arrival of traders and the involvement of Indians in international fur markets gradually undermined their subsistence economy. Construction of the Alaska Highway brought a flurry of activity comparable in magnitude to the Klondike gold-rush, and left behind a corridor that became the administrative axis of the Territory. More recently, the development of an unstable economy based on mining, an expanding government infrastructure centred in Whitehorse, and ongoing land claims negotiations have brought further disruptions.

Despite these changes, stories persist. Many stories told by these women in the 1970s and 1980s were recorded in some form in Alaska in 1883 and in 1904, and at Dease Lake, British Columbia in 1915.[4] Each ethnographer believed that he was working with the last native storytellers familiar with old traditions. While some details may have changed in stories told in the 1980s, plots and motifs are easily recognizable. Why have these stories persisted when so much else has changed? And how do women continue to use them to explain their life experiences? Both questions become clearer when we turn to the third issue raised here at the outset, the relationship of narrative themes to gender.

One genre of transformation story particularly intrigues me because women so often select stories with this theme when explaining some aspect of their life. Characteristically, a protagonist passes from the secular, material, temporal world to a supernatural, timeless domain where that individual undergoes a unique experience, and then returns to the human community transformed by the event and – ideally – able to bring new knowledge to the human community. The two domains are marked off in some physical way: the protagonist may pass under a log, into a cave, beyond the horizon, or may be given a slap, which causes temporary amnesia. The physical characteristics of this new domain are the reverse of those found in the more familiar world: it may be a winter world where everything, including people and animals, is white. In this world, wet logs make the best fires, and the food and habits of human beings are offensive to the inhabitants. Often the central organizing principle is a reflection of the human world from the perspective of animals. This view of the human social order is no mirror image, but one which – like myth itself – simultaneously unbalances and redirects the protagonist, revealing the ordinary in a new way.

More specifically, a man or woman meets a being with supernatural characteristics – usually an animal disguised as a person – who guides the protagonist on a symbolic journey to a supernatural domain. In the course of the story, the protagonist either learns or fails to learn about the abductor's culture, and eventually returns by complicated means to the world of ordinary reality. Of more than one hundred stories which I recorded, forty followed this general pattern. In twenty-five of these, the protagonist was male; in fifteen, the major character was a woman.[5] At first hearing, the stories about men and women appear to be quite similar. But as one hears more and more of them, the journeys taken by women no longer seem quite the same as those taken by men.

Stories about men begin with the hero demonstrating human arrogance by offending an animal species. He subsequently encounters that animal, disguised as a human, who guides him on a journey to another order of reality where spiritual knowledge is taught. His eventual return to human society follows a complex and difficult path. A shaman is called to assist the hero and the human community must participate in his return by fasting. The protagonist returns as the power bringer with new knowledge and with the permanent assistance of a spirit helper. Men, then, rely on supernatural intervention to acquire knowledge and on the community to socialize it.

The setting for stories about women is often puberty seclusion. A woman is accosted by a male stranger, is stolen and taken to an unfamiliar world. Instead of acquiring an animal helper as a man would, the woman focuses her mental energies on actively escaping back to the human community. In most stories, she manages to outwit her captors and to escape on her own, often actually assisting would-be rescuers. It is her powers of reasoning rather than supernatural assistance which save her. She relies on what she has been taught at puberty about dealing with supernatural power to think her way out of her dilemma.

One story I recorded, for example, was of a woman secluded while her husband is out hunting. (It was not uncommon for women to be married before puberty and consequently puberty seclusion could take place after marriage.) Two men kidnap her and taunt her husband who arrives home just as they are leaving. They take her by water to a point of land which lifts, and there enter a world where ordinary reality is reversed, a white world where everything is winter and even the animals are white. Her husband and brothers follow and ultimately rescue her, but initially it is she who saves them – first from starvation by stealing dry meat and smuggling it to them, later by occupying her kidnappers while rescuers raid the camp and kill everyone. The duality of the world is reflected throughout: the symbolism of opposing summer and winter worlds, the interdependence of husband and wife, the antipathy to strangers who may come from an unfamiliar world, steal human beings, and carry them away.

In another story a young woman is confined at puberty and is left at home while her brothers go hunting. Late at night, a being called Techa approaches the hut and enters through the smokehole. Instead of taking her away, he swallows her; however before he does so, he asks her how he should deceive her brothers when they return. She invents an elaborate ritual for him to follow; then he consumes her and dons her clothing. The brothers return, recognize the deception because of 'her' aberrant performance, kill the being and use their powers to revive their sister and parents. Again, the girl's cleverness and the brothers' shamanistic abilities appear in clear and complementary distinction.[6]

Narrators seem to find in the stolen woman a powerful metaphor for explaining individual life experiences. While versions of the same stories are told by different narrators, each tends to emphasize skills of her own which parallel those of the subject, both tangible, practical skills and less tangible knowledge about women's power. Traditional Athapaskan narratives are powerful because they are constructions rooted in general social concerns, even though they are refracted through individual tellers by the time we hear them. In the southern Yukon, they seem to do this in two distinct ways. The stories both explore social contradictions women have faced, and at the same time they dramatize a cultural ideal women recognize.

Structuralists have argued that myth arises in contradiction, rather than as a straightforward projection of a cultural ideal, so that we should look for interpretations of stories in areas of social life which seem problematic. One such critical area for Athapaskans in the past was the balance between individual autonomy and group cohesion. Self-sufficiency was essential to survival, and nearly every ethnographic description of Athapaskan society stresses the thorough training in autonomy that children received. A more problematic issue was maintaining the integrity of the group, because of the ongoing ecological pressure to reconstitute economic units in different seasons and during times of scarcity. Each hunting group needed a minimum number of providers – some male, some female – and could sustain a maximum number of dependants – elderly people and children.[7] But as children became adults and as adults married or grew elderly, the actual composition of groups had to change.

For women, this issue focused on their goal of remaining with their own family group at marriage. For a range of practical reasons, such a residential arrangement was not always possible. Sometimes a woman had to move to her husband's family at marriage, possibly to stabilize trading relationships or to balance the number of able-bodied adults in a group. Furthermore, a woman always faced the possibility of being stolen in a feud or war.[8] There was the additional possibility of being abandoned for antisocial activity and having to fend for herself. Stories dramatize each alternative, showing how a woman could activate all her training and skills to survive.

One example recorded was the Star Husband tale. This story is widespread throughout North America.[9] Two girls contemplate two stars and speculate about the possibilities of marrying them. To their surprise, their wish is granted; however, once in the sky they become lonely for their parents, even though their new husbands behave as ideal sons-in-law, sending back furs and food to their in-laws. The girls decide to work their way back home and do this by performing jobs every woman learns at puberty. They make babiche rope to climb back to earth, sew mitts and pants to protect them during their journey; then they puncture a hole in the sky and climb back to earth to return to their families. Their return indirectly mirrors the socialization of young women, the acquisition and demonstration of specific skills and knowledge.

Another story from the same teller, Kitty Smith, was of a young woman abandoned by her people and left to fend for herself with only a piece of flint and a knife. Using all the skills and knowledge she has acquired in her short lifespan, she manages to support not only herself but also an elderly couple whom she meets. They give her their deceased son's bow and she uses it to kill sheep high up in the mountains. Mountain Man appears and assists her hunting but only after it appears that she *could* live independently and even support others. He stays with her and supports the older couple as a son-in-law should. Describing the heroine of the story, the narrator commented, 'She's so smart she didn't even need a husband.'[10]

To interpret such stories simply in terms of social contradiction ignores individual talents and how narrators actually *use* the symbol of the stolen woman as a model. The stories in fact reflect a cultural ideal where acquisition of superhuman power was largely the domain of men while women relied more on their ingenuity in daily life. Men's power was based on individual access to a supernatural domain, ultimately translated into hunting capability; women's status was more dependent on practical knowledge, hard work, and discretion in discussing power. In stories, men cross to the supernatural domain, identify with a captor to the extent of taking on his physical characteristics, acquire a new name to symbolize new status, and return to the social world with the assistance of a supernatural helper. Women more often perfect their ability to live by their wits and escape to the human – matrilocal – community through everyday ingenuity.

Stolen women stories, then, seem rooted equally in an understanding of power and in the practical, empirical domain of observable, transferable knowledge which all women are expected to acquire by the time they reach adulthood. Both transactions with the supernatural and basic survival skills mobilize the same sets of abilities. For women, practical and spiritual knowledge are inextricably enmeshed.

These stories raise intriguing questions about gender models in narrative, because of their association of men and women with different kinds of knowledge, spiritual and practical. But it must be stressed that these are outsider categories. There is no evidence that an Athapaskan storyteller would make such distinctions, or see anything inherently more practical in such a woman's behaviour than in a male quest for the supernatural involving the mutually supportive relationship between hunters and game.

How then do these women use traditional narrative to explain their life stories? Each narrator has faced situations where she has had to make difficult choices about conflicting kinship obligations, or issues of supernatural power, or how to blend older ways with changing social and cultural constraints. The story makes its 'point' or takes its meaning from such a situation, and decisions are consistently explained by reference to traditional stories.

Oral traditions are never easily accessible to outsiders. They are cultural documents where much is implicit, where kinship terms, place names, metaphor, and symbol play a particular role in how the account is presented. Day-to-day communication in small kin-based subarctic societies assumes a larger body of mutually understood information, coded in metaphoric language. Because that metaphor is never formally explained, an outsider is likely to miss many implicit meanings. Nor is it easy to grasp how a story is 'organized'. Inevitably, even a careful listener can easily impose a meaning which makes sense in the cultural terms of the outsider rather than the storyteller.

This brings us to the issue of cross-cultural interpretations of gender and possible connections between story models and behavioural models. While Athapaskan Indian stories come from a very specific cultural tradition, a Western outsider's interpretation of the behaviour of women would probably be that they demonstrate what passes for practical knowledge. Women behave in ways closer to contemporary Western expectations about responsible women, while men seem to be searching for a kind of knowledge now much less respected. Yukon Indians account for only one third of the Territory's population, so they have to contend not only with Western institutions, but also with Western interpretations of Indian culture. In this cross-cultural setting, there is greater consistency in ideas about female than male roles.

Younger women who follow the model of women offered by these stories are precisely those rewarded by Western institutions. Government agencies identify them as 'more practical', 'more adaptable', 'more flexible' in coping with change than men. The stories seem to be more use for women than men, since women are rewarded by Western institutions for following traditional roles, whereas men are expected to make major behavioural changes.

But the patterns may equally apply to men. Successful native men in the Yukon, where success is defined in terms of economic and political influence in the Indian organizations, have almost invariably taken the difficult step of leaving the community to study at university or to take technical training in southern Canada. In other words, they have made the physical equivalent of the journey, have returned to the Yukon with new knowledge and have moved directly into careers or political positions of some influence. Successful women, defined in the same way, have generally stayed in the community, raised a family, and worked at a job while engaging in a range of social and political activities.

Native artists and musicians in the Yukon are often men whose art requires solitary creative activity. More women describe themselves as storytellers; an art practised with other people, particularly children. At a more tragic level, the majority of alcohol-related deaths and suicides involve men, particularly young men; women may face enormous social crises, but they continue to balance a whole range of familial and social responsibilities.

This 'adaptability' of Indian women in northern Canada has most often been explained in broad historical, economic, and institutional terms. The stories I have heard suggest we need to listen more closely to the women's own interpretations, rather than to disregard them as mythical fables. Storytelling is a universal cultural activity and may well be the oldest of the arts. We still have much to learn about how it may contribute to adaptive strategies in societies where oral tradition has always had a central role in sustaining culture. My suggestion is that elderly Athapaskan storytellers are using old narrative forms to think about new social problems. They are explicitly concerned about communicating these stories to younger women. The themes of their stories are archaic myths, yet the point made by a particular story depends very much on the context of its telling. And equally important, the points conveyed by these stories can have a real influence on social behaviour. In societies relying on oral tradition, such narratives provide valuable cultural resources for thinking about both past and present. This is best summed up in the words of one woman, Mrs Angela Sidney, who repeatedly comments on the importance of traditional stories in her own life, and her hope that they will continue to be important to her descendants. 'Well,' she concluded one afternoon when we had finished recording, 'I have no money to leave my grandchildren. My stories are my wealth.'

Notes

1 Funding for this research was provided for six months in 1974–5 by the Explorations Program of the Canada Council and for a total of thirteen months in 1978–9 by the Urgent Ethnology programme of the National Museums of Canada. It continued after 1980 as part of my work with the Yukon Native Languages Project, based in Whitehorse, Yukon.

2 Angela Sidney, Kitty Smith, and Rachel Dawson (1977) *My Stories are my Wealth*, ed. Julie Cruikshank, Whitehorse: Council for Yukon

Indians; Angela Sidney (1982) *Tagish Tlaagu* (Tagish Stories), ed. Julie Cruikshank, Whitehorse: Council for Yukon Indians and Government of Yukon; Kitty Smith (1982) *Nidal Kwadindur* (I'm Going to Tell You a Story), ed. Julie Cruikshank, Whitehorse: Council for Yukon Indians and Government of Yukon.

3 Catharine McClellan (1975) *'My Old People Say': an Ethnographic Survey of Southern Yukon Territory*, Ottawa: National Museums of Canada; Roger McDonnell (1975) 'Kasini society: some aspects of the social organisation of Athapaskan culture between 1900–1950', doctoral dissertation, Department of Anthropology, University of British Columbia; Robin Ridington (1986) 'Knowledge, power and the individual in northern hunting societies', paper presented to American Anthropological Association Annual Meeting, Philadelphia, p. 22.

4 Aurel Krause (1956) *The Tlingit Indians*, trans. Erna Gunther, Seattle: University of Washington Press (first published 1885); John R. Swanton (1909) 'Tlingit myths and texts', *Bureau of American Ethnology Bulletin* 39; James Teit (1917) 'Kaska tales', *Journal of American Folklore* 30 (118): 427–73.

5 Julie Cruikshank (1979) *Athapaskan Women: Lives and Legends*, and (1983) *The Stolen Woman: Female Journeys in Tagish and Tutchone Narrative*, Ottawa: Canadian Ethnology Service Papers 57 and 87, National Museum of Canada.

6 The four story summaries included here illustrate plots with female protagonists. They were told by two Yukon elders, Mrs Angela Sidney (b. 1902) and Mrs Kitty Smith (b. 1892). Each of these stories has been published separately in the narrator's words: the first in Smith, op. cit., pp. 29–32, the second in Sidney, op. cit., pp. 51–4.

7 McDonnell, op. cit., p. 216.

8 Catharine McClellan, 'Feuding and warfare among northwestern Athapaskans', and Richard Slobodin, 'Without fire: a Kutchin tale of warfare, survival and vengeance', in Annette McFadyen Clark (ed.) (1975) *Proceedings: Northern Athapaskan Conference, 1971*, Ottawa: Canadian Ethnology Service Paper 27, National Museum of Canada.

9 Stith Thompson (1965) 'The Star Husband', in Alan Dundes (ed.) *The Study of Folklore*, Englewood Cliffs, NJ: Prentice-Hall.

10 For the full text of the third story, see Sidney *et al.*, op. cit., pp. 73–9; for the fourth, see Smith, op. cit., pp. 103–7.

13

Stories to live by

Continuity and change in three generations of Puerto Rican women

Rina Benmayor, Blanca Vázquez, Ana Juarbe, and Celia Alvarez

Rina Benmayor

For Puerto Ricans, telling life stories is not a process of passing down treasured family lore to later generations who no longer share the same class position as their immigrant forbears. The 'rags to riches' stories of many older European immigrants depend not only on individual drive and achievement but on the collective upward mobility and social acceptance enjoyed by those groups as a whole. For Puerto Ricans, these stories are a sharp reminder of a persistent condition. They contain strategic and immediate value, giving historical perspective to current struggles and drawing out connections between oppressive conditions then and now. They provide important lessons, reflecting the strength and ingenuity developed through coping with adverse circumstances.

Four years ago, our Centre embarked on a long-term oral history to complement fourteen years of research on the history, politics, economy, and culture of the Puerto Rican migration to the United States. Our understanding of the history of the Puerto Rican working class during this century, in the context of colonial domination and economic upheaval, had up till then not included a systematic enquiry into how people themselves perceived their circumstances and acted upon them. Neither had we taken up issues of gender besides those of class and nationality.[1]

Our particular interest in garment workers arose from the need to know what impact the migration had on Puerto Rican women, about whom noticeably little has been written. We have drawn upon a growing body of scholarly research on women and work, particularly on garment production in Third World countries and the impact of this on female populations. The massive incorporation of Puerto Rican women into garment work, and into a wage-labour system, began during the early years of the century on the Island. However, this is but the initial chapter in an 80-year trajectory. The Puerto Rican case is particularly interesting in that it links the movement of offshore, capitalist expansion with the mass migration of workers to industrial centres, a phenomenon of serious, worldwide concern today.[2]

When Puerto Rican women began migrating to New York in the 1920s, they joined Jewish, Italian, and Irish women in the garment factories. They came with fine skills in hand needlework, a reflection of how extensive the cottage industry on the Island had become. Many had laboured since childhood over detailed embroidery and hand-stitching of garments. By the 1930s, needlework, although miserably remunerated, had become one of the major sources of family income on the Island.[3]

In the decade following the Second World War, nearly one million Puerto Ricans arrived in the metropolis, economic victims of an industrialization plan (Operation Bootstrap) that depended on reducing the labour force through migration and sterilization ('family planning'). By the 1960s, Puerto Rican women constituted over 25 per cent of New York's sewing machine operators, one of the lowest-paid jobs in the trade.[4] They entered an already deskilled industry as section workers, the most vulnerable to periodic or even long-term unemployment.

This has, in fact, become the reality since the 1970s. The exodus of over 200,000 jobs to offshore sites or non-unionized areas of the country has left thousands of Puerto Rican operators unemployed late in their working lives. Often they have become disqualified from pensions or medical benefits, and union strategies have not provided them with the necessary institutional support and job protection. Growing alienation from union activism has also reflected the exclusion of Puerto Rican and other minority women from top levels of union leadership, and thus, from policy representation.[5]

What we are witnessing today is an intensifying erosion of the economic base for women and their families. Puerto Ricans are suffering the highest poverty rates in New York State and an economic and social exclusionary trend of crisis proportions.[6] Young Puerto Rican women do not work in garment factories today. Rather, they typically hold low-paid service and clerical jobs in banks, hospitals, retail stores, and offices. Young Puerto Ricans are experiencing similar hardships to those their parents faced, as jobs continue to shrink.

Our study to date is based on ten interviews of varying length with women from two different stages of migration – the *pioneras* (pioneer migrants) of the 1920s and 1930s and those who came in the 1950s migration. They speak English with varying degrees of proficiency. Some have been leaders in union branches. But the narratives we gathered are not just about their working lives. Women speak of growing up in Puerto Rico, family contexts, resettling in the United States, poverty and discrimination, community connections, and the struggle to combine raising children with fulfilling some personal goals.

A special feature of our work was that among the women we interviewed were some who were also our own mothers. Our research team included three young Puerto Ricans, daughters of garment workers, born or raised in New York. While there was a strong collective dimension in our analysis, which drew on our diverse cultural and ethnic backgrounds, experiences, and disciplinary orientations, confronting the life histories of their own mothers was for the Puerto Rican women in our research team an intimate and sometimes painful process.[7]

The stories we collected provide raw material upon which the next generation constructs its own meanings, so we are presenting 'new tellings', mediations by daughters and granddaughters from the vantage point of their own histories. The accounts spark admiration for the fighting spirit maintained by these women in the face of tremendous hardship. They also call up constraints in female upbringing that continue to impinge on young Latinas today as well as the awareness of how each generation of women confronts and redefines inherited roles. And they bring out a sharper awareness of how historical forces affect the lives of one's own family members. This presents quite a different view to the inexorable reproduction of the 'culture of poverty' put forth by Oscar Lewis in *La Vida* (1966).[8]

The relationship of women to work was an entry point into considering broader issues of community and family, ideology and culture. In this study we have approached our narratives as cultural texts for understanding how and along what lines – class, gender, nationality, race, culture, age – Puerto Rican women are constructing identity and life strategies.

The sense of self shapes the very way the narratives are told. They are stories of small victories achieved in the face of severe social restraints. They run counter to images prevailing in the scant literature and media of the Latina as docile and self-sacrificing, exclusively family-centred, passive victims of domination, or alternatively, as overly aggressive.[9] None of the women we interviewed belongs to the middle class today; they still experience economic and social disadvantage. But, relative to the hardships they experienced as children, they have improved their lot and that of their children. As Doña Lucila puts it:

When you have children to raise ... to support ... and the man's salary is so low ... a woman has to find a way to help out. So that's been my life until now. I worked in the garment industry for thirty years. Thirty years sitting at a sewing machine is no small feat ... working so I could get to where I am and give my children an education. And I'm very proud of that because I was able to raise them the way I wanted and help them to get to where they are now.[10]

These women have learned how to negotiate – often on their own – in a hostile environment that has dealt them many blows but which they have met, in turn, with their strongest weapons: a keen sense of social justice and personal dignity and a steadfast commitment to their children. The positive images of self that they project serve to combat – for themselves and for their children – the disadvantage that working-class Puerto Ricans objectively experience in US society and the image that is cast of them from without.

Blanca Vázquez

The stories of María R. are drawn from the world of work, the arena in which she has been able to assert her selfhood despite oppressive conditions. María is a 55-year-old garment worker and mother of seven children, who migrated to New York from a rural area of Puerto Rico in 1948. Married at the age of 15, she had two daughters at the time when she and her husband decided they could not raise a family on the land and 'progress'. First her husband, then María, and finally her two daughters migrated to New York between 1948 and 1950. In her first story María explains how she learned to sew on a machine by going to school. Then after repeated rejections by employers because she doesn't sew well enough, she takes advantage of these trial periods in various factories to improve her sewing skills and then tells a foreman that she knows how to sew but not on his particular machine. The foreman assures her that if she can sew on a Singer machine, she can learn to sew on a Merrow and proceeds to give her the practice she needs.

This story illustrates María's resourcefulness and ingenuity. It is typical of other stories that she tells. She conveys forcefully that she has never been one to give up, regardless of the objective problems she encounters. María does not downplay the disadvantages she faces, her lack of sewing skills, or ability to speak English. In fact, she highlights these things because they set us up for a sort of punch line. These obstacles are precisely the things she will operate against and overcome. The constraints are clear, and that she will find a way around them, through them, or over them is an inevitable outcome of her stories. In this first story it is her determination, willingness to face rejection and ultimately a clever little lie that will see her through to her goal – a better-paying job so she can help to educate and feed her children.

The second story María tells takes place a few years later. Here we begin to see a change in her, a different sense of her own value as a worker and of her options in life. She starts the story by saying, 'I was very important on the job':

> I went to another place making panties. Then I learned to sew on another machine, the zig-zag machine. At that time I was earning about $40 a week. Only two people know how to work on that machine, an American guy and I. We used to start the garment and then we would give it to the other operators. So that meant that any day that we missed these other people doesn't have no work to do and they had to send them home. So I was very important on the job.
>
> Every time that a garment was new and it took me longer I had to fight for the price. So at one point [a new garment] came in and this work was very hard. I cannot make enough money for the hours ... and I said, 'No, I am not doing this.' He gave me a little more money but I said, 'No, no, I can't do this job at this price' and so he fired me. I never was fired in my life from no job. He told me 'If you don't want to do the work just go home' but at this time I had the protection of the union. So I said, 'O.K., I go home.' I get up, took my pocketbook, then my coat and left but I don't come here I went to the union place and I report him. [The agent] said, 'Don't worry about it. I'll be there tomorrow.' I'll never forget, it was a Friday. On Monday he came up with me and ... he talked to the boss and said, 'You're going to time her with a clock and you are going to see how long she takes with the garment and you're going to pay her accordingly.'
>
> He did that and it came out to be more money. So he paid me but inside of me I was mad because he had fired me, embarrassed me in front of 50 people. And I say, 'You are going to pay me one of these days.' I was very rebellious in that.
>
> And I waited ... that particular day, the work was piled up to the ceiling, work that only I and this man we have to work first. I wait for that moment [when] this fellow was sick. I worked on two days, I'll never forget. I worked Monday and Tuesday and on Wednesday I didn't report to work. I went next door and I find another job, this time in bathing suits. They paid me about 75 cents a garment which at that time, this was in 1956, was good money.

So on Friday when I was supposed to collect my money for the days I worked, the secretary told me that Al wanted to talk to me. So he came over and he told me, 'María, you can't do this to me. You know that we don't have nobody to operate that machine. How much you want?' I said, 'I don't want nothing. I don't want to work for you no more.' He said, 'You can't do that to me, you know I was paying good money.' I said, 'I don't care for your money.' He said, 'You don't find no job.' I said, 'I already have another job and I'll give you the address. I now work in Julia Sportswear.' He knew that place paid good money.

This story shows how by this time María has defined her status and worth as a worker with marketable skills, knows her rights as a union member and can fight in English as well as in Spanish. She does not fear rejection, but even invites it by challenging her boss on what she feels is an unjust and exploitative price. In a subsequent story, as a leader of the work team in another factory she stops the machines over an unfair piecework rate and calls in the union representative to back her up. At the end of each of these stories she leaves the job. Because of the relative ease of finding work in the boom era of the 1950s and 1960s, María had the option, as other women also did, to go from factory to factory, to shop for better salaries and working conditions.

Ana Juarbe

Growing up on the Lower East Side of New York City, 'one of the New World's oldest settlements', I felt fortunate to be part of its history of immigrants, pilgrims and turkey dinners. Yet, as I grew older on the same streets of the Lower East Side and learned my lessons on the Dutch, the English, and my immediate predecessors, the Jews, I longed to be included. And I longed for the day when we Puerto Ricans would be followed by another wave of immigrants. I naturally assumed that because we had come last we were suffering the consequences of being newcomers on the block.

However, thirty-five years later and after many waves of Puerto Rican and Latin American migration, I am dissatisfied with a society that includes or excludes its workers at whim, especially those of us who have different cultural and ethnic backgrounds. I am dissatisfied with the questions posed by the mainstream about why Puerto Ricans haven't made it or why 'they' continue to identify as Puerto Ricans rather than as Americans. I am dissatisfied with the colonial relationship that keeps us going in circles between island and mainland in search of the fruits of our labour. But most of all I am dissatisfied with the way historical, economic, and cultural differences are converted into negative stereotypes, which can make growing up Puerto Rican, Black, Native American, or Asian in this country so alienating.

In a sense, it is the recognition of this very alienation and the historical relationship to the United States that impel us to 'be Puerto Ricans' even when we are no longer directly nurtured by the culture our parents knew. There is a gap between the present lived by Puerto Ricans in the US and the experiences of our parents and grandparents. They represent an earlier generation and their ties to the Island and its culture, forged in another time, differ from ours today. At the same time, we still face, as our parents did, discrimination and a colonial context that determine so much of what we can be in this society. In this sense, there is an underlying link – a continuum – in our history, which has to be brought out. Our parents' untold stories hold a history we are still largely missing after living so long in this country. Their stories give us a sense of continuity even as they help us understand the real differences and contradictions in our experiences.

In interviewing my own mother, Anastasia Campos, I learnt that her ability to provide and cope is rooted in another context and struggle, which comes out in her stories of childhood and young adulthood in Puerto Rico. Furthermore, the early childhood stories provide intimate details of the cultural transformations our parents and we, as a people, have undergone in the process of migrating from Puerto Rico to the US. My mother's life history revealed episodes I had never heard as well as a very strong will and a determined sense of character I have come to understand and admire more.

The beginning of her story tells of her childhood in the coffee hills of Puerto Rico during the Depression on a small family farm. Family-owned coffee farms were still very much in existence throughout the 1930s in sharp contrast to the giant sugar *centrales* (mills) which were owned by North American corporations. The coffee farms were operated by individual families who depended on their own labour as well as the unpaid labour of their children in order to harvest the crop. In addition, landless peasants worked alongside family members in exchange for a portion of the coffee. My mother's memories of this work include joy and excitement as she describes discovering patches of beautiful red beans on the ground. However, her early years were marked, on the one hand, by resignation and the frustrated yearnings for an education, and on the other by a sense of determination and assertiveness.

The story is important for it is both a window into the past and a bridge to the future. My mother came to New York in 1951 during the great migration from a community which, although still bound by oppressive remnants of feudalistic and patriarchal culture, out of necessity lived more co-operatively. She came to find work and join her husband. In New York she immediately found a job and spent the next twenty-five years between the garment factory and home, rearing three girls and a boy. Her story provides Anastasia and myself with a point of convergence and reflection about the woman she is and the woman I've been striving to become. It highlights the work circumstances during her childhood and the socialization of women and children as well as the strategies young Anastasia developed to meet her needs then and later on as an adult.

We'd go pick coffee.... Father would make us miss school so we could pick coffee. I would tie a small basket [from] back here. I would fasten it on me with a piece of rope and then we would start picking coffee. We would walk with the basket hanging like that from the waist. Then wherever we'd spot a patch of coffee ... Oh, we'd get so excited .... 'So much!' .... Then we would begin, you know, to pick the coffee. But whenever Papa would say, 'Tomorrow you have to pick coffee ... no school tomorrow so you can pick coffee', oh, no, that was sad because I liked school. So, we would miss classes. And in those days there was none of that, 'Why were you absent', or anything like that. It was the most natural thing in the world [to miss school]. We would leave the house about eight in the morning for the coffee fields... and we would get back about two, terribly hungry and without having eaten a thing .... Two in the afternoon without having put anything into your stomach. In the morning there would be a bit of coffee but I didn't drink coffee. I would have some milk, sometimes with an orange leaf.

When we'd get back I would ask my mother, 'Mom, can I sell a half-litre of coffee?' And she would say, 'God forbid ... you are not going to sell anything!... You all know that Benito doesn't want you selling anything or see you going to the store or anything like that!' And, um, well sometimes we'd go by the store and those bread rolls there looking so pretty .... And our eyes would be popping out .... And we'd keep going. We wouldn't do it [take the coffee]. Then one day I told Mom, because you see I was the most precocious at home ... I told her .... 'Mom... ah... we get here very hungry and very late from the fields.... Don't you think we can sell a little bit of coffee?'

'No, no. They'll tell Benito and he'll kill all of you. You know how he is ... how he doesn't want you to go to the store or to get involved in any kind of business...' And I, well, I started to get ideas. I began to say, 'Oh, no. I'm going to do it secretly ... I'm going to sell.'

So the first year, the first grade ... in school, went like this. I was out a lot because of work and we'd go starved.

But then I was ... ah ... getting interested in things, you know, in eating better, in getting dressed better. Papa was a good person but ... he was ... ah ... totally ... ah ... well, he liked to drink and he would buy food whenever he saw fit and when not, that was that. Sometimes we'd go to bed without eating. In those days Mom couldn't;... If we didn't have any garlic at home, she couldn't go to the neighbours and say, 'Let me have a head of garlic or give me a little bit of salt.' If there wasn't any garlic, she had to cook without garlic. And if there wasn't any salt, she would cook without salt. But it was forbidden to ask anybody for anything. Papa didn't want it. And since he didn't want it, Mom wouldn't dare. But I was always a lively one. And I would talk to everybody. I would laugh, chat, you know .... But when we'd see Father coming we'd be afraid of him .... And if we'd be downstairs talking or laughing, Mother would say, 'Girls, come in. Benito is coming over there ... and get under the bed 'cause he'll surely come in fighting ...'. And we'd all run and get under the bed until he spoke. Father would always come in fighting.

When I finished the second grade in school Father said, 'You aren't going to school anymore', because I was supposedly a big girl. We kept going in that struggle that was everyday life during the coffee harvest. Every day we would go pick coffee. I would pick it from the trees, pick up coffee beans from the ground. That's when I started to keep a half-litre of coffee. I got smart. And I stopped being afraid. It's like there was a change in me. I would say, 'Mom, we're going to pick coffee. I'm going to sell a half-litre.' 'No, God forbid. You know how Benito is.' I said [to myself] 'OK... since she doesn't help me anyway ...'.

We would pass by the store every day. Then I would hide from Father and Mother. I would go to the store with the coffee and say, 'Ilio, I have a half-litre of coffee for some bread and butter but don't tell Mom or Dad because they're against it.' He'd give me my bread and roll and I'd go back to the coffee fields and we'd start to eat bread with whatever kids were around. Then, if you came to pick coffee in the family farm... if you'd pick two litres, one was for you and the other for Father half and half ... I started to sell a half-litre of coffee to get clothes.

Anastasia's story brought to life the harsh realities of growing up during the Depression in rural Puerto Rico. More importantly, it provided me with insights into the life of Puerto Ricans trying to survive in a decaying coffee-farm culture. Very different social relations are described here from those we know. The individual was much more subservient to the needs of the family unit and community networks. In some ways the old mode offered more protection and benefits while in others it locked people into more set, hierarchical relationships.

The stories my mother continues to tell of her work experience in the garment industry again reflect the familiar constraints next to active strategies for dealing with her bosses. There is the story, for example, of when she is made chairlady of her factory and the bosses do not want her to carry out her responsibilities to the other women. In this case, she does not allow the pressure from her bosses to keep her from helping the other women or bringing their complaints to the union. The exploitative garment industry of the 1950s was a key experience. It provided opportunities for employment, so that in the factory Anastasia engaged in more direct confrontation with unfavourable situations without fear of losing her family's livelihood. She could always find work in another shop.

My mother constructs the self-perception of an independent and assertive woman by telling stories that show she is making choices. On another level, old constraints are still there. On the one hand, her strategies serve as a force for making things happen. On the other, they avoid looking deeper at the conditions and circumstances that truly oppress her.

The poverty and exploitation my mother experienced in the colonial agricultural economy and again faced squarely in the modern, industrialized metropolis is what I now resist and consciously fight. The challenge for me is to create a future of equality for my own daughter Andrea and the children of her generation.

Celia Alvarez

Let us now look at what's happened to three women between adolescence and womanhood, as they moved from being single to women with children of their own, from Puerto Rico to New York.

Listening to these women's stories has served as a tremendous source of inspiration and validation of my own experience as a Puerto Rican woman. They captured and brought back to life the struggles of my own socialization during the 1960s. Though born in New York, I grappled with many of the same social contradictions and problems as Flor, Lucila, and Eulalia. While these women speak of the realities of Puerto Rican women during the 1920s and

1930s, the social and economic constraints that limit the possibilities for self-actualization for women continue to persist.

> *Doña Flor*: It was my idea to come here to study but it just so happened that within two months of my being here I got married. Shortly thereafter, I got pregnant and since I was never able to find anyone to take care of the children, I couldn't leave them alone. He never wanted me to study. I bought books. I bought *Master of English*, a set of books. I bought an encyclopedia and I educated myself that way, even though I couldn't go to school. He didn't want me to better myself.

These brief remarks capture the contradictions between individual aspirations and concrete realities which confronted most women upon coming to New York. Whether out of economic necessity, companionship, or as a way to get out of a confining family situation, women married. As a consequence, childbearing and working towards the support of their families had a tremendous impact on the future direction of their lives. The fact that women could bear children and had to be protected from that eventuality shaped the social milieu of their adolescence and courtship years.

This restrictive upbringing resulted in daughters rebelling against their parents:

> *Eulalia*: If they wouldn't let me go to a dance I'd take my clothes to a friend's house and go to the dance without their permission. You see they wouldn't let me go anywhere.

By being closely watched and kept away from men, daughters were externally protected from the perils of their gender. They were left to discover for themselves, however, the nature of their own sexuality. This left many unprepared for later sexual encounters in their relationships:

> *Lucila*: I knew nothing. To be more precise, I thought that women gave birth through their belly button and that is truly ignorance. And God forbid that some boy should touch you ... because 'I'll beat you up.' But they wouldn't tell you why ... then you didn't know any better.

It is in part from not having been informed of what to expect that she, like many other women, were vulnerable to the exploits of the men they married.

> *Lucila*: That's why the father of my kids took me for a fool all those years. I didn't know any better. I imagine he probably was saying to himself: 'I brought her from the docks untouched. With her I can do what I want because she doesn't know nothing from nothing.'

In addressing the issue of cultural transmission it is interesting to examine the extent to which old ways of being are replicated, reformulated, or transformed in the lives of individual families. In looking at the ways in which Doña Lucila and Doña Eulalia raised their respective children we get a glimpse of how divergent their strategies and approaches are in the socialization of their own daughters.

Lucila: I brought my children up in the twentieth century. I wasn't too free with them but neither was I too strict. Because if I was scared, if what they did hurt me, how was it not going to hurt them also?... I raised them without having to fight, without having to hit them ... and with my daughters little by little I went on explaining to them about sex because, you know, it's not good to live in ignorance.

We see in Lucila's life some continuity in the transmission of certain values, while at the same time some reformulation. For example, just as she had responsibilities for her household as a child, so do her children. But these responsibilities were not so overbearing as to deny them their youth. In addition, we experience some transformation in the positioning of parent and child within her family. There is a shift from a hierarchical relationship characteristic of her own childhood to a more egalitarian relationship with her children. In this context of mutual respect the channels of communication are more open between them.

Doña Eulalia, on the other hand, passes on to her own children the strictures of obedience and respect which she learned in her childhood. This is the only way she knows how to protect them from the unknowns of US society. Her daughter's rebelliousness replicates earlier scenarios in her own life revolving round the same issues – wanting to go out dancing.

Eulalia: I think I went a little overboard in disciplining my children ... and now I have a daughter that throws it all back in my face. How I behaved towards her ... that when there was a dance ... she had to be home in my house by eleven o'clock when the party was just getting started.

Eulalia reproduces in her own family the hierarchical and socially restraining behaviour of her childhood experience. In addition, she holds on to a clear demarcation of traditional male and female roles.

For women of each generation the socialization process is full of tension between individuation and connectedness within family structures. The family provides a social and cultural nexus by which to validate oneself – a particularly vital function in the US context, where Puerto Ricans are marginalized and alienated from the larger society. It also enables one to empower oneself, given the amount of control and responsibilities over the lives of other family members ascribed to Puerto Rican girls who take care of and support others from a young age. But, on the other hand, it also provides a context where limits are set on one's ability to be a separate, self-directing, and independent human being.

I grew up speaking Spanish, dancing *la pachanga*, *merengue*, and *mambo*, eating *arroz con habichuelas*, and drinking *malta y café*. It was hard to understand it all … to try to make sense of who I was – a Puerto Rican in New York.

The socially active local parish church became my refuge. It was there that I began to make connections with the poor whites, Blacks and Asians in my community and said there had to be a better way for us all. I got swept up by the energy of the civil rights movement and wanted to go to the march on Washington but my mother said, 'No!' She worried about me – didn't like me wearing my Martin Luther King button or getting involved in politics.

Tensions flourished when I turned 14 and told my parents I was going out with a Puerto Rican boy in the neighbourhood. Unfortunately, 'boyfriend' in America and *novio* in Puerto Rico did not translate as the same thing. In 1968 I was chaperoned and followed by my father wherever I went because of that grave mistake. Their biggest fear? That I would get pregnant. They even threatened to send me to Puerto Rico.

During this same period I started high school in a predominantly white school in the heart of Flatbush. I found myself desegregating the Catholic school system … one of five or six Latinas and Blacks in my class. I was known as one of the girls from the ghetto downtown and was constantly called upon to defend my race.

I never told my parents about the racist slurs – never had the heart. They were breaking their backs to send me to school; my father kept his job at a city hospital for thirty years and took on a second job at the docks. We would all go help him clean offices at night and on weekends after our day outings together. My mother went back to work in a paper factory down the street. Prior to that, she had taken care of the children of women in the neighbourhood who worked. I've also worked since about the time I was 14.

Nevertheless I graduated from high school with honours and planned to go to college. So I went to talk to my guidance counsellor. She always prided herself on being able to say a few words in Spanish … her way of 'relating'. I enquired about government grants programmes. All she could say to me was, 'Well, you're not the only one who needs money to go to school, dear.' No thanks to her, I managed to get to college with the help of ASPIRA (a Puerto Rican educational agency).

So I left home and landed in a progressive liberal arts college in New England. Ironically, it was there that I found my first Black and Puerto Rican teachers. I was relieved to know that someone understood the reference points in my life without having to explain, for the only formal mention of Puerto Rico in all my schooling up to that point had been in a geography class. I studied questions of language planning, bilingualism and education, and language, culture, and identity. I thought that knowledge of these areas would be useful to the Puerto Rican community. I always made it a point to keep my foot in both the community and the academe. I have struggled to stay integrated as a human being despite the efforts of academic institutions to take me over or deny my existence; for to survive means we have to deny who we are, where we come from and where we are going as a people.

This oral history project was a process of 'coming out' – not just for women of our mothers' or grandmothers' generations but for ourselves as well. In order to create an authentic connection with others, however, we must first deal with the sources of our own oppression;[11] we must break the silence of our invisibility; but we must speak in our own voice, first to ourselves and then to each other. For in moving beyond our own individual lives we can come to appreciate the connections between us, the continuity and the change, and dispel the fears that keep us apart.

Blanca Vázquez

Overall, the most striking pattern in these stories is one of omission. Missing is a sense of victimization. In spite of the hardships and discrimination these Puerto Rican women have faced, there is little sense of resignation or defeat. These stories of how María learns to sew and to get a better job, of how Anastasia claims her rightful earnings as a child-worker and decides she will come to New York, of how my own mother Juanita fights her shop steward for a higher piecework rate, all speak to that resourcefulness and resolve.

The women projected to us images of strength and combat in the face of the obstacles and constraints on their lives, images of truly mythical power. Certainly the constraints are real and shared as a community measurable by indices of poverty and disadvantage. But the constraints are also ideological and herein is the strength of these stories. In telling us these stories, the women give a clear message to younger generations about struggle and perseverance.

Embedded in them are positive images for women, for their children, and for all who care to listen.

The fact that these are stories of struggle and success is significant. I believe that on the level of symbolic meaning, these stories are the key to how we have survived as a people. We may not know the historical facts, what actually happened in those factory exchanges with the boss, how it would play back if we could recapture what actually happened. We are not looking at behaviour which can be measured objectively. We are listening to how people relate their lives – *what is of value to them*. Mythical or not, what we do know is that these stories have meaning for us as insiders; that there is a felt need to convey to younger generations what kind of people we are and need to be. The images and projections we get as women from women is that women struggle, wheel and deal, manoeuvre and confront, and do whatever they have to do to accomplish their goals. The message we get from these stories is that if we are to survive, we need to be like our mothers in fundamental ways.

The stories of migrant Puerto Rican workers empower us. This, I believe, is their intent. It is because we are excluded that these positive images are being conveyed from one generation to the next. They do what the larger society does not: they validate our experience and affirm our worth. Ultimately, underlying what our parents are saying is that they have not wholly internalized or accepted the terms of class and race that are meted out in this country. The underlying message we get then, is one of resistance and rebellion.

We have learned a renewed respect for the struggles of garment workers, for their steadfastness, ingenuity, and resolve in the midst of an alienating, oppressive, and often hostile environment. If these stories prepare us, a younger generation of listeners for anything, it is to understand how a colonized people survive: through persistence, perseverance, struggle, ingenuity, and hard work. If we are to go further collectively we must internalize these lessons, drawn from the everyday lives of common people, and struggle together across ethnic, language, and national lines to create true opportunity and equality. To ensure the better future for our children that compelled our mothers and fathers to go to work each day, we, too, must fight in countless ways to resist the lack of dignity in our lives. For us, that is the value and the legacy contained in these stories.

Notes

1 The following paper synthesizes a 70-page collection of essays published

as a Centro Working Paper in 1987. This is a first interpretive look at life stories of Puerto Rican women garment workers who constituted a significant portion of Puerto Rican working women on the Island, from before 1920 to the 1940s, and in New York City from the 1920s to the 1970s. The Centro has published extensively on the Puerto Rican reality in the United States and its linkages to the history and culture of the island. A complete listing may be obtained by writing to the Center for Puerto Rican Studies, Hunter College, 695 Park Ave. Box 548, New York, NY 10021.

2 See Frank Bonilla and Ricardo Campos (1986) *Industry and Idleness*, New York: Centro de Estudios Puertorriqueños; and Palmira Ríos (1985) 'Puerto Rican women in the United States labor market', *Line of March* 18.

3 For more detailed discussions see Lydia Milagros González (1984) 'Tras el mundillo de la aguja', *Claridad*, 2–8; Caroline Manning (1934) 'The employment of women in Puerto Rico', US Dept. of Labor, *Bulletin of the Women's Bureau* 18; and Blanca Silvestrini Pacheco (1980) 'The needlework industry in Puerto Rico, 1915–1940: women's transition from home to factory', paper presented at the 12th Conference of Caribbean Historians, Trinidad, West Indies.

4 Helen Icken Safa (n.d.) 'The differential incorporation of Hispanic women migrants in the US labor force', paper presented at the Workshop on US Immigration: Research Perspectives, National Institute of Child Health and Human Development.

5 Herbert Hill (1974) 'Guardians of the sweatshops: the trade unions, racism, and the garment industry', in A. López and J. Petras (eds) *Puerto Rico and Puerto Ricans: Studies in History and Society*, New York: Schenkman Robert Laurentz (1980) 'Racial ethnic conflict in the New York City garment industry 1933–1980', Ph.D. diss., SUNY Binghamton; and Altagracia Ortiz (1985) 'Puerto Rican women in the needlework industry of New York City: 1920–1960', in V. Sánchez Korrol *et al.*, *Immigrant Women in America*, Philadelphia: Temple University Press.

6 Governor's Advisory Committee for Hispanic Affairs (1985) *New York State Hispanics: A Challenging Minority*, Albany, NY.

7 Taking a cue from the late Barbara Myerhoff's treatment of 'insider' ethnography (1979), our intention is to produce interpretations that reveal the connections between what the speakers say about their lives and the impact their stories have on other members of the culture. See also, Popular Memory Group (1982) and Renza (1980).

8 Oscar Lewis (1966) *La Vida*, New York: Random House.

9 Sally J. Andrade (1982) 'Family roles of Hispanic women: stereotypes, empirical findings and implications for research', in Ruth E. Zambrana (ed.) *Work, Family and Health: Latina Women in Transition*, New York: Fordham University Hispanic Research Center Monograph No. 7.

10 Original of this and subsequent excerpts are in Spanish, with the exception of María Rodriguez's story.

11 Cheríe Moraga and Gloria Anzaldúa (1983) *This Bridge Called My Back: Writings By Radical Women of Color*, New York: Kitchen Table, Women of Color Press.

Part IV

Family stories

14

Ancient Greek family tradition and democracy
From oral history to myth

Rosalind Thomas

In ancient Greece, the past was preserved almost entirely by oral transmission and oral tradition. Even in the great classical age of 'Periclean Athens' (the fifth century BC), Greek history was known primarily through oral tradition. The written word was little used for recording the past until historians began writing down the traditions in the fifth century. Even then, oral tradition continued to be crucial. Classical Athens provides cases which are of wide significance for the study of oral tradition in general. We are faced unavoidably with the creation and transmission of myths and legends as part of what the Greeks accepted as their 'real' history. We are also forced to confront the processes by which memories change. Because we are so distant from them, we can also study the formation of political 'myths' with particular clarity. In Greece as elsewhere, oral traditions very often reflect as much of the present as the past, so they help us understand the contemporary societies which preserved them. But despite their importance, very little work has yet been done on oral traditions in ancient Greece.

I want to concentrate here on a particularly interesting group of oral traditions from the ancient Greek world, the family traditions of ancient Athens in the classical period (fifth to fourth century BC). In these we see how certain families remembered and reproduced their past history in the great period of Athenian democracy. They both illustrate how certain oral traditions grew up in the democratic milieu and suggest some general points about the development of oral traditions. For instance, we can see how Athenian democracy of the time encouraged certain memories and discouraged others. This eventually formed the family traditions themselves, and we can see how far they diverge from what originally happened. Secondly, family traditions bridge the gap between oral history and oral tradition in a striking way and are particularly illuminating because the train of transmission is relatively simple. While the way a family views its past is not studied much by anthropologists, it is essential, I think, for our understanding of the processes by which oral traditions gradually form from personal reminiscences and memory.

Family traditions start at the level of reminiscences from parent to child. This is especially clear in the ancient Greek world where oral communication was predominant and family tradition did not rely at all on written records.[1] Today oral tradition and oral history are often the preserve of different disciplines and their different methods. The material of oral history is usually the personal reminiscences of people still alive, while oral tradition is usually defined as information about the past which has been transmitted over at least one generation.[2] It is often the domain of anthropologists who have analysed how it may change according to present-day circumstances, and how the very reasons for remembering and passing down tradition may influence its content dramatically.[3] But for the Greeks there was no such division between 'oral history' and 'oral tradition'. Greek historians such as Herodotus and Thucydides relied largely on information which was communicated orally, not written down: sometimes from witnesses themselves, sometimes from people who had heard it from others. Memories and oral tradition formed a continuum. The historians distinguished carefully between seeing and hearing, what people saw themselves and what they had only heard.[4] But both forms of evidence were crucial.

Memory and the complex processes involved in memory surely link the two. Even individuals' own reminiscences can be complicated, and this complexity is increasingly studied by oral historians.[5] People do not just remember what happened to them. Deep and intricate processes of recall involve selection, formation, and re-formation of the original experiences. Our memories are complicated products of later alteration, structuring, selection, and improvement: they can be subtly changed by our later preoccupations. Memories of feelings and opinions are particularly unreliable.[6]

So what happens when personal reminiscences are passed on to the next generation? Is this oral history still, or 'oral tradition'?[7] If we imagine a man telling his grandson about what he did during the war, it is clear that his reminiscences are going to undergo further selection, further improvement, and reorganization – for example, he may tell his grandson only what he thinks will be admired. What then does the grandson pass on to the next generation, if anything?

By most definitions the grandson's knowledge about his grandfather would be 'oral tradition' – testimony passed on over at least one generation. So the continuity between personal reminiscences and oral tradition here is clear. But some definitions of oral tradition would not include the tales. It is worth examining why, since it touches at the heart of our understanding of oral tradition and memory. 'Oral tradition' is sometimes defined as generally accepted by the society in question. Its 'traditional' characteristics are stressed: hallowed by time immemorial, it expresses the general views of the society.[8] But we need to be particularly careful here not to slip into an over-romantic view of tradition. Traditions do originate somewhere, and they can form quite quickly. Often their origins are quickly forgotten and everyone assumes that they have always existed.[9] But at what precise point does some piece of information become 'oral tradition' by this definition? The mechanisms by which oral traditions are formed, the gradual processes of remembering, forgetting, or transmitting on which they depend, have been very well outlined by Vansina.[10] Oral tradition is 'the memory or memories'; as a testimony is passed on it is slightly altered for various reasons, which include the current interests and beliefs of the society. Individual testimonies are influenced by the more general views of the past and these help transform some of them so that they conform to the general traditions. Those which do not fit may gradually be lost or simply changed. That is where we return to family tradition.

In the Athenian family traditions we can see an extraordinary influence of the democracy and democratic organs of the fifth and fourth centuries BC. The democracy did, I think, encourage non-aristocratic families to remember their family's past: moreover it encouraged memory of the recent past, whereas aristocratic family tradition had preferred to dwell on remote legendary origins. For instance a family might boast proudly that their ancestors helped to expel the tyrants (at the end of the sixth century BC), that they had fought bravely for the city and that one had died in such-and-such a place, that they had always performed their financial duties for the city, and performed them well, and that they were thus good democratic citizens. At the same time the democratic conventions stressed a certain image of the past which was grossly simplified – and indeed falsified. Family traditions were also influenced by this, so that the very reasons for passing on traditions actually distorted them. It is possible by close analysis of the traditions to detect a very different original which has gradually been overlaid or obliterated. And in the end (most noticeably in the fourth century) the family traditions presented a seamless democratic past which conformed exactly to the conventional and orthodox view of Athens' history. The interesting and individual memories of different families with their different original experiences gradually became indistinguishable from each other and from the general views of Athenian society.

A basic difficulty is that our evidence for family traditions necessarily comes from those written texts which for some reason or other recorded a tradition and therefore preserved it for ever. But, as we have seen, family tradition was mainly passed on orally, not written down. So it is essential to concentrate on the evidence that reflects the traditions directly rather than, for example, on historiography, where the historian has reworked his material. Such direct evidence for a family's view of its past can be found in the poets, who refer to aristocrats; and also in those speeches made in the Athenian assembly and law courts, where a speaker gave his family tradition as part of his defence. We also have considerable general information about the ancient family to supplement oral tradition, though as is usual with the ancient world, it almost all concerns wealthy or aristocratic families.

So in what contexts and in what manner were Greek family traditions transmitted?[11] Family history was passed on in the most casual and fluid manner. In contrast to the set texts and formal rituals which have enabled some oral traditions to be transmitted relatively reliably, the Greeks seem to have had few formal occasions at which they related their ancestral past. Neither funerals nor poetry of praise dwelt on traditions about the ancestors or narrative of the past. On the other hand there are plenty of descriptions of people talking about their ancestors in informal conversation. For example in Plato's dialogue *Laches* the two sons of the famous Athenian, Aristeides ('the just') and Thucydides son of Melesias, tell their own sons about the grandfathers' deeds, in order to rouse them to emulation: the conversations simply take place at meals.[12]

The informal and fluid nature of transmission partly explains why Greek family tradition in general has so little chronological depth. Family memory seldom extends further than three generations back. In the Athenian law courts, a man might try to cite as many patriotic ancestors as he could. Even so, he could rarely go back beyond the third or sometimes fourth generation, hardly beyond living memory. Aristocratic families could sometimes reach back a little further, but they were most concerned with their legendary ancestors.

Against this background, however, Athenian democracy provided a strong reason for remembering and an opportunity for presenting more recent family tradition. It gave one of the few formal opportunities to rehearse family history. One of the most important institutions of the Athenian democracy was the democratic jury court. The law courts consisted of huge juries drawn from the ordinary citizens of Athens. They were closely identified with the assembly itself, the gathering of all citizens to decide and vote on the city's policy. The jury and assembly thus epitomized the popular and democratic political system. When an Athenian was prosecuting someone or defending himself in front of these juries, he had to *persuade* them. Ancient trials often neglected the question of whether the deed had been done or the law broken. They were frequently dazzling pieces of rhetoric intent on persuading the audience that the defendant should not be convicted. Amongst the means of persuasion was the man's service to Athens. It is perhaps hard for us to grasp how readily this was accepted. The service a man and his ancestors had rendered the city was so important a part of his defence that it would be stated quite blatantly.[13] One speaker, for instance, declares that he contributed more money to the various liturgies – financial duties for the state – than he had to, precisely so that if he was ever in a law court, the people (or *demos*) would grant him some favour.[14] A speaker often adds to his arguments his own 'democratic defence', a description of how he and his family have served the city.

Athens had an extreme form of direct democracy in which every citizen could vote on every decision: numbers were tiny by our standards and direct participation high. Family tradition now helped a man prove that he was a good citizen. Previously, aristocratic family tradition had laid most stress on the very remote legendary ancestors, such as Herakles, Ajax, or even the gods. Little was known about the more recent ancestors, and nobody cared. For instance a eulogy of Evagoras, ruler of Cyprus, describes his noble ancestors, but they are legendary heroes, not recent figures, and the orator jumps straight from Evagoras' father to the legendary ancestor. Recent figures slid quickly into oblivion because they were not so important. But the need for a democratic defence provided a powerful new reason for remembering recent family history and especially the contributions of ancestors to the city. I would argue that it actually created family tradition from the historical period. Aristocratic families also changed their family traditions in the new context. One aristocrat, Andocides, whose speeches are preserved, came from a very ancient family which traced its descent from the god Hermes and the hero Odysseus. But when Andocides was himself on trial before the people at the end of the fifth century, he had to present himself and his family in the conventional way to prove he was a good citizen. He says nothing about his legendary ancestors, who were irrelevant, but concentrates on a long and detailed description of how his ancestors helped overthrow the tyranny. Thus democratic family tradition from the recent past was born. Citizens would have remembered some of their patriotic services without the democracy: but oral tradition is what people deliberately repeat and pass on, not what they might remember casually of their experiences if an historian like Herodotus cross-questioned them. In that sense the democratic system encouraged a new kind of family tradition.

What, then, did these family traditions actually remember? Many speakers declare that they and their ancestors performed many financial services for Athens, one form of wealth tax in Athens. These were signs of patriotic duty, and some speakers point out that they provided more than they had to. Many other speakers stress military service. Greek armies at this period were still primarily citizen armies. They frequently cite the death in battle of their relations or ancestors. Little information is ever given except for the place of battle. We get the distinct impression that the simple fact of death in battle itself is enough for patriotic service: tradition need not remember more. This attitude actually conforms to the emphasis of the official traditions which dwelt on glorious heroic death devoid of historical context or significance.[15] So again the family traditions are partly formed by prevalent attitudes. We may contrast other societies which glorify death in battle with lengthy and moving narrative.

We do not get a coherent picture of Athenian history from these references, but rather a fragmented and usually very vague image. But one period is mentioned frequently, the overthrow of the Peisistratid tyrants in 510 BC, which was followed eventually by the establishment of the democracy by Cleisthenes in 508/7. Several speakers in the early fourth century told how their ancestors had helped 'expel the tyrants and establish the democracy'. There was a clear contemporary message, for at the end of the fifth century the democracy at Athens was itself overthrown, and two oligarchic systems were set up. The second in 404 was particularly savage: it was known as the rule of the Thirty Tyrants. Its end was intricately connected with the end of the long Peloponnesian War between Athens and Sparta. Democracy was re-established and, despite an amnesty, many were prosecuted for their part in the tyranny. Repeatedly we read in speeches from the early fourth century that a speaker 'had no part in the tyranny, nor did his father'. This was the necessary disclaimer in front of the people and the democratic assembly.

In these circumstances the past was dragged up as an example. Had one's ancestors had any part in Athens' previous period of tyranny? Antiphon the orator for instance was accused of having a grandfather who had been a member of the tyrant's bodyguard more than a hundred years before. Thus speakers had to assert that they had not been members of the oligarchy themselves and, what is more, that their ancestors had fought against the Peisistratid tyrants, expelled them and restored the democracy. Hence they and their family had an impeccable democratic pedigree: the speakers themselves had inherited ancestral service to the democracy.

So the end of the Peisistratid tyranny had vital contemporary relevance to the fourth century. How did these oral traditions remember it? Firstly, close analysis of certain family traditions suggest that in fact the family had very probably been on the side of the tyrants, *not* fighting against them; but that the traditions have gradually covered that up. Secondly, memories of the sixth century end of the tyranny are clearly influenced by the more recent late-fifth-century oligarchy and its downfall. The result is a gradual simplification of earlier memories to a neat unobjectionable and facile view of the end of the tyranny in which it has been partially assimilated to the better known and more recent events. We are fortunate in being able to compare this picture with the very complicated, detailed account written by the historian Herodotus at a time much closer to the original events, in the mid-fifth century. But if we did not have that, the oral traditions preserved in the later speeches would be our main evidence, and our view of the late sixth century would be extraordinarily different. History would seem in fact to have been repeating itself.

We will take one fairly lengthy tradition in some detail, that of Andocides, as an illustration.[16] His family tradition is clear and its historical falsity manifest. Andocides was an Athenian orator and aristocrat of the second half of the fifth century BC. He seems to have been lively and pleasure-loving, but probably a moderate politician. He was implicated in the scandal of 415, in which the members of a political drinking club blasphemously parodied the much-revered religious rites of the Eleusinian Mysteries. This and another similar incident had provoked a panic in Athens which had serious political and military repercussions (involving the general Alcibiades). Andocides was exiled. He pleaded unsuccessfully to be allowed back shortly after 411. He tried again in 399 BC, in the years after the Thirty Tyrants had been removed and full democracy restored. This time he was in danger of his life.

In this last speech Andocides used his patriotic family history as part of his defence. He refers to his ancestors' part in the end of the tyranny of the late sixth century and the return of the people (*demos*) and democracy. This is how he described it:

> In that time of great misfortune in Athens, when the tyrants ruled and the people were in exile, your ancestors [the Athenians] defeated the tyrants at Pallenion, and your generals were Leogoras, my great-grandfather, and Charias, whose daughter married Leogoras and bore my grandfather. They returned from exile to their homeland and they killed some of their enemies, exiled others and allowed some to stay in the city without citizen rights.

We learn a little more in the other speech:

> My behaviour today accords with the traditions of my family....For my father's great-grandfather Leogoras led a revolt [*stasis*] on behalf of the people against the tyrants. Though he had the opportunity to cease his hostility to the tyrants, marry into their house and share in ruling the city, yet he chose rather to share the exile of the *demos* and suffer the hardships of exile rather than be traitor to them.[17]

So his two ancestors went into exile with the *demos*, they engaged in *stasis* (factional strife) against the tyrants, and finally they returned in triumph with the people. A fine patriotic defence, an impressive tale of ancestral support for the *demos* as long as a hundred years ago. Yet unfortunately just about every detail in this account can be shown to be false. Andocides himself unwittingly gives us evidence to show that his ancestors probably behaved very differently. The oral tradition has retained some genuine memories of the original ancestors, but these have been transferred and utterly transformed in a totally different context.

For he is unusually specific about detail here: he gives the names of the two ancestors, their relation to him, and the name of the battle. This must surely represent some kind of genuine family memory, but it has been displaced. The battle at 'Pallenion' must be the same as the battle of Pallene, a battle mentioned by Herodotus and Aristotle in which the tyrant Peisistratus actually gained power in 545. The location of Andocides' victory against the tyrants turns out to be the site at which the tyrant actually defeated his Athenian opponents. So the family tradition must represent some actual participation in the battle of Pallene of 545, but it has been transferred to a quite different context, the expulsion of the tyrants which occurred nearly forty years later, in 510. The genuine memory can be picked out because it is inappropriate to the new context. This also leaves the ancestors' actual standpoint in doubt – were they fighting for, or against, the tyrants? We can no longer tell, for Andocides' statement is contradictory. We can never know. But what is clear is that this remarkably long-lived family tradition of 150 years is now hopelessly muddled. Other oral traditions suggest that defeats may often turn into victories for those remembering them. Andocides' only gives itself away because it is full enough to preserve anomalous details which can be checked against external sources.

There are other problems here. Andocides does not seem certain of the precise relationship he bears to Leogoras: the two passages give two different versions and though the manuscripts have often been amended, there is so much chronological muddle here that it is most likely that Andocides himself was unsure. For in our chronological terms, Andocides thought he was talking about an ancestor who was active around the end of the sixth century, but the battle of Pallene was forty years earlier.

What about the possibility that the ancestor *could* have allied with the tyrants through marriage, as Andocides says? This is also a suspiciously rhetorical disclaimer. We meet the same rhetorical point made about the tyranny of the Thirty: one man says his ancestor could have joined them but did not. So there might be more here than mere rhetorical force. We now know that some of the leading families who later claimed to have expelled the tyrants as 'democrats' had had some period of favour or even alliance with the Peisistratids – the Alcmaeonid family most notably. Given that Andocides' family tradition also had memory of the battle of Pallene, Peisistratus' great victory, it even looks possible that Andocides' ancestors could have had close dealings, even marriage ties, with the tyrants. Under the democracy, family tradition had to cover up that 'collaboration'.

Finally, what of the general picture of the tyrants' expulsion that we receive here? The impression Andocides gives is that his ancestors were the generals leading the opposition to the tyrants; there was a decisive battle – and only one – in which the tyrants were defeated; the people had been in exile all this time and now returned with the democracy. Andocides is not alone in giving this simple picture. Other family traditions and also the general city or *polis* traditions had a similar picture of exile of the *demos*, expulsion of the tyrants, and immediate re-establishment of the democracy. Luckily we can compare it with the very detailed account which the historian Herodotus collected in the mid-fifth century: though still from oral tradition, it was much nearer the time in question, and therefore more complex and more accurate historically.

As Herodotus shows us, the period of the tyranny was a complicated one of aristocratic faction.[18] The tyrant Peisistratus in fact had three periods of power. The third, after the battle of Pallene, was strong enough to enable his sons to succeed him. The other leading aristocratic families combined alliance with guarded opposition. The Alcmaeonid family later claimed it was in continual exile throughout the tyranny, and its member, Cleisthenes, was to found the democracy shortly after (508/7 BC). But we know for certain that he held one of the main offices under the tyranny and thus was certainly not in constant disfavour or exile. Moreover the expulsion, as Herodotus tells us, was very much more complicated, indeed messy. The Alcmaeonid family gained great influence at Delphi, the main panhellenic sanctuary of Greece and the seat of a prestigious oracle. They bribed the priestess to deliver false prophecies: so she repeatedly told Sparta, the rival state to Athens, that she should free Athens and expel her tyrants. Sparta succeeded in doing this only after a second try in 510, Athens then relapsed into renewed strife and aristocratic faction, mainly between a certain Isagoras and Cleisthenes the Alcmaeonid. Eventually in 508 Cleisthenes hit on the idea of enlisting the support of the people – he 'went into partnership with the *demos*', as Herodotus put it. He established very far-reaching reforms and the constitution which effectively gave classical Athens her democracy.

Herodotus' account is detailed and uncomplimentary enough to be fairly reliable. It was not an enlightening or inspiring series of events: Athens' great liberation had been achieved firstly through bribing Delphi – an irreligious offence which would have deeply shocked most Greeks – and then by the intervention of Sparta, Athens' main rival and, in the fifth century, her main enemy. It was not a tale suitable for so patriotic an occasion. The traditions of Athens could hardly remember the liberation in that form. What they in fact do is to omit both of these disreputable or undesirable elements. In the fifth century BC popular and official traditions stress one element or another in the tale. Wishful thinking and patriotism could do the rest: in the course of time, and certainly by the fourth century, certain elements were forgotten completely. By the early fourth century, over a hundred years after the original events, the roles of Sparta and Delphi had been obliterated. The great liberation from tyranny and establishment of the democracy were now a seamless, irreproachable, and totally Athenian affair. Her rival Sparta could be dismissed.

So the first element in the transformation of these general traditions is that of patriotic wishful thinking. The second element concerns analogy with more recent events, the so-called tyranny of the Thirty at the end of the fifth century, the brief period of extreme oligarchy that Athens underwent which left a deep scar in Athenian consciousness. After that more recent tyranny, the older Peisistratid period was brought up as an analogy, as we have seen. That one's ancestors had taken the democratic side then was further proof that the family did not favour tyranny now. Thus the neat and simple picture of the exile of the people in Andocides' version and several others seems to have been encouraged by the recent events at the end of the fifth century. For the democratic party *did* now go into exile (not the whole *demos*, but a substantial number); and their triumphant return did signify the return of the democracy – helped, one should add, by Sparta again. At the end of the fifth century it was appropriate to talk of a 'democratic party', but it had been less so at the end of the sixth century, when such political ideas were anachronistic. In other words the memories or traditions about the liberation of Athens in the late sixth century were in the fourth being rapidly assimilated to the salient characteristics of the late-fifth-century return of democracy. Patriotic feelings and assumptions, and the crucial analogy made with more recent, horrific events, combined to change the earlier memories drastically, to simplify the traditions almost beyond recognition, and to produce a rousing patriotic tale cleansed of disreputable elements, which could fittingly stand as the foundation myth, as it were, of the Athenian democracy.

Let us return to Andocides' family. His family tradition has the exile of the *demos* of the general city traditions, as well as its glorious return. But there are other elements which are clearly special to his own family. They fondly believed that it was *their* ancestors who had led the people against the tyrants, just as other leading families thought theirs had. The family tradition preserved a unique memory of the battle of Pallene. So we have to recognize that family tradition could preserve remarkable, individual memories which were not merely stereotypes conforming to the general traditions. But they have been amalgamated and assimilated to the wider picture held by the rest of Athens. The activities of Leogoras and Charias, whatever they were, have been shifted to some forty years later to form part of the great liberation in which everyone wished their ancestors had participated.

How does this happen? The need for a democratic past must be partly responsible: as you had to produce democratic ancestors, family tradition tended to remember – or invent – consciously or not, only those who were suitable, and forget those who were not. The common rhetorical tricks visible in different family traditions are not so much signs of identical family history, but of the same cultural pressures of the democracy to remember one's ancestors in a good light.

Then there is the influence of the wider popular or city (*polis*) traditions too. Here we come back to the unconscious processes of memory. Restructuring and reorganizing memory is particularly likely when certain memories are isolated, remembered without proper context, or when they take on a new significance later. This must explain how Andocides' family tradition has acquired the conventional stereotypes of the general patriotic traditions. The family had individual and genuine memories of their sixth-century ancestors, but they became isolated or displaced from their original historical context as time went on: this was bound to happen with oral transmission, imperfect memory, and no detailed historical knowledge. The memories then became subject to telescoping: both the events themselves and the chronology were amalgamated into a later more memorable and prominent series of events. These later events were part of Athens' most celebrated history, in a sense the foundation myth for her democracy. These more decisive traditions attracted the isolated, fragmented memories, which became set in the context of the wider traditions in order to make sense of them. As less and less information was preserved about the lengthy Peisistratid tyranny, the chronology and significance of Andocides' family history could only become less and less accurate or 'historical'. Each mistake or lapse of memory would add to the transformation, and the family's firm belief that their ancestors fought – of course – for the democracy would seem to confirm the transformation. Here interpretation combines with memory, and the transformation must largely be unconscious.

The analogy of recent events would also affect family memory just as it did the general city traditions. As these oral traditions could not help being relevant to the present, the characteristics of the present seemed to confirm the accuracy or plausibility of the 'history' so passed down.[19] Gradually family traditions lost memories peculiar to that family and came to conform more and more to the orthodox democratic canons: for if you mainly remember your past to prove your family has good democratic ancestry, then obviously that reason will select what you remember. But we cannot understand the formation and mechanisms of oral tradition without considering both the character of personal reminiscences and the processes of memory. Memory is not simply a passive process, and it is highly selective. With oral tradition the time-scale is so much longer, the opportunity to forget so much greater, that this selection and transformation operates on a huge scale. The traditions that are eventually left are those most valued by the whole society.

Notes

1 Very occasionally it was preserved through poetry which was then written down, but this poetry did not record family history as such.
2 See Vansina (1985), pp. 27ff.
3 See in particular Vansina (1985), Henige (1974) and (1982).
4 Herodotus II 99, 147, 156; Thucydides I 20.1, 73.2; VI 53.3, 60.1.
5 See for example 'Between memory and history', special edition of *History and Anthropology* (1986) vol.2, M. N. Bourget, L. Valensi, and N. Wachtel (eds).
6 See for example Halbwachs (1925) and (1950) on the social context of memory; psychologists such as Baddeley (1976) and, in more popular form, A.D. Baddeley (1983) *Your Memory: a User's Guide*, Harmondsworth, Middx: Penguin Books; A. Lieury (1975) *La mémoire, résultats et théories*, Brussels.
7 Cf. Henige's dilemma (1982), p. 108; cf. p. 106.
8 ibid, pp. 2 and 106.
9 For the modern world, see Hobsbawm and Ranger (1983).
10 J. Vansina, 'Memory and oral tradition', in Miller (1980), pp. 262–76.
11 For this, see Rosalind Thomas (1989) *Oral Tradition and Written Record in Classical Athens*, Cambridge: Cambridge University Press, Ch. 2.1.
12 179a–180b.
13 K.J. Dover (1974) *Greek Popular Morality in the time of Plato and Aristotle*, Oxford: Blackwell, esp. p. 230; A.W.H. Adkins (1960) *Merit and Responsibility: a Study in Greek Values*, Oxford: Clarendon Press, Chs 8, 10, and 11.
14 Lysias XXV 12f.
15 See also Thomas, op. cit., Ch. 4, where I discuss the strange facelessness or anonymity of the official tradition and its background in certain Athenian democratic ideals.
16 See Thomas, op. cit., Ch. 2.4. for further detail.
17 Andocides I 106; II 26.
18 V 62 ff.
19 Halbwachs (1925).

15

The power of family myths

John Byng-Hall interviewed by Paul Thompson

I first became interested in myths because I was seeing families in therapy who would behave as if something was true, while as an observer I quite often saw the opposite. For instance a family might be referred because their adolescent was seen as mad; but when I met with them, I would find that the mother was extremely strange, while the boy was absolutely on the spot and tuned into what was going on. I could see that this might be because they did not want to face that the mother was dementing: the fiction was serving a function for them. Using the common meaning of the term, I started to think about these misrepresentations as family myths with a purpose, and how they might be passed on through family stories. In this case, for instance, there could be a family story about a son who went mad in an earlier generation, encapsulating this belief which was now pointed at the boy. Family stories can give a feeling of continuity, of how the past led to the present, of rootedness and family tradition, and so help to make sense of a complicated and fraught family life in the present. But their power makes them dangerous too.

We need to distinguish family traditions, stories, and legends. Traditions are shared attitudes and customs, which may be supported by storytelling. Family storytelling is more than chance personal reminiscing, although it may begin with such memories: the main point is that a parent or grandparent wants to pass on that particular information about the past, feels it important that their descendants should know about it. Family stories that are repeated many times, or passed down over several generations become legends, which are closest to myths in the strict sense of the term. Once I became sensitive to the importance of this family storytelling for therapy, and came to see it as an essential part of family life which might need to be given a new meaning if I was to help the family, I decided I should look more deeply at one family story: and the first that came into my head was a 225-year-old legend from my own family.

Until then I had thought of it as just a family curio, not as a legend. It was the story of Admiral Byng, who was sent to Minorca to relieve the British garrison which had been attacked by the French. I tried to remember how I had been told the story myself, and wrote that down. Then I spent a long time exploring it from books and the documentary evidence. That was absolutely fascinating as an experience. I was working at the time with a psycho-historian, Howard Feinstein, and he pointed out to me, that as I found documentary evidence that my original version told to me by my father was not true, I was resisting change in the story. It was as if what I had been told as a child was such a powerful truth that the implications of changing it would be profound: I would have to change my image of myself and my family.

The differences were indeed very substantial. The story that I had been told by my father was that my great-great-great-great-uncle had been sent by Lord Newcastle, very late and under-equipped, to the Mediterranean, and encountered the French fleet there. And when he met them he realized he was going to lose the battle, because he was so grossly outnumbered. So, being a sensible man, he got some sort of distance from the French and fired a few shots at them, and then retreated, not wanting to lose his fleet. And he was court-martialled for this, and shot on his own quarterdeck for cowardice.

That was the story I was told. I found that there was virtually nothing in it that was supported by the documentary evidence. It is untrue that he kept out of range, because first-hand accounts from sailors describe how ships were dismasted in a raging battle. The only true bit of information was that he was shot. But not on his own quarterdeck, not even that! Not even for cowardice!

The account I have now is that Newcastle sent Byng to the Mediterranean partly because his father had been Admiral of the Fleet and Master of the Mediterranean before that, so he seemed the right person to go. When he got to Gibraltar he was not given any reinforcements. He does not seem to have been a strong character and he did not argue. When he met the French fleet, however, it was roughly the same size as his. They had a battle and in the course of it one of the ships sailing immediately ahead of him was dismasted. In order not to ram this ship he had to pull out of line, and he found the only way out, it seems from the evidence, and pulled backwards. Later that evidence was used to argue that he had run away. But I found a picture that showed how, when the lines were disengaged, the French fleet was also withdrawing, so it was a mutual disengagement. He then went back to Gibraltar for reinforcements and to re-equip, for he was certainly under-equipped. From there he sent, like all good generals and admirals, his own report of his great victory over the French.

Unfortunately for Byng the French admiral had likewise sent his report of his great victory over the English to Paris, and this report was intercepted on its way to Paris on horseback by British intelligence, so that the first account of the battle to arrive in England was the French version of their great victory. Newcastle, believing his premiership to be threatened by the defeat, set going a whole series of stories about Byng's incompetence and cowardice, which were then taken up in popular broadsheets and songs. When Byng arrived back in England he was immediately arrested and court-martialled. There was no evidence of his being a coward, but he was found guilty of a technical offence which carried a mandatory death sentence. The court martial expected George II to pardon him, but the king was so worried by the popular fury which had been stirred up that he refused: he did not want the public to feel he was condoning the defeat. These political reasons made more sense to me than the original story, that he was shot because he was defeated: there would not have been many admirals or generals left if that had been the custom. So Byng was shot to save a political crisis: but not on his own quarterdeck.

It is difficult to know how far the original version I had heard from my father had been handed down within the family. Certainly they were very supportive of Byng at the time. His brother went straight down to Portsmouth to meet him, although he was himself so ill that he died there; and his sister supported him through thick and thin. They put an epitaph on his grave implying that he was disgracefully scapegoated. I know too that my great-aunt, who was the matriarch of the family, had given my father a book about the battle which implied that Byng had been badly done by. But my father was a great reader and I do not know what else he may have seen. In fact my father's version had a double meaning. In one sense the story is after all a form of universal legend, a cautionary tale against running away: if you do that, you get shot. Byng's story had been recounted by many historians. It had also been retold by Churchill in his *History of the English Speaking Peoples*. It fitted with the wartime need then for an image of England as a country which fought against all odds, with Byng as the exception to prove the rule. It may be that my father had read Churchill's account. But it also fitted with our own family position at the time. My father needed a justification for not retreating himself.

He had gone out to Kenya when he was 18, and he farmed there until he retired at 65. We lived on a huge farm, in a very isolated part, a vulnerable and dangerous situation. We were far from home, far from England and, even if miles away from the sea, we were fighting a battle, a battle in a different environment. The farm became a very insecure and dangerous position from which commonsense wisdom might have said, we should have got out. When my father talked about Byng he seemed in a way proud that he had been sensible enough to retreat from an impossible situation. But the legend carried another message too: the danger of running away. In retrospect Byng would have been wiser to have gone into battle and lost. 'Look at what happens to you if you don't – and the shame of it.' I think the public shaming was the most powerful meaning in the legend. It helped to keep us out there.

Nor was it just my father whose attitudes were influenced. Bravery and cowardice was a central issue in our family through the period of empire. My father's father had faced considerable danger in Nigeria and others went out to New Zealand and Canada. There are lots of stories told about them in the family, which centre on bravery. Let me give two instances.

When my grandfather was Governor of Northern Nigeria, the story goes, he got news at a party late one night that there was going to be an attack in another place some distance away, the next morning at dawn. So he galloped through the night to the hill where this attack was to be, and when he got there he asked for a chair to be put out for him in front of the building. At dawn he went out there and sat, absolutely still, in his white tuxedo, unarmed, without even a firearm. But when the attackers saw this ghostly figure, they fled!

The second is a story my mother frequently tells about me. A leopard had been on our farm and taken some cattle, and the next day we were all travelling near where it had been. My parents, who were keen birdwatchers, got out of the car to look for an interesting bird, leaving my sister and me in the car. She was seven and I was five. They disappeared for such a long time that I said I was going to look for them, and I armed myself with a stick and a stone, and went off to rescue my parents from the leopard – and met them on their way back. But my sister wound up all the car windows and curled up on the back seat with her book. In reality I must have been anxious about my parents and being separated from them, rather than trying to rescue them. On one level this is a story about males and females: of how men have to go out and fight and brave danger, while it was all right for women to stay at home, and even to feel frightened. I think my mother must have spent most of her life in Kenya in some danger, and quite anxious. I was always colossally proud of my role in the story, but I took it that my sister was also shown up well as being much more sensible than me. I only very recently realized that for her the story has all the resonances of the Byng legend. My mother, who is now in her eighties, likes to tell it more and more frequently, and every time she trots it out my sister feels awful. For her the story is an insult: she is accused of being a coward. She is looking for ways of asking my mother not to tell it. I had not understood how powerful it is for her.

I think the legend has left us all with the anxiety that we are going to be cowards. For example when the Second World War was declared my father volunteered immediately, but he was told that because he was 35 and a farmer, he should go back to farming. He suffered terrible feelings of being a coward, even though he had no choice at all. He could not accept that he was not fighting.

It has left its mark on me too. I thought of going into the navy, which is interesting in itself – and although we lived 300 miles from the sea I went down to Mombasa and spent some time on a British cruiser. There was an incident there which I have always remembered but could not understand. I was standing on deck, and somebody told me I was on the quarterdeck, and I felt very frightened; and I remember watching the Second-in-Command, anxious that he would notice my fear. Later, the legend made sense of that for me. It also helped me understand other occasions when I had deliberately put myself in danger, like once when as an 18-year-old I went out with some local fishermen and dived off the boat to swim towards a shoal of sharks: as if I had a ghost to lay.

The most upsetting and powerful time for me, however, was soon afterwards, when I was returning from Africa to university, and I developed polio while I was on the liner. I was sleeping out on deck, I felt acute pain in my back and my legs were paralysed, and I began to imagine that somehow I had been shot in the back, because I had taken time off from the army to go to university: 'that's what happens to you if you run away'. It was the Byng legend again, feeding into my dream material, taken up in the nightmare delusions of the illness.

How do we explain this? In this and other family legends I would not want to overrate the significance of the particular story. What matters equally is the context of listening and the context of recalling. The stories and legends recounted by older family members provide powerful images, glimpses of action or energy, which can capture the minds of children, conveying a moral tale which will spring to mind in a comparable situation. You notice that all my three instances are in settings to do with ships. And it is not so much the story itself as the story-line which matters most, the family ethos which it transmits.

This is why I like to ask families for their legends. There is a vast variation in the number I find. But I think all families tell stories of some kind: you cannot really get by without telling at least everyday stories, about what happened at breakfast and so on. Some families talk about old legends, while others are just as rich in current, recent stories. I have found that the age of the story does not matter to the child who is told it: time means very little to children. In any case the stories of yesterday, in the telling and retelling, may be the legends of tomorrow. They cannot be rigidly distinguished. In general, I have found that legends about grandparents and their generation are common; and many families also have rather vague, simplified but in some ways more powerful and mythical images projected of characters from before that. For us, Admiral Byng was one of these characters. Interestingly there was another of whom we had many more stories: George Byng, first Viscount Torrington, who we were told had won many famous battles. For us he was a more straightforward family hero. But I think that if you really want to find stories about the past, most families have them.

What is more important, at least certainly to me as a therapist, is how important these legends are in shaping the family's mythology, its image of itself. Some families' myths centre on fables of the past, others on current distortions, like the family I mentioned at the start where it was clear to me that the mother was potty, but they said that the son was the only one of them who was mad. They conveyed this message to me through recent stories about the son. Other families may be more influenced by stories from previous generations. Let me give you three illustrations from other families of trans-generational stories.

The first family came to me because one of the children was insecure in his sexual identity. It turned out that concern about sexual identity was a major theme of the family's history. On one side the grandmother had been the eldest child, followed by two younger brothers. Her parents were so disappointed in having a girl first that they disinherited her and cut her off. She was of course deeply angry and upset by this. The whole psychological issue for the family was encapsulated in one story she told me, of how after she had married and left home, she lived in the same street as her elder brother, the son and heir; and one day she was washing up at the kitchen window, and suddenly she saw her father march past only a few feet away, straight past the window, towards her brother's house. And he never even glanced up. For the grandmother the story portrayed how fathers were not interested in daughters, especially once they had got into domestic roles. It is the story of a minute, an image, but it was the clue to the dynamics of the whole family. Its reverberations made sense of the behaviour of her small grandson, but now in reversed form. The boy felt that he could only get his mother's full attention when he dressed up as a girl, and so when he got into games and playlets with his brother, he would always choose the female role and get dressed up, while his brother would always play the man.

In the second family one of the daughters was not eating. Here food turned out to have been an issue for three generations at least. They told me the story of how the maternal great-grandfather had been a 'shilling soldier', away from the family most of the time, and his shilling was not enough to keep them alive. The great-grandmother actually died of starvation when the grandmother was about ten years old. The grandmother told me the story of how, when her mother was sick from malnutrition, she was sent to buy sausages for the family, and she bought them, but on the way back absolutely had to go to the lavatory: and while she was in it, somebody stole the sausages. For the family, that story encapsulated the moral that children had to be prepared to take their parents' responsibility, but however hard they tried they would mess it up. That grandmother still bore a terrible sense of failed responsibility: if only she'd got those sausages back home. In a way she felt responsible for her mother's death. Now that story has a mythical ring to me: it sounds larger than life. Stories that go so far back often have an epic quality, with a single act leading to tragic consequences. Of course the truth is that the great-grandmother is much more likely to have been malnourished, and died of a disease like tuberculosis, than literally starved; and as a daughter, the grandmother must have been involved countless times in the feeding of the family, and there must have been many many times when it did not go right. There are thousands of other events wrapped up in that single story. It encapsulates the essence of her childhood experience.

In this family too, the thread reverses between the generations. Once the grandmother was in a secure marriage, she became seriously overweight. One generation tilts one way and the next desperately tries to lean over to do the opposite. So when we came to the present generation, the granddaughter had taken the message that eating too much was dangerous, and was starving herself instead. She was anorexic. We were able to explore the fantasy with her that maybe her grandmother had actually eaten the sausages, and starved the rest of her family, and this hidden message in the story conveyed guilt at eating more than your fair share. The girl had picked up an ethos which suggested that eating could be wicked.

The third family had a daughter who needed a knee operation to save her from damage which was likely to be permanent without it. She was refusing the operation. I could not make any sense of this, until the father – who claimed there was nothing relevant at all in his background – told a story. As he told it, he suddenly came alive, as if he was talking of yesterday. It was in the Second World War. He was in the back of the house, and his father and brother were in the front, and a dive-bomber attacked. He heard a bomb whistling down – he made the whistling noise, so it was really as if he was there – and the bomb exploded, and he looked out of the window and saw his brother impaled on the fence, with a part of his arm hanging down off the rest, and his father on the ground, apparently dead. Earlier, he had told me, 'We don't have any disabled people in our family.' But his brother had his arm amputated, and his father had had multiple operations on his legs: acutely distressing, because, as a child, when the ambulance came to take him to hospital the family assumed he had died. In fact he survived, but afterwards he became totally hostile to any sort of medical care. This grandfather persisted in his attitude until he was an old man, and in the end he died from it. He had a thrombosis and lay on the floor for three days, refusing to go into hospital. By the time he did, gangrene had set in, it was too late to amputate, and he died. So suddenly, with the revelation of this rarely told story, it was clear enough why the father and this girl might find the need for her to go into hospital for a knee operation a very difficult decision to confront. Then I found that the father himself had a vascular condition in his leg for which he urgently needed consultation, but refused to have it. I worked with him first until he was able to get a consultation and accept advice from it. It was only then that the girl was able to think of having her own operation.

This family raises an interesting issue: why are certain stories handed on, but others, which may prove equally significant, are kept very nearly secret. You might say that in this case I helped the family by making a shared secret into an open legend. I have found other instances in which people have told me of terrible events, tragedies and deaths, which they had not told their spouses or their children: yet nevertheless the theme behind the tragedy is re-enacted by the children. The story is kept secret, yet somehow the imagery is so powerful for the person who holds it that the rest of the family picks up that imagery and ends by re-enacting it. It is a very fascinating process. It looks as if the family ethos is being transferred through a mute unconscious.

At the other end of the spectrum, it may become an explicit part of the family tradition that dad tells stories or mum tells stories.

Families often have their own historian, perhaps an aunt who is invited to family events and given space there, and people will go to her to ask what happened about something in the past. When she dies, someone else in the family will find themselves put in her position, and indeed as people come and talk to them about it, may become genuinely interested in family history.

In these families where storytelling is more open, it may take place quite often in the evenings at dinner, or on outings such as to the theatre. Others tell stories mainly at family gatherings, at Christmas or at weddings or funerals. Stories can also be sparked off by anniversaries. Some may be reinvoked by points in the life cycle: when children reach a particular age, parents will think of how they were themselves then. Visiting relatives, or returning to where you were born, can also bring a flood of stories. Although it is not a common custom, as it is in Scotland or France, for English families to take their children to look at the family graves, I have sometimes done this as a therapist. It may give a chance to settle unfinished business with the dead person. Sometimes the survivors will take up the conversation they regretted never having had with a dead parent, and by talking aloud about the past, settle old debts. By reconnecting with the past they can forgive, and put it to rest.

As a therapist I need to have a much more active relationship to these family stories than you would as an historian.[1] If I find a family suffering from a disabling legend, I need to help them. I see my task as helping them to re-edit their legend. If I get them to retell the stories at the end of the therapy, they tend to do so in a different way, which is less moralizing, less rigid, less splitting into good and bad. We end up with a more real picture of people with both strengths and weaknesses. In a way, the legend becomes less mythical. Sometimes I probably kill the legend altogether. Or I might help them to build an alternative story: of how they got into their current difficulties, and how they came out of it. It would hopefully be a healthier and more real story about why they had to go to see a psychiatrist, and what transpired there; because there are plenty of mythical images of what goes on in psychiatry. But that again is another story.

Note

1 See John Byng-Hall (1982) 'Family legends: their significance for the therapist', in A. Bentovim, G. Gorell, and A. Cooklin Barnes (eds) *Family Therapy: Complementary Frameworks of Theory and Practice*, London: Academic Press, vol. I, pp. 213–28.

16

Changing images of German maids during the inter-war period in the Netherlands

From trusted help to traitor in the nest

Barbara Henkes

In 1960, the leading socialist Hilda Verwey-Jonker, discussing the shortage of women working outside the home, suggested that women from Germany might be willing to supplement the Dutch workforce. Her call evoked a flood of indignant responses, ranging from anonymous abusive letters, signed 'a patriot', to a comment in a provincial paper that 'it might be a solution, but we do not believe that it will kindle much enthusiasm. We are still troubled by our memories of the German maids of the thirties.'[1]

Fifteen years after the Second World War people continued to think of German women as traitors, spies, or even a 'fifth column'.[2] Today, almost half a century later, these beliefs will appear unchanged. From the start of my investigation into the migration of German women during the inter-war years, I have frequently been confronted with statements about 'German spies'.[3] These concern the often young, unmarried German women who came in large numbers to the Netherlands during the 1920s and 1930s in search of work.

Here I would like to discuss how the image of the German maid in the Netherlands changed from a very positive to an extremely negative one, and how far this still affects the collective memory of those who lived through the war. For this, I shall use documents from the period and interviews with two different groups of women: first, women who came from Germany to work in the Netherlands as domestic servants and stayed; and second, Dutch women who worked alongside them as maids.

My interviews with these Dutch women were originally undertaken for another research project, in collaboration with Hanneke Oosterhof, about the life and work of Dutch domestic servants from 1900 to 1940.[4] Eight of the seventeen women whom I talked to told me spontaneously about the presence of German colleagues at that time, which is remarkable, especially as there is a conspicuous silence about them when the period is discussed nowadays. I have used the recollections of these eight women here.

All except one of the other group of women who had left Germany before the Second World War to work in the Netherlands were interviewed only last year. Here I have used interviews with nine women who stayed in the Netherlands. I also spoke with women who returned to Germany before the outbreak of the Second World War, but I have decided to refer to their memories only in passing as I want to concentrate on the past and present images of German maids in the Netherlands.

This material is not intended to establish the extent to which the images do or do not accord with 'reality', for instance by checking if there is any evidence of treachery. I have limited myself to the image-building itself, which I will present in two sections. In the first I trace the changing images of these German women during the 1920s and 1930s as revealed by documents of the period and confirmed by statements during the interviews. In the second I use principally the interviews, to discuss how far the images still play a part in the collective memory.

After the First World War tens of thousands of young, unmarried women left their battered native country to try their luck in a more prosperous neighbouring country. Since they did not have a home there, most worked as resident servants in private households or hotels.

According to official figures, around 9,100 foreign women were employed in the Netherlands in 1920. By 1930 the number had risen to 30,500. This indicates that one resident servant in five was of non-Dutch origin. After 1930 the figure rose further, to about 40,000 in 1934. From then on it fell: by the end of 1936 the number of foreign female servants was estimated at 22,000; by the end of 1938 it had fallen as low as 15,500. The majority of these foreign housemaids were German. Of 30,000 maids employed in the Netherlands in 1930, 24,000 came from Germany and 3,300 from Austria. There were also over a thousand Czech, Polish, Hungarian, and Yugoslavian maids, as well as a thousand from Belgium.[5] Because of the shortage of Dutch female domestics[6] the German maids were at first received with open arms. Their *Tüchtigkeit* (industriousness) and gift for 'accommodating themselves quickly to their circumstances' were generally praised, and a number of women's organizations soon set up an agency 'for the recruitment of German domestic servants'.[7]

In 1930 the Dutch government itself responded by setting up a special women's section in the Dutch labour exchange in

Oberhausen (Germany), 'in order to arrange for an appropriate supply of German maids to enter the Netherlands'. During the first half of the 1930s this section helped hundreds of girls to find situations on the other side of the border.[8] But most managed to find posts in Dutch households by themselves, through their own efforts.

The virtues that were ascribed to the German domestics were quite often contrasted with the deficiencies of their Dutch colleagues. The daily paper *Het Vaderland*, for instance, published a letter from a lady from The Hague on 18 August 1933 about the 'endless trouble' she had had with her Dutch maids:

> Either they were lazy or untidy, or they brought suspicious men into the house, or stole ....No, as long as the Dutch servant has not learned that there are such things as good manners and devotion to duty, I will keep my German maid (who, as a matter of fact, gives me the opportunity to 'keep up' a foreign language), who is polite, civilized, never grumbles, and who shows gratitude for extra kindness, which is extended with joy to such a diligent, nice girl, who in short has her heart in her work.[9]

The Dutch servants displayed less enthusiasm at the arrival of their German colleagues, who were often prepared to do more work for less money. The Dutch Union of Domestic Servants called on its members 'to convince the German servants that they are making their own situation worse than need be and are causing the wages of Dutch servants to be lowered'.[10] But even if they had managed to transmit this insight to the German maids –in so far as they were not already aware of it – to act on it was quite a different matter. Their vulnerable position, as foreigners living in their employer's home, made most of them cherish the image of *Tüchtigkeit* and obedience.

> The German maids were cheap, because they were glad to have work; they were dependants and had no one they could lean on. Dutch maids greatly resented this, because these German maids did everything those Dutch maids refused to do. They didn't have a choice, because they couldn't go home, they'd nowhere to go, and so they did it, and for little pay.[11]

This is how Mrs Rieff describes the position of most of the German maids who, like herself, had come from Germany to the Netherlands during the inter-war period. Her former Dutch colleagues recall a similar deadlock:

> It was exactly at the same time when we'd formed our Union of Domestic Servants that those German maids came. We wanted

to establish regular working hours and things, and the arrival of those German maids was indeed ...eh well... how shall I put it ... something of a nuisance. They destroyed the things we stood for. They had to find work, no matter how. And they put up with a lot more because ... they were simply under a lot of pressure.[12]

Looking back on this period, former German as well as Dutch servants recall the *tüchtige*, obedient German maid who was prepared to work for low wages while neither the German nor Dutch maids could see a way of changing the situation. The employers had it all their way.

Nevertheless, the initial enthusiasm with which foreign servants were welcomed into Dutch families gave way to a certain reserve during the 1930s. As unemployment grew, people were urged – especially by the government – to replace their foreign servants by Dutch maids.

Gradually the image of the obedient, hard-working housemaid began to change:

Dutch women are shamed by the fact that almost 30 to 35,000 women from abroad are assisting in the management of our households, while there are tens of thousands of girls in the Netherlands who have too much time on their hands, or who help to increase unemployment among men and compete with men in the labour market. In view of the lamentations about employment and bad times it seems ironic that in our country approximately 40,000 foreign servants have taken the place of Dutch maids, and that they get more than 20 million guilders a year in the form of wages, board and lodging, of which several millions go to foreign countries each year.

Thus wrote Th. Van Lier, Head of the Rijksdienst der Werkverschaffing en Arbeidsbemiddeling (the Government Department of Job Creation and Relief Work for the Unemployed), in 1936.[13] The Depression caused a new emphasis on national identity: non-Dutch, German servants came to be regarded as 'foreign' women, who were responsible for the precious national 'good' (i.e. currency) disappearing across the border.

The Dutch government intervened: the women's section of the Labour Exchange in Oberhausen was closed by the end of 1934, and in the same year the Wet op de Vreemde Arbeidskrachten (Foreign Workers Act) came into force. This Act imposed restrictions on the employment of foreigners in the Netherlands by means of work permits, though foreign domestic servants were – owing to campaigns of women's organizations – at first excluded from this Act, because of the alleged scarcity of satisfactory Dutch servants.[14]

In order to solve this problem the government took a number of measures: it decided to finance a programme of free training courses for housemaids throughout the country. These were set up with the help of regional labour exchanges and various women's organizations.[15] In addition, the Minister of Social Services and Employment made two abortive attempts to prohibit the employment of women in factories and workshops.[16]

These measures were meant to persuade Dutch girls to enter domestic service. This would reduce the rate of unemployment among men, and the reason for allowing the 'foreigners' – who 'interfered with Dutch domesticity'[17] – to stay, would no longer exist. From June 1936 the Foreign Workers Act also included domestic servants, which made it more difficult for German maids to live and work in the Netherlands.

The employment of German domestic servants was also restricted by the developments in Nazi Germany, which helped to bring about a rapid decline in the total number of German servants in the Netherlands.

With the arrival of Hitler, the necessity of leaving Germany for economic reasons became less imperative, because war preparations brought employment and a certain prosperity. In the mean time, the growing threat of war contributed to the return of many German servants to their native country. They feared being cut off from their families in Germany, as much as they feared possible retaliation by the Dutch in case of a German invasion.[18]

In addition, a number of measures were taken which made many young women feel obliged to leave the posts they had obtained in the Netherlands. In September 1935, for instance, the Nuremberg Acts came into force. Under the provisions of these Acts 'female subjects of German or related blood under forty-five' were not allowed to work in Jewish families.[19] Although, officially, these Acts were not operative outside Germany, it appears that German girls working in Jewish households in the Netherlands were also pressurized into resigning their posts:

> When asked why they wanted to leave, they said that pressure had been exerted on them from Germany, by means of threats against relatives or parents living there. These threats had taken the form, for instance, of dismissal from work or discontinuation of old-age pension, boycott etc. Naturally the result of this was that the family had asked the daughter to leave the Jewish family.[20]

Three years later the authorities in Berlin recalled German women working abroad to *die Heimat* (the homeland), where war preparations had created a shortage of workers. By then the number of German maids in the Netherlands had fallen to about 35,000.[21] Their stay was *Amtlich gekürtzt* (officially terminated) on 2 February 1939 by the German consulate.[22]

Among the women who were summoned back to their native country there were many who moved heaven and earth to be allowed to stay in the Netherlands. A number quickly married, while others 'addressed a flood of appeals to all conceivable kinds of official bodies, numerous appeals even to the Führer's chancellory'. To Mr Butting, Head of the Reichsdeutsche Gemeinschaft (the German community abroad) in the Netherlands, who reported this to the Head of the Ausland Organisation (Foreign Service) in Berlin, 'the mentality of these girls' was 'a mystery'.[23] He suggested that the aim should be

> to induce all German girls to return, if they are not employed in German households or are of an age to need financial support in Germany, or in isolated cases, those girls employed by a political person who might be of special interest to Germany.[24]

This reveals the intention of using a small number of women as spies, even though there is not even the slightest piece of evidence that this ever in fact happened.[25] On this point L. de Jong, in his extensive work on the Netherlands during the Second World War, concludes repeatedly that the idea of espionage or fifth-column activities of Germans in the Netherlands 'was a projection of Dutch fears, which did not correspond with the facts'. But neither the prestige of this renowned historian, nor the wide circulation of his work, have managed to erase the image of German servants as German spies in the Netherlands.

The sparkling image of the German maid, which had already faded under economic pressure, became daubed in Nazi brown in the collective memory as soon as Germany invaded the Netherlands. The fact that the majority of those who stayed behind had become Dutch subjects through marriage did not alter this. From the moment the German occupation became a fact, this group of women of German origin – married or not, and regardless of their political preferences – were suspected of treachery and espionage.

What images of these German maids are remembered today? Let us take their own memories first. In 1923 Mrs Alwine Rieff came from the Ruhr to the Netherlands. In 1935 she married a Dutchman, with whom she was working as a caretaker in The Hague when the German army invaded the Netherlands:

When the war had finally become a fact and those Germans had invaded the country, the Dutch soldiers were spread all over The Hague. They had to keep watch everywhere. And at night those boys slept in the shelter below our buildings. One night I brought them some coffee, but they didn't take it. They said to me: 'After all, you could poison us here.' I said: 'Why should I do a thing like that?' They said: 'You're German, aren't you?!' I said 'I'm not at all German.' 'But where does that accent come from then?'

I didn't know what to say, so I fetched the manager, and he told them: 'You can drink that coffee, there's nothing wrong with it.' Well, from that time on they always protected me, when I was stopped in the street. Because then you had to say 'Scheveningen', you know, so that they could find out if you were a German, because German people can't pronounce that. [Laughs]

It must have been hard for you during the war...?

At first it was, but later it wasn't, because later everyone knew .... We had many evacuees at the office, and they were a great help to me, and then we also took in the Red Cross. When the Germans wanted to confiscate their gear, they went into hiding in our office ....But after the war it *was* unpleasant: I had a Dutch deposit book, and because I was from Germany, I was summoned to the director of the Rijksspaarbank (National Savings Bank). He asked me if I'd in any way been involved with the Nazis. I said: 'Not me, I'm Dutch.' I said: 'And if you don't believe me, talk to our manager.' I hid the Red Cross from the Germans and I helped an awful lot of young men. I was so angry![26]

The fear of betrayal did not exist solely in the Netherlands. Mrs Marie Ton experienced this during a visit to Germany in 1938:

Then I went home in September, because my stepfather had died unexpectedly. In the train I sat with a couple of soldiers on their way to the barracks. They were talking about the various drinks that exist in the world. They mentioned saki and arrack and *jènever* [Dutch gin]; *jènever* they said, and they claimed it was distilled from maize. Then I said: 'You're wrong, it's distilled from grain', in perfect German, you bet. 'Where did you get that idea?' one of them asked. *He* knew for certain: maize. I said: 'No, really, I should know; I am from Holland.' 'You're from Holland? I don't believe that.' So I produced my passport: silence. Not a word was said any more. They were dead silent. And I'd seen at the stations: '*Achtung, Feind hört mit*' [Be careful, the enemy is listening too]. So I was also a possible spy. Not another word was said. Then I thought: 'Why, you're no longer a German.'[27]

For Mrs Ton this was a 'key event': 'At that moment, somewhere a door was shut.' But when she returned to the Netherlands, she was likewise confronted with the prevailing fear of betrayal by foreigners:

> Of course, I have this accent, so in this country I had to prove myself again and again. But that wasn't too bad, because the people I knew, well, that was okay, and strangers – were strangers. It was much harder after the war.
> *After the war? Why?*
> Well, you know, there were an awful lot of people who were overcautious, who all of a sudden had become oh so patriotic, so small-minded ....After the liberation we stood in the schoolyard. Then the headmaster arrived, I didn't know him very well. He walked up to me and said: 'Are you free?' I said: 'What do you mean, free?' 'Haven't they interned you? You're German, aren't you?' And Elly, a Dutch friend with whom I'd worked for the resistance – that didn't amount to much, mind you, the things I did: I had a small paper round and did a little courier work, but then, we were at least doing something – that Elly got furious. Those things did indeed happen.[28]

Mrs Rieff and Mrs Ton were not the only women who described how, just prior to the outbreak of the war, they were approached as potential traitors and – regardless of their attitude during the war years – were subsequently confronted with renewed mistrust. To this day suspicion continues to play a role in the Netherlands. When Klara Neumann – at the age of 82 – went into a home for the elderly, the first thing her fellow residents said to her was : 'You're a Kraut; you don't belong here; you've got to go.'[29]

With every change of environment these women were held responsible for the events of the Second World War. Characteristic of this repeated necessity to explain their war roles is the response of one woman to a notice about my research. She sent me ten written portraits of former German and Austrian housemaids from her immediate neighbourhood. Every new portrait was introduced with a fictitious Christian name and the entry, 'not a Nazi' or, in the case of two women, 'became a Nazi', followed with the remark that they were not 'vicious people', but 'ignorant all right'.[30]

The memories which former Dutch housemaids have of their German colleagues partly contradict and partly reinforce this overriding image of treachery.

During the 1930s Mrs Aagtje Kuipers worked as a parlour-maid with a German kitchen-maid called Tekela. She recalls:

In those days there were many German maids. Times were bad in Germany then. Germany was going through the kind of economic depression we're having today ....That is why that Hitler came to power. Those German people didn't have any money or food, because social security didn't exist in those days. And so their maids all went to the Netherlands to work for wealthy people. That's why Tekela was there, with her sister, but she went back I think, and then they hired me.

Tekela was really an expert cook, she could bake fine cakes, she'd learned how to do that ....She had to do the cooking in the afternoon, and I'd sit there polishing the silver and things like that, so then she'd teach me all kinds of things while at work ....

Tekela was a Roman Catholic, very, very strict. Once in a while she'd make a very nice pudding, and if there was still a bit left in the pan, 'you should leave a bit more in it', I'd say. You know, you were young and you could do with a bit. 'No', she said, 'I can't do that, because that's not allowed.' She would have had to go to confession, because then she'd have sinned. 'Well, leave something in it for me then, because I don't have to go to confession'...

We slept in the same room, with a fitted basin. Oh, that was ever so nice! At night she'd kneel in front of the bed, wearing a very long night-gown, and then she'd pray. I'd been taught at the Rode Valken [Red Falcons]:[31] 'Show respect for each other's honest conviction, even if it isn't ours.' She used to wear her hair in a long blonde plait, and at such moments I thought she looked like a little angel.[32]

So far Mrs Kuipers' story evokes the image of the hardworking, respectable, skilled worker, which I have already discussed. But her memories also reveal the intimacy she experienced in her relationship with her German colleague, which formed the basis for reconciling their different outlooks on life. This is revealed even more clearly as she continues her story:

It's said about those German girls – well, not really nice things. Did you ever notice any signs of this?
You mean in the days of the Nazis, whether they were spies? Well, I do think that Tekela had friends – there was a friend of whom I thought: 'You've had so much schooling, I bet you're not a real housemaid.' I don't know, there was something about her – you simply feel these things ...

Later, when the war had more or less begun, I met that woman
again at the station and she turned her head away from me; no,
she didn't have a clear conscience, that one didn't. She must have
been one too ... But Tekela also said *'Heil Hitler!'* She'd sit in the
kitchen with her friends. Sometimes I stayed at home and would
also be there. Then she'd say *'Heil Hitler!'* I didn't like it when
she said that.
Did you ever talk to her about this?
Yes, because there wasn't a war going on yet, and when we were
doing the dishes, Tekela and I, we'd talk about the poverty in
Germany and things like that. And then I'd say: 'Tekela, Hitler
brings war.' *'Nein, nein'*, she'd answer, *'denn als wir Hitler nicht
gehabt haben, dann hätten wir Kommunismus gehabt.'* [No, no,
because if it hadn't been for Hitler, we'd have had Communism.]
That's how she'd talk. I said: 'Just you wait, there'll be war.' You
noticed it, we got information about it in the youth movement. I
was afraid to tell her. Funny, isn't it? Can you imagine: I didn't
tell her I was a member of the Arbeiders Jeugd Centrale
[Worker's Youth Federation].[33]

Mrs Aagtje Kuipers recalls how she put her own views, formed in
the Social-Democratic youth movement, cautiously alongside
Tekela's ideas, avoiding a direct confrontation. As a young resident
servant from the country in a strange city, she was greatly
dependent on her friendship with her German colleague. Because
Tekela displayed an intense hostility to Communism, and since
Catholics at that time made little distinction between Communism
and socialism, Aagtje did not reveal her socialist identity.

She does not judge Tekela less favourably because of this. By
making a distinction between personal integrity and political
sympathies, she places Tekela outside the image of the traitor, but
does not question the image itself. On the contrary: a German
woman with whom she did not have a personal relationship can at
the same time serve to confirm the current image of the German
spy.

Like Mrs Kuipers, Mrs Vandervelde came from the country to a
strange town in the 1930s, where she became friends with Liesel.
This German maid took her to meetings of a German organization
where she built up a close circle of German friends. In her memories
we find a similar distinction between the personal character of her
friends and their political ideas:

There are also stories dating from that time about German
servants who came to the Netherlands to spy....
Well, I really don't believe it. But they *were* mad about their

Führer then. Their parents were ever so poor in Germany and then came that Hitler. She'd sit in front of the radio and then, '*Heil*!' But I can't believe – those girls I tagged along with, not one of them would ever have done such a thing.[34]

Both women emphasize the good character of their personal German friends, and both point to the miserable circumstances in Germany to account for the extreme ignorance of these German women.

Mrs De Groot, on the other hand, belongs to the group of Dutch servants who felt wronged by the German maids' presence. For years she had been working for the Wijnberg family as a resident parlour-maid together with a kitchen-maid, when Mrs Wijnberg suddenly decided to reduce her domestic staff to a single living-in servant:

I said: 'Alone?!' O God, I'd become so used to working with another maid, that was always so pleasant. I said: 'I really won't do that.' And then I told them that I'd leave. Oh, how sorry I was later on!

Then they hired a German maid. And they are such climbers, you know. And later she [Mrs W] said to me about that German maid: 'They're far more obedient than Dutch servants.' When Missus planned to go out, she'd already be waiting with her coat, to put it on and things like that ....We didn't do that, because it wasn't necessary. And so they thought that these German maids were much more capable. I had heard that already before that time, when there were visitors, you know, ladies having tea together – that those German maids were far more capable.

The image of the capable, hard-working German servant emerges from her recollections too, but with this time a more competitive and critical tone. Entirely of her own accord, she went on:

Goodness, yes, they were said to be far more friendly, and things like that. They were real climbers. And meanwhile perhaps keeping their eyes open here and – and betraying things perhaps. That's what some people said, that special girls were sent from Germany to ...
Don't you think that's a bit far-fetched? After all, what secrets were there to betray to them?
Well, I don't know. Maybe there were indeed a couple of crafty ones among them....[35]

Thus a striking feature of these interviews with former Dutch servants who described German colleagues during the inter-war years is that they all confirm the image of the hard working, *tüchtige* German servant, though they evaluate it in contrary ways.

So there is more diversity of opinion in the current image of German maids as traitors. In the general view, one myth has been supplanted by another: the trusted servant has been transformed into a spy. But this myth has to be fitted alongside personal memory. Thus Dutch women who had no personal relationships with their German colleagues tend to endorse the image of the German spy without being able to link this to actual incidents. Women who did have personal relationships with colleagues from Germany placed them outside the image of treachery, but without questioning the image itself.

As for these women who lived and worked either as German maids, or as Dutch-naturalized housewives in the heart of Dutch society – the family – they denied the myth, but could not get away from it. An image of untrustworthiness and treachery came to prevail, even though both contemporary documentation and the direct memories of personal relationships with German maids produce an entirely different picture. Within a single decade economic and political developments had produced a fundamental change in the general image of German maids, on which the women themselves were unable to exert any influence. Their influence remained restricted to their immediate circle of friends and acquaintances, as appears from both their own recollections and those of their former Dutch colleagues. Outside their immediate circle they always had, and still have, to define their position with reference to a negative image of themselves and their German background. For them, personal memory is a vital weapon against a myth they need to fight to keep the respect of both others and themselves.

Notes

This paper was translated by Marianne de Rooy.

1 Letter 26 April 1960. 'Vrouwentekort', article in the *Gooi-en-Eemlander* of 25 April 1960.

2 The 'fifth column' is a concept which dates back to 1936 when, at the beginning of the Spanish Civil War, one of the rebel generals in a radio speech pointed threateningly to the operation of four military columns marching on Madrid, and added that the attack on the centre of the republican government would be opened by a fifth column, who were already secretly mixed with the citizens of Madrid.

3 'In Hitler's time many of them [German maids] were put to spying, especially on German Jews. This matter would merit your attention!' (L. Wolters, letter, 7 March 1987). There were many more similar oral and written responses to my research activities.

4 Barbara Henkes and Hanneke Oosterhof (1985) *Kaatje ben je boven? Leven en werken van Nederlandse dienstbodes, 1900–1940*, Nijmegen: SUN.
5 Statistics from the Centraal Bureau voor de Statistiek (Dutch Central Statistical Office), published in C.A.H. Haitsma Mulier-van Beusekom (1947) *Hulp in de huishouding gevraagd*, Amsterdam, pp. 77–8.
6 With growing industrialization and mechanization during the twentieth century, more women came to be employed in factories and workshops, as a result of which fewer female workers were available for domestic service, while the demand for domestic servants did not diminish. It is true that the arrival of running water, gas, and electricity made household chores somewhat easier, but at the same time people began to have higher standards of hygiene. Moreover, the presence of a servant was a sign of apparent wealth and functioned therefore as an indispensable status symbol.
7 *Christelijk Vrouwenleven* (magazine of the Christian Women's Organization) (1921), p. 66 and (1922), p. 258.
8 *De Arbeidsmarkt* (practical magazine of the organization of labour exchanges in the Netherlands) (1930), p. 147 and (1931), p. 69.
9 *Het Huispersoneel* (magazine of the Dutch Union of Domestic Servants), January 1934.
10 ibid.
11 Interview, Mrs Alwine Rieff-Broekman, 13 December 1981.
12 Interview, Mrs Trui Luider-van Zanten and Mrs Trijn Mekel-van Zanten, 28 February 1982.
13 *Tijdschrift der Nationale Vereeniging tegen de Werkloosheid* (theoretical magazine of the organization of Dutch labour exchanges) (1936), pp. 135–6.
14 Article in the daily paper *Het Handelslad*, 21 February 1934.
15 Henkes and Oosterhof, op. cit., pp. 33–9.
16 In August 1935 the Minister introduced a bill which prohibited the employment of young women in factories, workshops, and offices. In February 1936 a second bill followed to establish a maximum percentage of women workers to be employed in factories and workshops. Both bills were rejected, thanks to effective opposition from the women's rights movement.
17 Letter to the editor from 'a patriot' in *Het Vaderland* 16 August 1933, cited in *Het Huispersoneel*, October 1933.
18 As appeared from the conversations I conducted, with a group of students from the University of Oldenburg (Germany), with twelve women from East Friesland, who had been employed in the Netherlands during the inter-war period and had returned to Germany before the outbreak of the Second World War.
19 Nuremberg Acts, ch. 3. 'Juden durfen weibliche Staatsangehörige deutschen oder artverwandter Blutes unter 45 Jahren nicht in ihrem Haushalt beschäftigen'.
20 *Het Huispersoneel*, January 1939.

21 L. de Jong (1953) *De Duitse Vijfde Colonne*, Amsterdam: Meulenhoff, p. 245.
22 *Het Huispersoneel*, January 1939.
23 Letter of 2 February 1939 from Butting to the Head of the Ausland Organization, cited in de Jong, op. cit., p. 245.
24 Letter of February 1939 from Butting to the German ambassador in the Hague, Zech von Burkersroda, cited in de Jong, op. cit., p. 245.
25 de Jong, op. cit., p. 246.
26 Interview, Mrs Alwine Rieff-Broekman.
27 Interview, Mrs Marie Ton-Seyler, 20 October 1986.
28 ibid.
29 Interview conducted by Hans Meulenbroek, cited in his article (1982) 'De Duitse Dienstmeisjes', *Vrij Nederland* supplement, 13 November: 38.
30 Letter from Mrs A.J. Zandtstra, March 1987.
31 Youth section of the Social-Democratic Youth Federation.
32 Interview, Mrs Aagtje Kuipers-Staal, 15 May 1982.
33 ibid.
34 Interview, Mrs Trui Vandervelde-van Dijk, 3 March 1982.
35 Interview, Mrs Harmpje De Groot-van Bergen, 1 January 1982.

17

Stepchildren's memories

Myth, understanding, and forgiveness

Natasha Burchardt

Those working with stepfamilies in difficulties have no doubt of the force of myth in their lives. The wicked stepmother of the past, still annually evoked in pantomime performances, is echoed today not only in the 'monster' figure of the abusing stepfather but also in the heartless figure of the child-snatching social worker so ruthlessly harried by the tabloid press. But the stepfamily does not only suffer from negative myths. Some therapists have pointed out how many real difficulties in the reconstituted families of second marriages spring from myths about naturalness of family bonds: the 'myth of instant love', for example, which so many over-optimistic step-parents expect to experience from a stepchild as soon as they take on the parental role.[1]

One of the most widespread of current beliefs about stepfamilies is that their recent growth in the Western world is a unique phenomenon, in itself a sign of the collapse of family values. In fact stepfamilies were as present throughout the nineteenth century as in contemporary Britain. The proportion of broken marriages after twenty years has been estimated for the 1826 cohort as 36 per cent, and for the 1896 cohort still 30 per cent, while the projection for the 1980 cohort is 32 per cent. It was only in between that the rate fell dramatically: the figure for the 1921 cohort is as low as 17 per cent.[2] In retrospect, the inter-war years appear as a brief interlude of exceptional marital stability, an aberration in the long-term pers-pective. What has certainly changed is the reason for breakup: no longer almost always death, but now principally divorce.

We do not know the number of stepchildren in Britain today, although since one in three current marriages are remarriages, it may be nearly as high as in America where it has been estimated that one child in every six is a stepchild.[3] Not surprisingly, figures for the past are still vaguer. In addition, English historians face a particular lack of records for earlier centuries, since divorce was not legally possible between 1540 and 1857 except for the very wealthy, by special Act of Parliament. Work on pre-revolutionary French legal documents, however, has found little mention of children, except as a cause of marital conflict: typically through the resistance of adult stepchildren to a new father – 'il avait epousé la veuve et non pas les enfants'.[4] English legal disputes over the custody of children begin with the personal campaign of Caroline Norton, which led to the 1839 Infant Custody Act. But legal records are a very misleading source for understanding normal patterns, for they only concern families so conflictual that they came before the courts.

What other sources of information do we have for the history of stepfamily relationships? Personal documents – letters, diaries, and autobiographies – undoubtedly contain evidence for earlier periods, but very little use has been made of these. Houlbrooke mentions a reluctant Norwich widow, Katherine Andrews, who in 1532 told her widower suitor that she would have been glad to marry him, but 'I will never be a stepmother, for I understand ye have children, and that should cause us never to agree.'[5] And we know that by the late eighteenth and early nineteenth century some extremely complex families had developed, especially among the liberal Whig upper classes. For example, Lord John Russell (1792–1878) married a widow with four children, had two children with her and after her death remarried and had four more children.[6] According to Lord David Cecil, the children of the Countess of Oxford, the Harley family,

> were known as the Harleian Miscellany on account of the variety of fathers alleged to be responsible for their existence ... 'Emily, does it never strike you', writes Miss Pamela Fitzgerald in 1816, 'the vices are wonderfully prolific among Whigs? There are such countless illegitimates, such a tribe of children of the mist.'[7]

A second important source of information on stepfamilies is myth and folklore. There is a contemporary belief that the popular perception of the undesirability of 'step' status may itself shape the self-image and experience of people in stepfamilies.[8] I want here to look at the evidence from a representative national sample of life story interviews collected in the 1970s from people born at the turn of the century, who had the experience of living with a stepmother or a stepfather.[9] How far does the remembered experience of stepfamily life deviate from the myth or accord with it? And is there any evidence that the myth itself shaped that experience or the way it is recalled?

The popular images of stepfamilies come to us principally through fairy stories, of which by far the best known are Grimms'.

Although stepfathers sometimes figure, it is stepmothers around whom an aura of dread is created in relation to the fate of the children of the family. The nineteenth-century German ideology of motherhood encouraged the notion of the sweet, pure, self-sacrificing woman at the centre of the home. The image of the wicked stepmother can be seen as the reverse of this, the person-ification of evil, arising in the shadow of bereavement.

Perhaps the three best known fairy-story stepmothers are to be found in Hansel and Gretel, Cinderella, and Snow White. In each of these stories the stepmother is powerful and cruel, the father weak, the children helpless victims. For example, from Hansel and Gretel:

> In a little hut near the edge of a deep, deep forest lived a poor woodchopper with his wife and his two children, Hansel and Gretel. Times were hard, many people were starving. One evening after they had gone to bed, the man said to his wife, 'I don't know what will become of us.' 'You are right,' said his wife, who was not the children's real mother, 'and there is nothing for us to do but take Hansel and Gretel into the woods and let them shift for themselves'. She was a hard-hearted woman and did not much care what became of the children. But the father loved them dearly and said, 'Wife, what are you saying? I would never have the heart to do such a thing!' 'Oh well then,' snapped the stepmother, 'if you won't listen to reason, we'll all have to starve'. And she nagged and scolded until the poor man consented. 'May heaven keep them from harm,' he sighed.[10]

The *Oxford English Dictionary* defines 'to stepmother' as 'to behave as a stepmother, especially with a suggestion of unfairness or cruelty'. The myth of the wicked stepmother is well known in all Western cultures, and in some, like France, it is linked to dramatic games which children play about the haunting danger of finding themselves, as orphans, in such harsh hands.[11] The prefix 'step' which came into the English language as the Old English *steop* is indeed derived from a common Teutonic root meaning 'orphan', with all its connotations of deprivation and neglect, often retained in modern metaphoric use. In the Middle English of the fourteenth century, 'stepchild' could mean either simply 'orphan' or 'stepson' or 'stepdaughter'. The term 'stepdame', in use from the second half of the fifteenth century, possibly had fewer overtones than 'step-mother', by then already loaded with negative meaning. But step-dame did not survive in the language, giving way to the present, powerfully evocative 'stepmother'. In Italian *matrigna* has even more strongly negative connotations, for example *la natura gli fu matrigna*, translated according to one dictionary as 'nature was cruel to him'. The term *patrigno*, as with the English 'stepfather', is more neutral.

Turning to the interviews, it is clear that there is a qualitative difference in memories of stepmothers and stepfathers. Whereas stepmothers consistently provoke strong emotion, both positive and negative, reactions to stepfathers are more mixed. In some cases the stepfather appears hardly to have impinged on the life of the family, so that he may be mentioned but dismissed from the story, or altogether ignored. Overall, whereas an equal number of stepmothers are remembered either strongly positively or strongly negatively – six in each case – of the sixteen stepfathers, seven are remembered positively, five negatively and four are disregarded.

Sex and age when the parent died and the step-parent came into the family were important in determining how the step-parent was experienced – those children who were younger were more likely to be receptive to a step-parent. But there is no simple relationship. Among the four interviews in which stepfathers are barely mentioned is one with a man, the youngest in a family of five, who was 3 when his father died and still only 11 when his mother remarried. But his stepfather is referred to only in passing in a memory of his funeral. And though none of the women with positive memories of their stepmothers were old enough when their fathers remarried to retain any memory of their own mother, the two women whose stories most closely resemble the 'wicked stepmother' myth were also only small children when their father remarried – both still under five.

Factors besides age and sex were important: for example, position in the family, the attitude of other siblings, the relationship to the surviving parent, the quality of the new marriage, whether further children were born, and whether authority in the family remained with the natural parent, passed to the step-parent, or was shared.

The theme of poverty on the father's death resonates through the interviews. For this reason, no matter what the age of the children when he joined the family, the key quality for an Edwardian stepfather appears to have been his capacity to bring about an improvement in the family circumstances. Sometimes poverty was relative, but nevertheless keenly felt. A woman from a middle-class family tells of the changes in her life when her naval father died suddenly when she was 12. She and her sister had to give up learning the piano, which she loved, and she remembers the bitter experience of having to leave their select all-girls Admiral's school to go to the Board school, costing only a penny a day. But her mother's remarriage brought about a transformation. She was 16 when they all moved into her stepfather's house: 'But – of course we were made then. When he bought us a bike each. I don't mean to say he wanted to buy his popularity because – he – we knew him all our lives ... his first wife was a great friend of my mother's.' For this woman, and even more so for others for whom a mother's remarriage could bring an end to a time of dire poverty 'Well, it was a good thing for my mother when she married again, and for us really.'[12]

Conversely, in every case where there are negative memories of stepfathers, the root cause was drunkenness. Moreover, drunkenness is also by far the commonest problem associated with negative memories of fathers, so that sometimes the positive memory of a stepfather is contrasted with that of a despised, drunken father. A man whose father had died when he was about eight says:

He wasn't a father I should say that I could have – ... he never looked after mother as he should have done. He was very fond of drink and – whenever he was out of hospital – well, he was just having a – a drink outside and very – very often there was arguments with – mother or father.

But when he was nearly 17: 'Well – you see – my mother married again – that was a different thing altogether you see. Well that's when we enjoyed ourselves.' He recalls his stepfather was a better parent than his father:

He was a good man. He was. Extraordinarily good man ... more happiness in the family when she got married for the second time. Because she enjoyed herself. He took her on holiday. And he – and now and again they used to go and have a drink together. They were – enjoyment in the family then.[13]

One woman has contrasting memories of two stepfathers. When her father died when she was one week old, her mother was left to bring up her two children 'with nothing'. They were so poor that even as a small child she had to work with her mother in the shop: 'It used to be awful coming home from school and not being able to go out and play ... course me mother couldn't get through on her own, you know.' In speaking of her stepfathers, she dismisses the first, who married her mother when she was ten, with a few words: 'I think they were only married about 5 years. He killed himself with drink.' But she goes on to conjure up a vivid picture of the pleasures of family life when her mother remarried for the second time, when she was 15. The second stepfather 'was very good to me'. She tells of his love of music in the home, how he would play the organ and how on a Sunday evening his sister and her husband and their daughter would come round and the neighbours would pop in for a sing-song; and the enjoyment in her later teenage years when her stepfather would take her to the theatre, her mother then being too ill to go. Her brother, two years old, did not like the idea of their mother's second remarriage, but for her it was different: 'Well, it didn't bother me. Because, I mean, he was always kind to us, and he was good to me mother.' Later her stepfather looked after her mother when she became bedridden until his own death, when she took on the task.[14]

Stepmothers sometimes played a protective role in relation to fathers who treated their children harshly. One seaman father is remembered entirely negatively, frequently violent and drunk. This father beat his children, the girls as well as the boys: 'Oh yes, he hit – them just the same. He hit me brother with a bottle end and he put a big bump on his head. Oh he was cruel – yes.' Not surprisingly, the children were glad to see the back of him. 'Well – we used to – we used to wish him to go away to sea, yes. We were glad when we see them packing his bag.' The stepmother is remembered with affection by this man – although she too had turned to drink by the time he was 12, with the result that he left home to live with his elder sister, who had by then married.[15]

One of the most glowing accounts of stepmothers in the interviews is that of a woman who was an only child. Her own mother had died when she was only 6, but she has an idealized memory, almost like a fairy godmother.

> From what I hear from my father she was a lovely woman. Golden hair. Hair always looked beautiful ... we used to have a neighbour here ... she knew my mother – and she said what a lovely woman she was, she always had fair hair. And always a white starched apron. But that's all I can – I don't even remember her.

She speaks equally favourably of her stepmother: 'Two good mothers I've had ... my stepmother, she was one of the best in the world.' She praises her stepmother for the moral guidance she had received from her when she was poised between the worlds of childhood and adulthood: 'Now you're going out to work. But you're going to mix with different people. Got your eyes to see, your nose to breathe – keep your mouth shut' – advice which she says helped her throughout her life in that she never divulged the many secrets that were confided in her.[15]

Of the six stepmothers who are positively remembered, only two had children in the new marriage. In both cases the families are described as 'united', a description which does not occur elsewhere in the step-parent interviews. In one case the woman, herself the second of two girls and two boys in the first family, with four younger half-siblings, introduces them in this way: 'We were a family of eight, you see, well four girls and four boys.'[17] She makes it clear that no distinction was made between the two sets of children within the family and that, for her, both father and stepmother were equally important influences in her life.

In the case of another woman, the insistent repetition 'of course we've always been a united family' begins to arouse suspicion that this might represent a mythical ideal rather than reality. But as the story unfolds from childhood to adult life, the description 'united' rings true. This woman was the youngest of the four in the first family, with two younger half-brothers. Her mother had died at her birth but it was not till many years later that she discovered this, and that her 'mother' was, in fact, a stepmother.

> Some children at school told us, told my brother and I. When I said something about – me mother – me brother and he said, 'Not your brother, it's your stepbrother' – I said 'No it isn't.' Of course we had – we had a bit of a fight ....And when we get home I asked mother straight out and father said 'Come here', and told me what had happened, and that was the first I knew of it and – and her own boy was only a year and ten months you see younger.

Her devotion to her half-brothers emerges as her story unfolds. She tells of her sorrow when the brother closest in age was killed in the war; and how she kept the promise she had made to her 'mother' (that is, her stepmother) to help her younger brother, whose parents had both died by the time he was 15. She went to Australia to be with him and his wife when they had their first baby, even though this interfered with her own chances of marriage until much later in life.[18]

Idealization of others is a theme encountered in many of the life stories, and in all three cases where mothers had died when the children were older, passionately loving memories of the mothers are retained. For example, a woman whose mother had died when she was 14 extols her for her domestic virtues:

> My mother was – I – there's nothing I can say – I can't speak too highly of her altogether in every possible way. She was absolutely admirable. She seemed to do everything, she made clothes and mended clothes. And baked eternally. She never – we never bought anything to – to eat, it was always home made.

In speaking of her father's remarriage, this woman uses the language of the fairy stories: 'Father had – inflicted a stepmother upon us.'[19] And even the manner of telling takes on a magical quality, contrasting with the factual way she relates other details of her life elsewhere in her story. It is as if the tenderly preserved memory of the mother effectively blocks any re-evaluation of the stepmother, frozen in the reverse image of the idealized mother.

One interviewer touches an uncomfortable, even shameful cord. He asks: 'How did you get on with your stepmother?' and has the reply: 'Oh no. No. She was his first sweetheart and all. He'd never seen her from being married and she – she moved up when me mother died and – she got married again.' This woman refuses to be drawn further: 'I got on with her all right but – it just – a family affair, that's a thing you keep to yourself.' The unforeseen result of the remarriage of her caring and affectionate father was that the whole family split up. 'Me brother went to live with me auntie and ... our Hannah went to service and – our Nora was brought up with me auntie.' Only she remained at home, but her strength of feeling was such that she ignored her father's fears about her frail health and took a job straight away: 'He was married on the Saturday then I started work in the Co-operative factory on the Monday ....Me father was against it, he'd have had me at home but ...'. And, for her, early courtship was another means of avoiding the new family situation: 'I was only in me teens when I got to know Bob ... I was only in at nights. Then I got married when I was 23 and got a home of me own.'[20]

Sometimes it was the boys rather than the girls in the family who idealized the mother and resisted her displacement by the stepmother. One man, only 4 when his father remarried, and himself the seventh in a family of eight children, tells how his older brothers refused to do anything for his stepmother. 'The older ones seemed to think that no-one could take your mother's place, isn't that about the size of it?' He holds to the stereotype in explaining his own poor relationship with his stepmother, much like his younger brother's, contrasting with the more positive but still ambivalent attitudes of his sisters:

> And – well I don't know – I can't say I ever liked her, my brother Richard never said he liked her. My sister Janet and my sister Nellie – thought there was nobody like her, until they fell out over the shop and my – oldest sister left home and went to keep house for a gentleman. And I don't think she cared much for her after that either....[21]

But when the reactions not only of those interviewed but also of their siblings are taken into account, it becomes clear that the most consistently difficult of all step-relationships was that between older girls or young women and their stepmothers. Fathers were likely to remarry within two years of the mother's death, unlike mothers, who often remained single for many years before remarriage. A stepmother might find herself in unwitting competition with a mother not long dead, the unresolved grief of the children turned to anger at the outsider. Moreover, stepmothers were inevitably cast as intruders, displacing older girls in their care-taking role, and sometimes also from a relationship with the father remembered as especially close.

Closeness to the father and pride in the role often compensated for the burden of housekeeping. One woman, the oldest of four surviving children, whose schooling had come to an abrupt end when her mother died when she was 12 remembers, 'It didn't matter what we spoilt, he never discouraged you ... I was only 12. Did the baking, washing, anything when I was 12. And then when I was 13 I were like a little old woman.'[22] Another woman gives a graphic account of how her 20-year-old sister, who had looked after the family for fifteen months after their mother died, found she could no longer intercede on her 10-year-old sister's behalf with their father after his remarriage. Rather than accept this humiliation, her solution was to go into a convent, with the result that from that time she had little contact with any of the family:

> And I remember I wanted to go swimming after school hours and – I daren't go without permission. So – of course I was in bed when father came home, so I said to my oldest sister – all evening I must have been on about 'I'm going to ask me dad if I can go', and so she asked him. And the stepmother took umbrage. It was her place to ask, not mine, not Annie's. Yes, oh yes, well I felt – no wonder she joined the church, was there?[23]

In another family a man who himself thought of his stepmother as 'wonderful' knows that he was favoured as the youngest boy. He recalls the friction between his older sisters and their stepmother, herself only one year older than the oldest sister and nicknamed by the sisters 'The Duchess'.[24]

Among the stepmother interviews, two stand out in depicting stepmothers who come near to the image of the fairy stories. But in one case it was only when the tape-recorder was turned off that the woman recalled how when she was only five her new stepmother punished her for waking in the night by bonking her on the nose, and drawing blood. For her, the stepmother coming into the family meant that 'I got estranged from my father. Estranged.' As the only girl in the family, and the eldest, she was expected to take the brunt of the housework, so that she was often in trouble for being late for school. Her stepmother died when she was 11, leaving her with the full care of the household, her two younger brothers and her half-brother 'the wee boy', still only 4, but himself to die when he was 15. It is a surprise when she gives her view of her stepmother: '... she was a very good stepmother. But no love.'[25]

Much closer to the Cinderella story is another of a woman, also from Scotland. Here we find the weak father and the rejecting stepmother, who accepts the powerful projections of wickedness on to herself, in the fantasy that she has murdered or driven out the mother or previous caretaker. In this family, the mother had died when the woman was only 5 months old and her sister 2. They were cared for by a good aunt who came to live with them until their father remarried five years later. The aunt returned to her home and from that time 'we were very – under the – stepmother's thumb you know.' She explains that her father 'had a difficult life and he was a very quiet man and he always took the line of least resistance, and my stepmother was – was far better to us when he was in than when he wasnae.' She and her sister were not allowed to play in the house and hardly dared say a word. They were often kept back from school to scrub floors and do the washing and the stepmother would thrash them for misbehaviour. She showed no affection and 'often used to say she dinna like us – and – we would never get married and we'd faces – like – and oh she said some terrible things to us when I think of it' – treating them quite differently from her own two children. The better educated half-sisters later both became clerical workers, but:

> it was a sort of understood thing – by my stepmother that whenever we were old enough we were to go into service. Into service. To get out of the house, to get away, yes, mm. Would – wouldnae be bothered with us.

When this woman found herself at the age of 14, a servant in the imposing house of a medical officer of health, she was in no doubt that the drudgery there was better than her life at home: she stayed for two years, much longer than other young girls, whose mothers would not allow them to stay more than a few months because their health suffered from the work. But for this woman:

> I – I quite enjoyed – being with other girls in the place, there were a few of us you know, of course I was young – besides then and – they treated me awful nice you know, they sort of made a fuss of me, and I never had any fuss made of me when I was young. Never was petted or anything like that. But they were sort of awfully good to me you know and – I just knew the difference and – enjoyed it, mm.

In her adult life the story departs from the myth. For in spite of the antagonism between this woman and her stepmother during her childhood, by the time she herself came to marry they had achieved sufficient tolerance of each other for the stepmother to help with the wedding. But later on, when children were born, the stepmother again reacted coldly – she provided no comfort when the first child died, and rather than welcome the second, she fiercely rejected the role of grandmother: 'When I – when he was born, a cousin came in – and she said – to my stepmother, you'll be a granny now. "Oh", she says, "I'm not – not a granny, and I don't want to be called granny."'[26]

Time may give a changing perspective but sometimes myth shapes the understanding, lending doubt to the storyteller. For one man, who describes his stepfather as 'quite a nice man', the image of the neglected stepchild persists. He tells of the first introduction of his future wife to his mother and stepfather:

> Yes – 'course it was my stepfather, it wasn't my own father. And – yes, he – he was – he was very very – so was my mother, but he was extraordinarily friendly; it's rather queer ... rather unusual for a stepfather to treat a stepchild as his own.[27]

Yet sometimes even when the image held from childhood is entirely hostile, with the passage of time the stepchild as an adult may be able to develop understanding and compassion for a step-parent, in the same way as for a parent. One woman blames her stepfather for luring her mother away from her father and family, refers to him throughout her story as 'Tom Brown', never recognizing their kinship. But she acknowledges that towards the end of his life she felt sorry for him: 'I couldn't bear to see him – you know – the suffering he did suffer – he was punished – really punished. Whatever he did to us he was punished.' By that time too her relationship with her mother had changed. Her mother often left her to her own devices as a child while she 'pursued her own pleasures', but 'later in life she would have given me the world'. Although she never grew to respect her (unlike her loved and revered grandmother), she forgave her, and in the end she can say, 'I – I loved her – in my way.'[28]

What part, then, does myth play in these life stories of step-families? Certainly myth weaves a thread, helping to shape the memories both of parents and of step-parents. But reality is more various, less tidy than myth. Time and again real personal experience breaks through, at times negating the myth, taking the story in unexpected directions and finally giving its own substance to every life story.

Notes

1 Emily B. Visher and John S. Visher (1982) 'Children in stepfamilies', *Psychiatric Annals* 12 (9): 832–41, and 'Stepfamilies and step-parenting', in Froma Walsh (ed.) (1982) *Normal Family Processes*, London: Guilford, pp. 331–53.

2 Michael Anderson (1983) 'What is new about the modern family: an historical perspective', OPCS Occasional Paper 21, *The Family*: 5.

3 One in three marriages today involves remarriage for at least one partner, and one in six for both partners. L. Rimmer (1980) *Families in Focus: Marriage, Divorce and Family Patterns*, London: Study Commission on the Family.

4 Roderick Phillips (1980) *Family Breakdown in Late 18th Century France: Divorce in Rouen 1792–1803*, Oxford: Clarendon Press, pp. 121–2.

5 Ralph Houlbrooke (1984) *The English Family 1450–1700*, London: Longman, p. 211.

6 His eldest son, John, Lord Amberley, married Kate Stanley. The eldest child of their 'open' marriage was Bertrand Russell, himself three times married.

7 Lord David Cecil (1939) *The Young Melbourne*, London: Constable, pp. 10–11.

8 See, for example, Brenda Maddox (1980) *Step-Parenting*, London: Unwin; Margaret Robinson (1980) 'Stepfamilies: a reconstituted family system', *Journal of Family Therapy* 2: 45–69

9 Paul Thompson (1975) *The Edwardians*, London: Weidenfeld & Nicolson, pp. 7–8 describes the sample. Since his interview survey was not designed with stepfamilies in mind, no special thought was given to structural differences between intact and stepfamilies. In a few instances parent and step-parent are not clearly distinguished, or the interviewer asks about either the natural or the step-parent but not both. Twenty-eight of those interviewed had step-parents, of whom nine women and four men had a stepmother and nine men and six women had a stepfather, in one case two stepfathers.
I am grateful to Paul Thompson for permission to use the transcripts of the Family Life and Work Experience interviews at the University of Essex, for his advice on the earlier history of families in Britain and Europe, and for his help and encouragement in focusing my thoughts on stepfamilies and their history.

10 *Tales from Grimm* (1937) trans. and ill. Wanda Gag, London: Faber & Faber, pp. 23–4.

11 J. Flandrin (1979) *Families in Former Times*, Cambridge: Cambridge University Press, pp. 40–3.

12 Interview 349.

13 Interview 88.

14 Interview 87.

15 Interview 103.

16 Interview 407.

17 Interview 66.

18 Interview 227.
19 Interview 187.
20 Interview 195.
21 Interview 364.
22 Interview 195.
23 Interview 217.
24 Interview 275.
25 Interview 366.
26 Interview 363.
27 Interview 428.
28 Interview 92.

Bibliography

Baddeley, Alan D. (1976) *The Psychology of Memory*, New York: Basic Books.

Barthes, Roland (1957) *Mythologies*, Paris: Seuil.

Barthes, Roland (1981) *Le Grain de la voix*, Paris: Seuil.

Beer, Gillian (1983) *Darwin's Plots*, London: Routledge & Kegan Paul.

Bernhard, Ernst (1969) *Mitobiografia*, Milan: Adelphi.

Bloch, Marc (1974) *Apologie pour l'histoire*, Paris: Colin.

Bloch, Maurice (1921) 'Réflexions d'un historien sur les fausses nouvelles de la guerre', *Revue de synthèse historique*, republished (1963) *Mélanges historiques* 1: 41–56.

Canary, Robert and Kozicki, Henry (eds) (1978) *The Writing of History: Literary Form and Historical Understanding*, Madison: University of Wisconsin Press.

Cohen, Stanley (1972) *Folk Devils and Moral Panics*, London: MacGibbon & Kee.

Cru, Jean Norton (1930) *Du témoignage*, Paris: Gallimard.

Figlio, Karl (1988) 'Oral history and the unconscious', *History Workshop Journal* 26: 120–32.

Fraser, Ronald (1984) *In Search of a Past: the Manor House, Amnersfield, 1933–45*, London: Verso.

Freud, Sigmund (1921) *Massenpsychologie und Ich-Analyse*, Leipzig; English trans. (1960) *Group Psychology and the Analysis of the Ego*, New York: Bantam Books.

Grele, Ronald (1979) 'Listen to their voices: two case studies in the interpretation of oral history interviews', *Oral History* 7(1): 33–42.

Halbwachs, Maurice (1925) *Les cadres sociaux de la mémoire*, Paris: Alcan.

Halbwachs, Maurice (1950) *La mémoire collective*, Paris: Presses Universitaires de France; English trans. (1980) *Collective Memory*, New York: Harper & Row.

Hall, Stuart (1978) *Policing the Crisis: Mugging, the State and Law and Order*, London: Macmillan.

Henige, David (1974) *The Chronology of Oral Tradition: Quest for a Chimera*, Oxford: Clarendon Press.

Henige, David (1982) *Oral Historiography*, London: Longman.

Hewins, Angela (ed.) (1982) *The Dillen: Memories of a Man of Stratford-upon-Avon*, Oxford: Oxford University Press.

Hillman, James (1979) 'Senex and puer', in *Puer Papers*, University of Texas: Spring Publications, pp. 3–53.

Hillman, James (1983) *Healing Fiction*, Barrytown, NY: Station Hill Press.

Hobsbawm, Eric and Ranger, Terence (eds) (1983) *The Invention of Tradition*, Cambridge: Cambridge University Press.

Johnson, Richard (ed.) (1982) *Making Histories: Studies in History-writing and Politics*, London: Hutchinson.

Jonas, Hans (1956) *The Gnostic Religion*, Boston: Beacon Press.

Joutard, Philippe (1977) *La légende des Camisards: une sensibilité au passé*, Paris: Gallimard.

Jung, Carl Gustav (1940–1) *Einführung in das Wesen der Mythologie*; Italian trans. (1972) *Prolegomeni allo studio scientificio della mitologia*, Turin: Boringhieri; English trans. (1970) *Introduction to a Science of Mythology*, London: Routledge & Kegan Paul.

Le Bon, Gustav (1895) *Psychologie des foules*, Paris: Alcan; English trans. (1895) *The Crowd: a Study of the Popular Mind*, London: Unwin.

Lefebvre, Georges (1932) *La Grande Peur de 1789*, Paris: Colin; English trans. (1973) *The Great Fear of 1789: Rural Panic in Revolutionary France*, London: New Left Books.

Maranda, Pierre (ed.) (1972) *Mythology*, Harmondsworth, Middx: Penguin Books.

Miller, Joseph (ed.) (1980) *The African Past Speaks: Essays on Oral Tradition and History*, Folkestone: Dawson and Archon.

Mink, Louis O. (1978) 'Narrative form as a cognitive instrument', in Canary and Kozicki (1978).

Moreno, Mario (1969) *Psicodinamica della contestazione*, Turin: Edizioni Radiotelivise Italiane.

Morin, Edgar (1984) *Sociologie*, Paris: Fayard.

Myerhoff, Barbara (1979) *Number Our Days*, New York: Dutton.

Okpewho, Isidore (1983) *Myth in Africa: a Study of its Aesthetic and Cultural Relevance*, Cambridge: Cambridge University Press.

Olney, James (ed.) (1980) *Autobiography: Essays Theoretical and Critical*, Princeton, NJ: Princeton University Press.

Passerini, Luisa (1979) 'Work ideology and consensus under Italian fascism', *History Workshop Journal* 8: 82–108.

Passerini, Luisa (1987) *Fascism in Popular Memory: the Cultural Experience of the Turin Working Class*, Cambridge: Cambridge University Press.

Patlagean, Evelyne (1980) 'Storia dell'immaginario', in *La nuova storia*, Milan: Mondadori, pp. 289–317; French edition (1978) Jacques Le Goff (ed.) *La nouvelle histoire*, Paris: CEPL.

Pompa, Leon (1982) 'Narrative form, significance and historical knowledge', in David Carr *et al.* (eds) *Philosophy of History and Contemporary Historiography (Philosophia no. 23)*, Ottawa: University of Ottawa Press.

Popular Memory Group (1982) 'Popular memory: theory, politics, method', in Johnson (1982).

Portelli, Alessandro (1981a) 'The peculiarities of oral history', in *History Workshop Journal* 12: 96–107.

Portelli, Alessandro (1981b) '"The time of my life"; functions of time in oral history', *International Journal of Oral History* 2: 162–80.

Porter, Dale H. (1981) *The Emergence of the Past: A Theory of Historical Explanation*, Chicago: University of Chicago Press.

Propp, Vladimir (1984) *The Theory and History of Folklore*, trans. from Russian (from various originals 1946, 1969, etc.), Manchester: Manchester University Press.

Renza, Louis A. (1980) 'The veto of the imagination: a theory of autobiography', in Olney (1980).

Samuel, Raphael (1981) *East End Underworld: Chapters in the Life of Arthur Harding*, London: Routledge & Kegan Paul.

Samuel, Raphael (1982) 'Life histories', paper presented at the International Oral History Conference, Amsterdam.

Schrager, Sam (1983) 'What is social in oral history?' *International Journal of Oral History* 4: 76–98.

Sherzer, Joel and Woodbury, Anthony C. (eds) (1987) *Native American Discourse*, Cambridge: Cambridge University Press.

Tedlock, Dennis (1983) *The Spoken Word and the Work of Interpretation*, Philadelphia: University of Pennsylvania Press.

Thompson, Paul (1988) *The Voice of the Past: Oral History*, Oxford: Oxford University Press, 2nd edn (1st edn 1978).

Thompson, Paul with Natasha Burchardt (ed.) (1982) *Our Common History: the Transformation of Europe*, London: Pluto Press; New Jersey: Humanities Press.

Tonkin, Elizabeth (1982) Review article, 'Steps to the redefinition of "oral history": examples from Africa', *Social History* 7: 329–35.

Trevi, Mario (1987) *Per uno junghismo critico*, Milan: Bompiani.

Vansina, Jan (1985) *Oral Tradition as History*, Madison: University of Wisconsin Press.

White, Hayden (1973) *Metahistory*, Baltimore: Johns Hopkins University Press.

Index